ENTERTAINING WITH TOVEY

ENTERTAINING WITH TOVEY

HOW TO STAR IN YOUR OWN KITCHEN

JOHN TOVEY

Photographs by Mick Duff
Drawings by
Ray and Corrine Burrows

Macdonald General Books
MACDONALD AND JANE'S · LONDON AND SYDNEY

First published in Great Britain in 1979 by
Macdonald General Books
Macdonald and Jane's Publishers Limited,
Paulton House
8 Shepherdess Walk
London N.1

ISBN 0 354 04433 8

Designed by Janet James

Photographs by Mick Duff of savoury cheese peach, chocolate roulade, Marsala and almond cake, shortbread and orange mousse, reproduced by courtesy of *The Caterer and Hotelkeeper*

Filmset in 'Monophoto' Century Schoolbook by
Servis Filmsetting Limited, Manchester

Printed in Great Britain by
Purnell & Sons Ltd, Paulton, Bristol

CONTENTS

Contents *continued*

LIST OF ILLUSTRATIONS

Colour plates

MEASUREMENTS

The recipes in this book were originated in pounds and ounces, and the metric equivalents are based on the approximations most commonly used:
1 oz = 25 g, 1 fl oz = 25 ml.

Conversion Tables (Britain, Australia etc.)

Weight		Capacity	
Imperial	*Metric*	*Imperial*	*Metric*
1 oz	25 g	1 fl oz	25 ml
2 oz	50 g	2 fl oz	50 ml
3 oz	75 g	4 fl oz	100 ml
4 oz (¼ lb)	100–125 g	5 fl oz (¼ pt)	150 ml
5 oz	150 g	6 fl oz	175 ml
6 oz	175 g	7 fl oz	200 ml
7 oz	200 g	8 fl oz	225 ml
8 oz (½ lb)	225 g	10 fl oz (½ pt)	300 ml
9 oz	250 g	15 fl oz (¾ pt)	400 ml
10 oz	275 g	20 fl oz (1 pt)	500–600 ml
11 oz	300 g	1¼ pt	700 ml
12 oz (¾ lb)	350 g	1½ pt	900 ml
13 oz	375 g	1¾ pt	1 litre
14 oz	400 g	2 pt	1.1 litre
15 oz	425 g	2¼ pt	1.3 litre
16 oz (1 lb)	450 g	2½ pt	1.4 litre
1½ lb	700 g	2¾ pt	1.6 litre
2 lb	900 g	3 pt	1.7 litre
2½ lb	1.1 kg		
2¾ lb	1.3 kg		
3 lb	1.4 kg		

Conversion Tables (America)

If you are using standard American cup and spoon measures when cooking from recipes in this book, the following measuring equivalents will be useful for reference. They have been very slightly adjusted for ease of calculation.

Liquid

1 Imperial pint = 20 fl oz = $2\frac{1}{2}$ cups
$\frac{1}{2}$ Imperial pint = 10 fl oz = $1\frac{1}{4}$ cups
$\frac{1}{4}$ Imperial pint = 5 fl oz = $\frac{5}{8}$ cup

1 Imperial gill = 5 fl oz = $\frac{5}{8}$ cup

1 standard UK tablespoon = $1\frac{1}{4}$ standard American tablespoons
1 standard UK teaspoon = $1\frac{1}{4}$ standard American teaspoons

Dry

Imperial/Metric		*American*
1 lb (450 g)	almonds, slivered	4 cups
	whole	3 cups
1 lb	breadcrumbs, fresh	16 cups
1 lb	butter or margarine	2 cups
1 lb	cheese, fresh grated	4 cups
1 lb	cherries, glacé	$2\frac{1}{4}$ cups
1 lb	coconut, shredded	4 cups
1 lb	cooking fat	2 cups
1 lb	dried fruit (average)	3 cups
1 lb	flour, all-purpose	4 cups
1 lb	honey	$1\frac{1}{3}$ cups
1 lb	meat, ground	2 cups
1 lb	mushrooms, sliced	5 cups
1 lb	rice, cooked	6 cups
	uncooked	2 cups
1 lb	sugar, confectioners'	$3\frac{1}{2}$ cups
	demerara	$2\frac{1}{4}$ cups
	granulated	2 cups
1 lb	syrup	$1\frac{1}{4}$ cups
1 lb	walnuts, halved	4 cups

1 oz flour = 30 g = 2 level tablespoons
1 oz sugar = 30 g = 1 level tablespoon

Terms

biscuit crumbs ...graham cracker crumbs
cornflour ....cornstarch
double cream ......heavy cream
flour ....all-purpose flour
grill ....broil
icing sugar ....confectioners' sugar
minced meat ......ground meat
rich shortcrust ...rich pie pastry
shortcrust ....pie pastry
single cream ......light cream

PROLOGUE

BACKSTAGE
THE SCRIPT
THE SET
THE DRESS REHEARSAL
THE FINAL TOUCH

Theatre means joy and sorrow, laughter and tears, comedy and drama. Cooking, too, contains all these elements.

Just as the actor delights in the pleasure of his audience, so the cook and his or her guests can share the pleasure of a carefully directed performance.

The art of entertaining, whether in the theatre or in the kitchen, means knowing just how much to give the audience; means getting to know the short cuts, the ways of 'sharpening' the act; means making the most profound effect on the audience with the use of a pause; means developing the technique of timing – for to overdo a dish is like 'milking' a line, and to underdo it is to throw it away.

Cooking itself is interpreting a recipe in much the same way as an actor interprets a part, each cook or actor producing a subtly different and, in fact, unique result.

But cooking, too, is confidence. The rehearsals are the time for experimentation, and the actual performance should be given with the confidence and familiarity, if you, the creator – the cook – are to share the pleasure of your guests. And with this very strongly in mind, the recipes in this book have been very carefully planned so that the confidence of familiarity does not turn into the 'same old act'. Each basic recipe has many variations. Once one approach is perfected – when you have found a recipe that you enjoy preparing, find easy to serve, and your guests love to eat – stick to it; its variations will lend infinite variety to your performing skills.

Cooking and entertaining should be a pleasure shared by all concerned and this book outlines to you my own ideas – born of long and hard experience – on how this may most effectively be achieved.

Be the star in your own kitchen!

BACKSTAGE

Although the kitchen or backstage may never be seen during the performance, it is here that everything begins and ends.

For me, the kitchen has to be simply operational. It is the place where the ideas for the meals are conceived, the area where the meals are prepared, cooked, served, and cleared away. My own kitchen is divided into 3 areas – Work, Cook and Wash.

The work area should be as spacious as possible with much thought given to storage – cupboards with revolving shelves, doors fitted with racks for small items, easy running and easily cleaned drawers all help the cook. Be as methodical as possible in your storing of provisions and utensils. For instance, I have one section for baking where I store all the various flours in one cupboard, and next to it is a revolving corner cupboard, one shelf of which is full of the many items needed for baking – cherries, sultanas, silver balls, mixed peel, icing sugar and so on.

Also ensure that you have enough jets or rings on which to cook the dishes, enough oven space, sufficient warming areas, adequate fridge space for the build-up of dishes. If your backstage area isn't effectively designed for the purpose, the performances may never run as smoothly as they could.

Props

An essential ingredient of efficient backstage work is the right props. **Knives** need not be many, but should be as sharp as possible (the blunt ones do the most damage!). The Swiss Victorinox knives are my personal favourites. Palette knives are useful, too.

Electrical equipment can be very much overdone, and you could find yourself surrounded by a hundred-and-one gadgets such as electrical can-openers, carvers, knife-sharpeners, auto-stir saucepans. . . . I have only a Kenwood Major, a Magimix, and a small electric hand mixer, as I firmly believe that any chore that can be done more quickly and as well by machine saves me, the host, time and energy. The rest of the array are a waste of time and money.

Spoons of the right sort are a must. My collection of wooden spoons is enormous, as every time I pass a junk shop I look for those pre-war spoons which are so much better than the modern ones. The matured wood of the older spoons is always so beautifully shaped at the back – essential when beating out sauces. Modern spoons are cut out of unmatured timber, and tend to take on odd shapes in the heat of the kitchen; indeed, they are often straight-backed which does not allow you to beat out the flour in a sauce, for instance, or get food through a sieve quicker.

Large metal spoons are also essential, one perforated and one plain.

I wouldn't be without measuring spoons, and I find the plastic sets the easiest to work with, but do check them first before you use them. On one occasion I experienced much trouble in the bake-house only to discover that the new metal set of measuring spoons (imported from Australia) were miles out! The new Melamine spoons available from chemists' shops are good, but rather confusing as they're metric at one end and avoirdupois the other. But the notes on measuring on page viii will help.

Sieves are another necessity in my kitchen. I most often use a round plastic sieve and a fine mesh metal sieve (ideal for sieving gelatine as you can warm it prior to putting the mixture through).

Trays and tins can be used for so many different things, that I can never have enough of either. I use metal trays for baking and preparation, and white plastic trays for storing garnishes, etc. Loaf tins can be used for a variety of purposes, not just for baking bread, and the new non-stick ones really are excellent and actually do not stick. But do be sure that you buy sensibly. I'll never forget giving a demonstration of how to make a roulade (see page 46), when I stressed continually that I was doubling the usual quantities in order to acquire a special effect for a Christmas buffet centre piece. One of my audience insisted on knowing the size of the tin and, on being told, went and bought a similar sized tin, made up the recipe, and found that the tin wouldn't fit into her oven!

Flan tins come in many different guises. For pies and tarts I always prefer to use the loose-bottomed fluted flan tins. They conduct heat very well and the actual dish when presented at the table minus its outside casing looks so much nicer. Do beware of the china flan dishes which look so pretty and eye-catching with their recipes printed on the base! If you use them you will end up with soggy-bottomed pastry, and it is sheer hell getting the first portion out.

When buying the loose-bottomed fluted flan tins, do take particular notice of the bases. You want them to be perfectly plain. There are some tins on the market with a slight rim round the outside (sometimes quite noticeable) but these are difficult (or practically impossible) to get pastry out of, too.

Spatulas made of rubber which are 'built' into metal handles are the best to buy. Rubber spatulas with wooden or plastic handles tend to get soft when used and then do not fit the handle and can fall off just when you come to scrape out a dish. A small point, but important, I think.

Rolling pins of the right length and the right material are a must for anyone who bakes. I always use a rolling pin about 18 in (46 cm) long and 2 in (5 cm) diameter, made from well-seasoned wood which won't warp. There are some very gimmicky rolling pins on the market – made from plastic (into which you can pour iced water), or even glass. Avoid them like the plague, use the one I suggest (even though it might cost just that little bit more) and it will prove more beneficial in the long run.

Scales. Yes, I know metrication is in, and pounds and ounces are officially out, but for me, the old-fashioned balancing scale (one with weights on one side and a pan in which to weigh the material on the other) is easily the best. To actually *see* the scales balance equally is satisfying and reassuring. Many of the spring-balance modern scales don't always work out. But I did acquire from a curio shop a lovely 'thirties sweet-shop spring-loaded scale with a large sweeping arm that goes from left to right. It weighs up to 4 lb (1·8 kg) which, for a normal kitchen, is rather large, and it does take up a bit of room screwed to its surface in the bakehouse, but the weekly chore of polishing it with Brasso and oiling it is a labour of intense love.

Oven thermometers, for me, are a *must.* Although they can easily be damaged, they are worth the repeated expense. Gas and voltage pressures can so often be erratic, but the thermometer does tell you just what your oven is doing at that very minute and, more important still, *where* it is being done. For goodness' sake, don't assume that if the middle of the oven is 400°F (200°C) Gas 6, the bottom shelf is going to be the same. If you *do,* you have more faith than I in modern mass-produced gadgets!

The thermometers I like are like a clinical thermometer but mounted sideways on to a metal stand that can be stood or hung on your oven shelves. They tend to get dirty quickly but are easily cleaned with a bit of detergent powder. When my team and I travel around the world cooking in other hotel kitchens, this piece of portable – and essential – equipment is much appreciated.

Timers are another must for me as, like most people, once I have something in the oven or on the top of the stove I immediately find a dozen other jobs to be done and occasionally forget what I have cooking. I must admit to my fetish of having *two* timers in my own kitchen as the older I get the more absent-minded I seem to become. I set one for 5 minutes prior to the dish being completed and one for the exact timing. I always hear one going off and so seldom have problems.

But don't stand them on an oven shelf or on the top of the stove as the heat can damage their plastic mountings. On the top of the stove they can be easily knocked off into pans of bubbling food, which does nothing for the clock or the dish (I know from experience)!

One gadget I am proud of is a Swiss pocket timer which was a present from a close friend who knows my memory only too well. You set the gadget for the time you want and either clip it on to your apron or put it in your pocket and it goes off wherever you are (handy if you decide to do some gardening whilst your dish is cooking merrily away).

Egg slicers are egg slicers, you might think, but do take care in buying the right one. There are 2 on the market, one which cuts your boiled egg into 6 or 8 wedges, and the other which actually produces egg slices. I bought a slicer lately only to find it not only cut very thick slices of egg, but was so badly made the 'piano wire' snapped very quickly. It's only a small point, I know, but do watch for rubbishy slicers on the market.

Fish kettles are perhaps a slight extravagance when setting up a kitchen. I use mine for many things other than cooking salmon and trout – if you take the fish rack out, you can cook dishes in ramekins, keep vegetables hot in tinfoil, or cook your Christmas puddings. But for the best poached salmon or trout I find a fish kettle essential and the notes in the Fish section (see page 68) will support my suggestion.

An **asparagus pan** isn't vital, as you can improvise, but I feel that as asparagus is so expensive, it does warrant this additional expenditure. The *ease* alone with which you handle the vegetable when cooking it in an asparagus pan demonstrates the wisdom of such a buy. I have cooked asparagus in a jam-jar immersed in simmering water, but it is never quite the same. I also tried to rationalize by using the basic pan as a base when doing sauces in a bowl, but it was quite rightly pointed out to me that the cost of boiling the vast amount of water asparagus pans hold, just to do a sauce or essence, was rather crazy!

THE SCRIPT

The most important part of any performance is, of course, the menu. It is the script, the programme, as well as the plot. It is also the most difficult to manage, as so much thought has to be put into it – including the shopping, which can be a nightmare.

Careful planning and lots of preparation beforehand will ensure a performance as near-perfect as possible. Seasonal considerations should be foremost – making full use of what is available, making stars of the freshest vegetables or seasonal fruits. Do remember, too, that sweet should follow sour; dry, wet; sharp, delicate; rough, smooth, and it is so much easier to serve cold dishes to make a meal 'flow'.

The main course, for me, is the backbone of the show, and as I prefer to sit down course by course with my guests and enjoy the evening, I normally do a simple seasonal roast, or a dish that can be prepared well in advance. By buying extra bones of the meat for the roast, the gravy can be made in the morning (no last-minute frantic stirring), and many of my main course recipes are enhanced by a sauce which can also be made hours in advance.

Shopping

I think the most difficult part of entertaining is the actual shopping! For me at Miller Howe life is a never-ending battle with suppliers who seem to have been 'tamed' for months on end and then suddenly – and unsuspectingly – deliver inferior goods which throw the whole pattern of work out of gear.

At home it is tricky sitting down planning menus for the week, or just one for a night of entertaining, as you are completely in the hands of the shopkeepers who, in turn, are in the hands of the market traders. I have often thought I would do a certain dish as a starter and something else as a main course, and finish up with such and such as a dessert – all of which should be in season and in the shops – and how often I am proved wrong.

So the first thing you must do when planning a menu is, naturally, to consider what is best for the time of year. Salmon is unheard of in my repertoire in October (but so often found on menus), just as parsnips are in June. Fresh, in my mind, being the keyword to success with cooking, do bear in mind constantly what is on the market month by month and buy accordingly. But be sensible. Of course raspberries and strawberries are summer fruits, but extravagantly so for the first 10 to 14 days of the season, and tailing off miserably towards the end. Get to know your local suppliers – those who are fairly dependable and selling good-quality goods – and stay clear of those scallywags who endeavour to lure you into their 'caves' with tempting signs showing 'special offer' this and 'special offer' that. A greengrocer with a small display of good quality (even if limited in selection) is a better bet than one having mountains of fruit and veg on show outside – more often than not backed up by tips of veg and fruit that have worked their way down from the outward polished array, and which might come into the shop days later for actual sale.

A butcher is much respected by me if he has a cold room (*not* freezer) where he hangs his meat to mature, but so often these days I am told by butchers that their clients like bright red, blood-running meat. Beware of that, and get clearly in your mind that dried, shrivelled-up outside pieces of legs of lamb or sirloins are a sign of maturity. OK, they often cost more as they have shrunk and taken up valuable storage space for many days, but when cooked, you will soon know the difference.

My Nan, in days when fridges were more likely to be at the morgue than in everyday household use, had a rickety wooden cupboard lined with wire gauze underneath the cold slab in the larder. On both shelves were old, large, cracked and slightly chipped meat-serving dishes, on which she would store the cuts of meat (bought as late as possible on Saturday from the local market where traders – in just as desperate straits as my Nan – started to knock off the odd penny per pound in order to avoid having to take stuff back home). I clearly remember her covering the exposed ends of beef with dripping from the enamel basin, and pork was rubbed with

olive oil. I must admit that occasionally in the summer bluebottles might hum around the rickety cupboard, but I never had tough or tasteless meat in her house.

You might be asking how, if she was so poor, she could buy joints of meat when so many people in the early thirties had stewing meat once a week and that was their lot. Well, she used to cook in every spare moment she had from her cleaning, washing and ironing jobs, and many of my Grandad's mates used to have their lunch bait supplied by Leah. I'm sure that by the time she had prepared the food, put it into blue enamel containers inside a large square wicker basket, and had walked to the shipyard to be there for 12 noon when the buzzer blew, and returned home to her many chores, she was barely in pocket. Money, I know only too well, she did not make in those days, but her hard efforts meant she paid her way and her family lived well.

Nowadays we have it so much easier in so many ways, and whilst we would never wish to return to those harsh days of the depression, I think most people are the poorer for not spotting a bargain when shopping for food, or not having the ability – through necessity – to buy really well. There is hardly a way of cooking or serving belly pork, for instance, that I don't know, and I still get a kick out of pinching a large bit when it comes out of the oven after being cooked for pâté or terrines. And roast belly pork with mushy marrowfat dried peas is still high on my personal list of feasts.

But this side-steps the point of how important buying is. In the section on Main Courses in Act Two, I tell you what to look for when buying meat.

Fish is another tricky item to buy really fresh. Here you *don't* want it well hung! But suppliers have a tendency to ship fish from the docks so abundantly surrounded by ice that the flesh will never rise to the occasion. A fishmonger with a display on a Monday is immediately suspect to me.

THE SET

I feel the set for any performance is almost as important as the performance itself. If a theatre curtain goes up on a magnificent set which takes the breath away, the battle is half-won already. So it is in the dining-room too: a clever combination of lighting, atmosphere, visuals, music, can create an ambiance of pleasure before the food makes its appearance.

Nothing need be lavish, or beyond the capabilities of your purse or home, but the *right* combination, carefully directed, can be especially effective.

I usually lay the table the day before – even to putting the glasses on the table upside down (then one of the last and easiest jobs is to get a dish of boiling water and hold each glass over it in turn and polish with a soft cotton cloth). Obviously this advance preparation is not always possible for a family dining-room, but it does save energy and a last-minute rush.

Flowers add so much to a stage setting, and they need not be costly shop-bought varieties. At most times of the year, some sort of wild or garden flower is available, and it can always be presented attractively, even if not strictly professionally, with masses of green foliage, especially ferns. Simple and unobtrusive is the keynote, though, and do watch the fragrance. I once went to a dinner party where the table was a mass of lilac, freshly picked roses, and sweet peas. A feast for the eye, but not for the nostrils and palate!

Lighting has an important part to play too. It should be low enough to lend an intimate atmosphere, yet bright enough for the guests to easily see what is put in front of them. Candles are delightful, but can add to the heat of the room and, occasionally, leave lovely smoke rings on the ceiling. Nowadays dimmer switches can easily be incorporated into an existing circuit, and make it easy to get the desired effect. If the room has lots of windows, and it is still light at the start of the party, do keep an eye on the lighting during the course of the evening.

THE DRESS REHEARSAL

It is the basic prior organization that takes the strain out of the evening for the host and hostess. Get as much as possible done beforehand rather than leave everything to the last moment. All the Intermission menus throughout the book can be prepared, cooked and served with leisure and pleasure provided you *do* get yourself organized.

When the curtain goes up on my productions, I make certain the table is laid, the flowers are watered and fresh, and don't smell too strong; the lighting is as I want it, the tapes or records are ready for background music, and the room temperature is just right; the white wine is in the fridge, the red wine opened, the soup bowls warming, and the croûtons are ready in a small dish; the main course plates are warming, and servers are ready for the vegetables; desserts on the sideboard with plates nearby or, if an ice, with the serving dishes in or close to the fridge. The bread should be sliced and buttered and covered. Have the coffee ready to percolate, a jug of cream out of the fridge (there is nothing worse for coffee than a dollop of chilled cream), the tray set with coffee cups and sugar and any after-dinner mints etc you might be offering your guests. Then you will have a relatively easy, free-flowing party.

Your guests will invariably offer to help serve and clear the meal but if you have everything organized before their arrival there should be no need. Just before the start of dinner I fill a large jug with boiling water and detergent to pop the cutlery in as I clear, and have a basin to hand for scraping in any leftovers from the plates. Leave lots of space near the sink or dishwasher (the latter filled with detergent). If you don't do this, when you come to do the actual washing-up later on it is harder work.

Sometimes during the meal do remember to just go back into the lounge or sitting-room to collect any dirty glasses, empty the ashtrays, adjust the temperature of the room and double-check the lighting. Also have a quick look at the lavatory and cloakroom. A couple more hand towels may need to be put out, a quick flush of the loo, and a quick clean of the washbasin may be called for – and don't forget the toilet paper!

THE FINAL TOUCH

A lesson that was well and truly taught me once, ages ago, was that when you invite people for dinner do find some pretext to speak to them on the day.

'Do you have a copy of last month's so and so? When you come tonight would you mind if I borrowed it?'

'Do you have any fresh parsley in your garden going spare? I would love a few sprigs for tonight's party.'

'When you come tonight, could you possibly pick up such and such for me?'

At least they will turn up in the flesh. I once cooked for a family of four. When they were 15 minutes overdue, I became concerned. After 30 minutes my anxiety was turning to temper, and when they still hadn't appeared after 45 minutes my blood was boiling. A telephone call produced shrieks of horror as they were sitting at home, having had supper, and watching the telly!

Lastly, what to do if some of your guests are late? Start without them. I really do mean that. When a vegetable or a quiche is ready, it is ready. When it is time for the curtain to rise, rise it must.

This is the first (and probably last) time I have written a cookery book, and I have found it very difficult. Certain sections have simply flowed from my head to the typewriter; others have had to be worked on over and over again. Without the forebearance of my loyal band of permanent staff at Miller Howe, this never would have been achieved, as the book has been written during our busiest-ever season when we have played to full houses night after night. It is to them I dedicate this book, for the future of my profession is bright when I know they (and so many others in this country) will be spreading their own version of my Gospel soon! I wish them, and my readers, luck and happiness with their cooking.

OVERTURE AND BEGINNERS PLEASE

WINE
BEFORE THE SHOW
SNACKS

WINE

Wine is a fascinating subject I am only beginning to scratch the surface of, and the more I get to know, the more I realize just how much there is *still* to know, and how little I *do*!

In my opinion, *honesty* is the basic requirement. Wines are just as personal as food, so when tasting a wine, do seriously think about what effect it has on you before expressing an opinion. If you think a wine tastes of black boot polish, say so. I once tasted a white wine in Beaune itself that I thought reeked of garlic – to this day I am positive that close by that particular cluster of vines a farmer was growing a healthy crop of garlic – but nobody agreed with me! The correct words to describe wine are often elusive, but do try to ascertain what your immediate sensations are; liquorice, peppermint, blackcurrant, gooseberries, fennel and sour plum are all epithets which now feature in my wine vocabulary.

Don't be afraid of making a fool of yourself if asking, or asked, a question about wine, as if you are completely honest, your acquisition of knowledge will be much speedier and more reliable than if you repeat parrot-fashion the 'in' thing about particular wines. I always remember a particularly pleasant luncheon party when I was rude and rash enough to taste a wine before my host and hostess. One of my fellow guests – the most respected female wine writer in this country (dare I say hemisphere?) – quietly asked me to say what I felt about this new wine she had discovered. If the floor could have opened up at that moment, I wished it had! I played for time, imagining the silence becoming more obvious and oppressing, and then said what I truly thought. Fifty per cent was correct, twenty per cent not far off the mark, and thirty per cent utter rubbish. But I was given full marks for tackling the problem, and I learned in those few awkward moments that nobody was going to ridicule me.

There are, of course, lots of golden rules attached to wines and wine drinking – white wine with white meat and fish only; red wines with red meat; sweet wines with dessert – but all rules are made to be broken! For instance, I love a small glass of well-chilled sweet Sauternes on the very infrequent occasions I daringly order a portion of Foie Gras (see the eyebrows of the sommeliers in restaurants going up to the ceiling at such a peasant request), and I also like a chilled Beaujolais with a piece of baked cod, and a glass of chilled Alsace wine is lovely with a plate of fatty cold lamb!

How contrary all this must sound. But what I am trying to say is, serve what wine *you* like with what *you* think it matches. And do think carefully about it. I have known Pamela Vandyke Price to spend hours, no, days, selecting wines for a particularly lavish banquet I was doing, and although on paper there was one I found hard to accept, on the evening in question the food was completely enhanced by what turned out to be perfect wines for the occasion.

That was true professionalism, I think – wise men (or women) never rush in.

Never buy the special offers that sometimes fall in through the letter box with credit card bills, and beware of the ever-popular and highly advertised wines. To me they are poor value, as I am constantly aware of how much has been spent by the maker on promotion rather than on production. Learn to follow and know the style and taste of a particular wine writer in one of the numerous magazines or newspapers with features on wine, and when he or she recommends a case lot, have confidence in that judgement and put pen to cheque! Also seek out your own wines (supermarkets often have interesting selections on their shelves), but one point I should like to stress is that I personally always steer clear of any foreign-produced wine which is bottled in this country. I think it never tastes the same, but I'm sure that is not a hard and fast rule for everyone to follow.

Wine need not be expensive either, and higher cost certainly does not mean higher quality! In fact, the reverse is often the case. Over the years I have experienced great delight in asking wine merchants to send me mixed cases of wines (for which I pay), and these are drunk at leisure and studied. Most are dismissed, but when you do come across one that seems to make your day – it's inexpensive and you *like* it – buy a case of it.

One old wives' tale I do believe is that you should never mix the grape and the grain, so I always serve wine as a pre-dinner drink (it's so much simpler to serve the same to everybody and it sets the pattern for the evening).

In the summer, any sparkling white wine or particularly a sparkling white Burgundy, is delicious alone (to many people they're reminiscent of champagne, and therefore start the evening off on the right foot!), but in the summer I like to make up a drink called Kir – the favourite tipple of one Canon Kir who was a Resistance worker during the Second World War and also Mayor of Dijon. You should mix one part of Crème de Cassis (Ribena is no substitute) to seven parts sparkling white Burgundy – but I, despite my sweet tooth, am very sparing with my use of Crème de Cassis. Usually I pour out a generous sherry glass of wine and fill the bottle up again with Crème de Cassis. This way, everybody gets the same mixing and you aren't messing about with two bottles when serving. Cork the bottle, top and tail it once or twice, and return it to chill.

In November I often serve the gimmicky (but occasionally good) Beaujolais Nouveau well chilled as an aperitif, or a full-bodied Alsace, but my favourite is a dry white Burgundy or a glass of the ever-popular Muscadet. This wine – produced around Nantes at the mouth of the Loire – is lovely and light, and very pleasant as a pre-dinner drink.

The pâtés in the book – if served as a first course – are particularly delicious accompanied by a glass of well-chilled *dry* Madeira (sometimes difficult to find but well worth the trouble).

I will never ever forget my first introduction to Sancerre – a *marvellous* wine. I was told it tasted like freshly-picked gooseberries, which I found rather odd. But as soon as I sniffed it and tasted it, I fully realized what my hostess meant. Although I have drunk every vintage since, never have I recaptured the glorious memory of that initial introduction.

South African wines are excellent value for money and have a distinct flavour which grows on you. Some of the Californian wines compare very favourably to the classical French wines. But both these types of wine are, for me, better for being drunk in their own homeland! When travelling, I think you must always – but always – drink the wine of the country you are in. I have sipped, with pleasure, Russian, Chinese, Mauritian, Rhodesian, Canadian and Moroccan wines, and provided you *never* attempt to compare them to your own favourite wine, you will find them interesting. Let *them* tell *you* with their own bouquet and flavour, what they are offering. Some I like very much, and others I dislike with as much intensity. But once again, if you are honest with yourself over your selection and serving of wine, your guests will be impressed with this approach.

Of course, your wine depends on your food! Wild horses wouldn't make me serve anything with a Curried Apple Soup (mind you, I *might* be tempted to serve a small glass of Scrumpy!) and Gewürztraminer would murder beef. I think there is, however, quite a lot to be said for the basic saying, 'Red for red meats and white for white'. I still cannot accept salmon poached in red wine and served with a chilled young red Beaujolais, which many people say is excellent.

There is a lot of nonsense spoken about opening a bottle to let it breathe, and there are horrifying contradictions in the length of time it should do so before being served. I wish someone would clearly tell me why this should be done, as the amount of wine surface actually exposed to the air is so minute considering the volume of booze in the bottle. I also think there is a modern tendency to serve white wines too chilled, so that all you seem to get is shivers in the sensitive areas of your mouth. I do think, though, that most wines are better after being poured into a glass for several minutes. I find it disturbing at the Chevalier du Tastevin Banquets held at the Clos Vougeot in Burgundy to see the French swigging the red Burgundies immediately they are served, while the British cherish the beautiful glasses in their palms, lovingly trying to bring on the bouquet with a little heat. For me, good wines reach a peak in their actual drinking time just as food does in the cooking time.

When I give a dinner party, I try to have one wine that will make people sit up and take notice, and surround that by less unusual wines which go well with the dishes. And if you serve a cherished wine to guests who are indifferent, for goodness sake never repeat the mistake. There are some people's company I like but whose palate I abhor, so I entertain accordingly. Also, never serve an expensive wine with ceremony bordering on religious awe, thereby making your guests feel they should drool over their glasses and not their plates! It is much more dramatic to answer a question with a quiet and calm, 'I'm lucky enough to have got hold of a '64 Chambertin which I'm sure you'll recognize', than to preach a sermon!

On my dinner table there is always a bottle of chilled Malvern water and one of sparkling water, and sensible guests will use this for quenching thirsts, and thus savour the wines.

BEFORE THE SHOW SNACKS

I adore nuts in any shape or form, but I always have to hand a supply of baked spiced and baked curried nuts. Provided you store them in airtight containers, they will keep (if you have any left at the end of the evening) for several months, and are very good to serve instead of canapés with drinks, before a dinner party.

Baked Spiced Sweet Nuts

$\frac{1}{2}$ lb (225 g) castor sugar

$\frac{1}{2}$ teaspoon grated nutmeg

2 teaspoons powdered cinnamon

2 teaspoons powdered ginger

2 teaspoons powdered allspice

4 egg whites

1 lb (450 g) mixed raw nuts (cashew, pecan, almond, macadamia, pistachio etc, with skins removed)

Sieve the sugar with all the spices. Lightly beat the egg whites and put in a bowl. Using a strainer that fits into the bowl, dip the nuts, a few at a time, into the lightly beaten egg white and transfer them to a wire tray until you have done the remainder.

Coat liberally with the spiced sugar and then lay the nuts out on baking sheets which are also coated with the sugar. Bake at 200°F (100°C) Gas oven just lower than $\frac{1}{4}$, for $2\frac{1}{2}$ hours.

Baked Curried Nuts

To the above quantities of nutmeg, cinnamon, ginger and allspice add:

$\frac{1}{4}$ lb (125 g) fine ground oatmeal (use a blender to get it really fine)

$\frac{1}{4}$ lb (225 g) castor sugar

4 teaspoons Madras curry powder

4 egg whites

Dip the nuts in the lightly beaten egg whites as above, then coat the nuts with the sugar, oatmeal, spice and curry powder all mixed together. Bake as above.

ACT
ONE

ACT ONE

SCENE ONE
STARTERS

SCENE TWO
SOUPS

SCENE THREE
FISH

The bustle of excitement reaches a crescendo in any theatre as the warning bell begins to ring. The orchestra tunes up, the spotlights and footlights come on, the house lights dim, the overture plays and the curtain goes up. I find this moment personally very exhilarating as a new experience commences. I always hope by the end of the evening to have been entertained, to have learned something, to have laughed a little, and to have been made to think. It is the sheer glow of joy that invariably comes to me in the theatre that makes the evening as far as I am concerned. So it should be when cooking and entertaining.

When I was in repertory, I used to love to hear the gasps when the visual impact of the opening scene reached the audience. All these frustrating moments for the stage manager of borrowing this or wheedling that, begging furniture, or asking for the loan of pictures, seemed worthwhile when, occasionally, our efforts were rewarded by an immediate round of applause. This was always a marvellous start to the evening's performance.

The same applies when entertaining at home. As I have already said, the lights, flowers and your basic set are *all* terribly important to your entertaining, and when the guests are seated at the table, the impact of your starter sets the scene for the rest of the meal.

I always try to serve a cold starter that can be decorated with radish flowers, sprigs of watercress or orange or celery twirls. Brash and vulgar? Not at all. Clever entertaining, like clever conversation, needs encouragement to flow. A well-experienced host or hostess, however, could choose to play down the starter – which I occasionally do if I am serving a cold main course – and it is then fun to sit back and see how the evening progresses. So be aware of the impact you are about to create, and plan accordingly.

SCENE ONE
STARTERS

The most important starter recipes to me and my staff at Miller Howe are the 3 basic pâtés. They're easy to make and easy to serve in a variety of delicious ways.

Because of our set menus at the hotel, we make the pâtés up on the day they are to be eaten, but they can keep for up to 10 days in a good refrigerator. I have even frozen them for use at home in the winter, but they are never quite the same: the cheese tends to lose its smoothness, the mushroom its richness, and the liver its flavour.

PÂTÉS

The majority of the recipes in this section magnificently fulfil all the basic points I make about entertaining in the book: they can be prepared well in advance, and once the basic recipe is mastered, there are an infinite number of ways in which to use it – as you will see from the selection of recipes below, and thereafter throughout the other sections.

Miller Howe Cheese and Herb Pâté

5 oz (150 g) butter

1 lb (450 g) cream cheese

3 cloves garlic, freshly crushed with a little salt

1 tablespoon chopped chervil

1 tablespoon finely chopped parsley

1 tablespoon finely chopped chives

Melt the butter slowly in a saucepan. Mix the other ingredients together in a mixer bowl (or by hand), making sure that the herbs are evenly distributed.

When the melted butter has cooled, pour it gently into the cream cheese mixture. Fold it into the cheese gently (*do* take care, as the mixture could curdle), and transfer the pâté to a loaf tin, or leave it in the bowl, to cool and set.

There are numerous uses for Cheese and Herb Pâté. Here are a few delicious starters:

Cheese and Herb Pâté on Tomato and Orange Salad

Transfer the pâté to a bread tin to cool and set, and simply serve a slice of it, about $\frac{1}{4}$ in (5 mm) thick, on a well-dressed sliced Tomato and Orange Salad (see page 130). I prefer to make the salad in the morning (alternating tomato with orange on the dish) and sprinkle on a French dressing made with walnut oil, then lots of very finely chopped onion and parsley. A spiced bread cob served with this turns it into a substantial starter, or a snack meal.

Cheese and Herb Pâté in Puff Pastry Cornet with Hot Burgundy and Cranberry Sauce

For 4

4 puff pastry cornets (see page 36)

about 3–4 oz (75–100 g) Cheese and Herb Pâté

2 walnuts, halved

8 oz (225 g) frozen cranberries

$\frac{1}{2}$ pint (300 ml) red wine

rind and juice of 1 orange

1 tablespoon sugar

arrowroot to thicken

Cook the puff pastry cornets well. Just before serving, fill them with the pâté, garnishing the tops with half a walnut.

For the sauce, scatter the frozen cranberries on a baking tray and leave to gently warm through, but *do not cook* them as they split and look unsightly. Reduce the wine in a pan with the finely grated orange rind, juice and sugar according to taste. Thicken with the arrowroot. Just prior to serving – and while the sauce is hot – fold in the cranberries.

You can garnish the cornets by putting the narrow end through a thin slice of cored fresh pineapple, and a sprig of watercress adds colour.

Another way of serving them is to put each cornet on a bed of fresh cherries (about 4 each portion) and chopped walnuts which have been marinated for 2 hours in the fresh juice of 1 lime and about 4 tablespoons walnut oil.

Cheese and Herb Pâté in Tomato

Small sweet English tomatoes stuffed with Cheese and Herb Pâté are delightful. Serve on a cucumber and yoghurt salad. Stuff the huge Continental tomatoes too, and serve them cut into slices.

Cheese and Herb Pâté with Walnut in Red Pepper

Cut both ends off the red peppers and clean out thoroughly. Dry, then stand on end and pipe the soft pâté in and then force walnut halves down the middle. Chill well, cut into sliced portions, arrange these on a plastic tray and cover with fresh chopped herb fennel, lime wedges, black olives and coat with aspic made with dry sherry (see page 211).

Cheese and Herb Pâté in Cucumber

Peel, cut in half and remove the seeds from a cucumber. Pipe in the cream cheese pâté using a 6-point star nozzle and garnish with stoned black olives and chopped walnuts. When actually serving the portions, slip circles of red pepper over the cucumber portions to add colour.

Miller Howe Mushroom Pâté

4 oz (125 g) butter

8 oz (225 g) minced onions

2 lb (1 kg) minced mushrooms

generous pinch of sea salt

freshly ground black pepper

2 pints (generous 1 litre) red wine

Melt the butter in a large saucepan over a gentle heat, then add the minced onions. Simmer for approximately 10 minutes, then add the mushrooms, salt and pepper and stir well. Add the red wine and leave to simmer over a low heat for 2 to 3 hours, stirring occasionally. The idea is to let the liquid evaporate until the mixture is fairly dry. When cold, it can easily be stored in a suitable plastic container in the fridge or freezer.

This pâté, which is delicious to eat by itself, can be used in many different ways. You'll find variations popping up all over the place, but here are a few to start with:

Mushrooms in Marsala Sauce Pastry Tartlets

tartlets (see page 42)

1 lb (450 g) Mushroom Pâté

$\frac{1}{2}$ pint (300 ml) double cream

pinch of sea salt

$\frac{1}{4}$ pint (150 ml) Marsala wine, reduced

freshly chopped parsley to garnish

The given quantity of Mushroom Pâté (see above) will fill generously about 8 × 3-in (7.5-cm) tartlets (1 per portion as a starter), or 30 smaller individual tartlets for cocktails.

Make savoury tartlets and bake off blind. (I normally do this at 325°F (170°C), Gas 3, for up to 45 minutes and then leave in the oven with the heat turned off for a further 30 minutes. This makes a dry crisp pastry.) For the sauce, reduce the double cream by half – watching carefully as it has a tendency to boil over on the lowest of heats – having added the pinch of sea salt. This extremely rich creamy mixture is then mixed into the Mushroom Pâté. Reduce the Marsala to a tablespoon's worth, practically an essence, and stir into the creamy Mushroom Pâté.

When serving, lightly warm the pastry cases through and add the rich mixture just before serving so that the pastry remains lovely and crisp. Garnish liberally with freshly chopped parsley.

Miller Howe Marsala Mushroom Puff Pastry Cornets

The above mushroom, cream and Marsala filling can also be served in puff pastry cornets (see page 36), and for a contrasting sauce, I use a good reduction of onions, freshly crushed garlic, tomatoes and a little tarragon (see page 211). Once again, the cornets should be filled at the last moment.

Tomato Stuffed with Mushroom Pâté

As with Cheese and Herb Pâté, stuff small, sweet, locally-grown tomatoes with Mushroom Pâté and serve cold on a salad made with sliced orange and cucumber and coated with yoghurt. I have also used the enormous North African tomatoes during the limited period they are available, and served them stuffed with the pâté and cut in thick slices. Accompany with thin buttered slices of wholemeal bread (see page 185).

Deep Fried Cob with Mushroom Pâté

A cunning way to use up stale dinner cob rolls is to hollow them out from the bottom removing as much dough as possible and so ending up with a cup-like object. This can be deep fried if you have the luxury of a deep fryer or simply dipped in melted butter and then baked in the oven on a baking tray at 350°F (180°C), Gas 4, for about 30 minutes. Leave to drain on kitchen paper and then fill with at least 3 oz (75 g) Mushroom Pâté per cob. Serve hot or cold.

You can also stuff the deep fried cob with Cheese and Herb Pâté or any of the liver pâtés in the next few pages.

Miller Howe Duck Liver Pâté

¾ lb (300 g) belly pork

1 medium-size onion

4 oz (100 g) butter

1 lb (450 g) duck livers

¼ pint (150 ml) Marsala wine

2 cloves finely crushed garlic

fresh marjoram to taste

freshly ground black pepper and salt

Put the belly pork in a roasting tray and cook at 425°F (220°C), Gas 7, for 1 hour then take off bone, remove skin and cut up into small pieces. Sauté the finely chopped onion in the butter and then add all the other ingredients and simmer until cooked and slightly reduced. This takes about 2 hours. When both the belly pork and the liver mixture are cool, liquidize together and pass through a sieve. Adjust the seasoning, pack into a terrine or dish, and chill.

Miller Howe Duck Liver Pâté with Marsala Aspic

Using a 6-point star nozzle, pipe the pâté on to a plastic tray into shapes resembling those old-fashioned nut twirls, garnish with a thin slice of stuffed olive and small sprigs of parsley, and then coat with Marsala aspic (see page 211) just as it is setting. The best way to do this, is to pour about a dessertspoon of the aspic over each twirl and then put them back into the fridge. Keep the aspic at the soft runny stage and cover the twirl 2 or 3 times more. If you try to cover it all at once you end up with a very thin coating of aspic on the actual pâté and a thick layer on the base of the tray. Serve with Tomato and Orange Salad (see page 130).

Miller Howe Duck Liver Pâté in Red Pepper

Stuff a pepper in exactly the same way as described on page 30; but you can soak some dried morilles in brandy overnight, clean them thoroughly, and stuff them down the middle (or, if you are very extravagant, truffles).

Miller Howe Duck Liver Pâté in Pastry Tartlet or Puff Pastry Cornet
Make up the tartlets or cornets as described in the relevant pages (42 and 36), and then stuff them at the last minute with 3–4 oz (75–125 g) pâté.

Miller Howe Chicken Liver Pâté

Make Chicken Liver Pâté in exactly the same way as the above Duck Liver, but use $\frac{1}{4}$ pint (150 ml) brandy instead of Marsala.

Miller Howe Pâté Terrine

Terrines are comparatively simple to make, economical, tasty and an ideal dish to start off a dinner party. They can be made the day before, sliced and served at the last minute, invariably impress guests, and are quite filling!

Don't rush out and buy an expensive steel terrine dish if you haven't one, as 1 or 2 one-pound (450 g) bread tins will do to start off with. If you do use the professional terrine moulds with lids, all you do when cooking is put the lid on and bake the terrine for the time stated in the recipe. However, if you are improvising with bread tins, I usually wrap each tin with 3 layers of aluminium foil, measuring the foil out first and putting the 3 sheets on top of one another. Place the tin in the middle and draw up the sides and edges to the top, which makes for easier testing when the terrine is cooked.

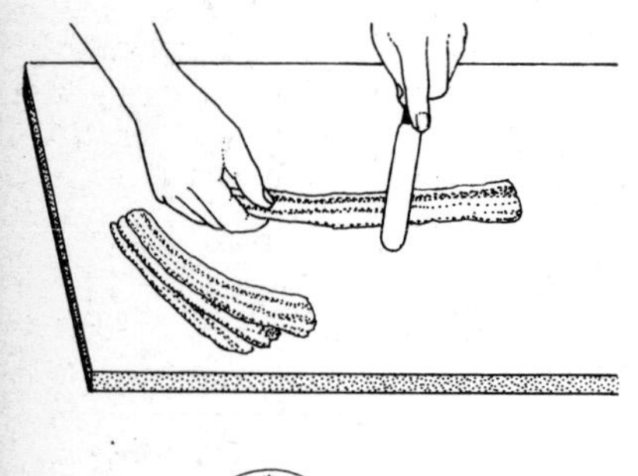

Terrines need not necessarily be lined with bacon (the most common lining). You can also use cooked pancakes, and I once even used quadruple layers of blanched spinach (very time-consuming and not always worth the effort). But do use good quality and flavour bacon, as your terrine will be more tasty. I use the best smoked middle cut.

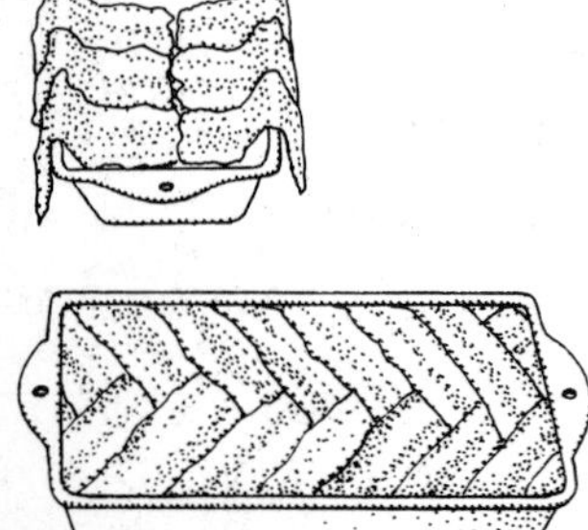

Lay slices on a work board and, using a small knife, stretch and flatten them individually. Place your container with the narrow end in front of you, divide the inside lengthwise in two, and start placing your bacon pieces along half of the bottom and up the side of the wall, the balance coming over the edge of the tin. Do this down both sides and then finish off the top and bottom ends similarly. Now put in the filling. When the tin or dish is full, start at the top left and flip the end flap of bacon over (slightly at an angle) and immediately do the flap opposite it likewise. You eventually finish up at the end nearest you with a tin that looks like a laced-up shoe. The top and bottom bits are then just pulled over and across, and the dish is ready for the oven.

Place the tin or tins on a baking tray and cover with a further baking tray on which you have placed a couple of 1-lb (450-g) or 2-lb

Triple pâté mille feuille with celery and spring onion twirls.

A savoury swan filled with cheese and herb pâté

(1-kg) weights. Bake for the stated time in a bain marie (a roasting tray, filled with hot water which comes half-way up the sides of the terrines). The water should not be too near the top as you don't want it either to boil up into the terrine or, worse still, to slop into the terrine when you take the cooked dish out of the oven.

Line the terrine with de-rinded slices of good smoked bacon, then alternate layers (each $\frac{1}{3}$ thickness of the terrine) of the 3 pâtés interleaved with stoned olives, shelled pistachio nuts (chopped bacon is also nice if pre-cooked well, then sprinkled onto the Cheese and Herb Pâté; cooked prunes are quite delicious with the Duck Liver Pâté).

Bake in a bain marie (the roasting tin again) at 350°F (180°C), Gas 4, for about $1\frac{1}{2}$ hours. Leave to cool with weights on top. Turn out and slice when cool.

SAVOURY CREAMS

Thinking of a name to give these dishes was quite difficult as the end result is like a soufflé but not as light, it's as tasty as a mousse, and it's served piping hot like quenelle, but it isn't quite as airy! So I settled for Savoury Creams.

These can be made for a dinner party provided your guests sit down when you ask them to, and don't linger over extra drinks (such people should be immediately struck off your guest list). You need to have a liquidizer or – better still – a Magimix (I've prepared hot creams with an electric hand whisk, but didn't get quite the same result, although they were edible!)

Before you go on to read the basic recipe don't be horrified to see that you need one pint, yes, one whole pint, of double cream, Bear in mind, you will get up to 16 × 3-in (7.5-cm) starter or fish portions from the recipe or 8 more-than-adequate main course portions (serving 2 per person). If you are very budget-conscious, work out now what the dish is going to cost and whatever answer you come to, do try it once. You will do it a second and third time, I know.

Savoury Fish Creams

1 lb (450 g) fish (lemon sole is the best)

$\frac{1}{2}$ teaspoon salt

pinch of ground nutmeg

4 eggs, lightly beaten

1 pint (600 ml) double cream

Cut the fish into approximately 2-in (5-cm) square portions, place in the liquidizer or Magimix with the seasonings and whizz round until the mixture is smooth, and then stir in the lightly beaten eggs. Turn the mixture out into a bowl and chill well for at least 6 hours. After this resting period the mixture will look rather gelatinous. Put back into the Magimix or liquidizer and whisk in the cream.

Butter the ramekin (or dariole) moulds very generously and season them well with freshly ground black pepper and some salt. Preheat the oven to 375°F (190°C), Gas 5, and check that it is actually registering this temperature! Put the cream mixture into a piping bag and pipe with a 6-point star nozzle to about two-thirds of the way up the ramekin or container. Put into a bain marie, with about 1 in (2.5 cm) of very hot water in the base, and place in the oven. Cook for 30 minutes.

To turn the creams out you require a pair of rubber gloves and a small sharp knife. Run the knife round the edge of the cream, turn out into the palm of one hand and then transfer onto a warmed plate. They need not necessarily be turned out, of course, and if piped into nice ramekins they can come to the table straight from the oven. Serve on a ferned and doyleyed plate.

Hollandaise Sauce (see page 207) goes well with every single savoury cream and there are, of course, numerous flavourings that can ring the changes – in particular, chopped watercress and chopped fennel herb.

Savoury Meat Creams

See Savoury Fish Creams for the basic method.

Meat for Savoury Creams, whether chicken, veal or fillet of pork, is all the better for being marinated for at least 24 hours in natural yoghurt. Roughly dice the meat, coat it liberally with yoghurt, and leave in the fridge, turning from time to time. When you want to use the meat, take it out of the yoghurt, but don't bother to drain or wipe off the small amount still clinging to the meat.

Thereafter, the preparation and cooking is exactly the same as for Savoury Fish Creams.

Serve with plain or flavoured Hollandaise (see page 207). Calvados apple (page 211) or chopped tarragon mixed with the Hollandaise are nice with chicken savoury creams; tomatoes or walnuts are good flavours for pork, and pear brandy in the Hollandaise is magnificent with veal.

MY NAN'S ROUGH PUFF PASTRY

This is a rough puff pastry that does away with the endless resting in between turns. It can be made up in about 10 minutes (a 1-lb (450-g) mixing produces 60 small mince pies at Christmas), and it can be done in a kitchen at any temperature. The only process you will develop skill in is the use of the rolling pin, but I am quite confident that even on your first attempt you will be onto a winner.

I normally prepare two separate 1-lb (450-g) mixings as I find the short rest one mixing has while I work on the other gives a slightly better edge to the end result. So I suggest you double up the following basic recipe, and use two separate bowls.

1 lb (450 g) *strong* plain flour

generous pinch of salt

$\frac{1}{2}$ lb (225 g) *soft* margarine

$\frac{1}{2}$ lb (225 g) *soft* American lard, or shortening

1 tablespoon lemon juice made up to $\frac{1}{2}$ pint (300 ml) with very cold water

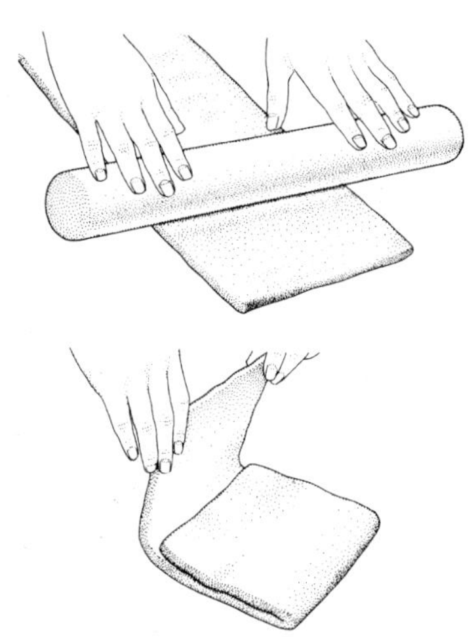

Having sieved the two lots of strong plain flour into the two bowls, you break up the fats into $\frac{1}{2}$-oz (15-g) pieces and dot them about over the flour. Shake the bowls separately in order to coat the pieces of fat with flour, and then gently make a well in the centre of each. Into this you pour the very cold water and lemon juice. Using a palette knife, mix together your two basic doughs. They certainly don't look very attractive at this stage, and look uneven with pockets of flour and glaring areas of pure fat showing through. But don't worry.

Lightly flour a large rolling area and turn out the first dough mixing taking care to scrape out *all* the ingredients, however untidy this may look. Shape this basic dough gently into the shape of a house brick with the short end of the brick nearest you and the long sides running down from your left to your right side.

Now you must take care. Hold the rolling pin at each end – never in the middle – and treat it with delicacy. If you attack the dough like a steam roller pounding over asphalt, the end result will be similar. Just tap the merest outline of the rolling pin in the middle, top and bottom of the 'brick' and then, starting at the impression immediately in front of you, just lightly – oh so lightly – give the rolling pin a good gentle push and remove your hands. (Imagine you are helping to start off a large snowball from the top of a hill.)

Never bring the rolling pin back towards you with any pressure. *Always* make sharp, soft movements away from you, slowly but surely stretching the pastry out into a shape roughly measuring 16 × 5 in (40 × 12 cm). Picture this long rectangle in three equal parts and fold the piece facing you up and over the middle third and bring the top third down on top of these two thirds.

You want this pastry to be as light as possible, so trap the air at this stage by gently tapping down on the three open layers at the short ends at your left and right. Give this piece of dough a *quarter* turn – imagine your dough is the hour hand pointing to 6 o'clock, and turn it to 9 o'clock. Put it to one side.

Now repeat the process with the second mixing of dough.

At the end of this first rolling the dough will have a slightly smoother consistency and will be easier to handle. Repeat this process three more times, flouring your work area well between each rolling so the dough does not stick. You may find when you turn the bottom third of dough up over the middle third there is a surplus of flour. I find a household 6-in (15-cm) paintbrush useful here to brush the surplus flour away.

With each rolling, the texture becomes smoother and smoother. On the fourth and last rolling, the dough is even slightly resistant, so *don't* force it in any way. Sometimes it just will not roll to the above measurements so, whatever you do, don't force it to this size at the expense of knocking the air out!

Pop the two doughs into separate polythene bags and leave to chill.

Rolling and Baking Rough Puff Pastry
When you take the rough puff pastry out of the freezer or fridge, make certain it comes back to a workable consistency before you start rolling it (out of a normal fridge, this should take 20 to 30 minutes, longer from a freezer).

You need a clean flat surface and a large rolling pin. Flour both of these well and roll the pastry out to about $\frac{1}{8}$ in (3 mm) thickness. Cut out your shapes – squares or rounds – place them on slightly dampened metal trays, and put back in the fridge to chill. When you wish to cook them, remove them from the fridge and put a piece of well-buttered greaseproof paper on top (greased side down on to the prepared pastry). Prick through the paper and pastry with a sharp pointed knife (about 6 pricks to a $3\frac{1}{2}$-in (9-cm) vol au vent) and put immediately into a hot oven at 450°F (230°C), Gas 8. Unless I know the exact size of pastry you are cooking, it is impossible to tell you how long it will take to cook, but after about 12 minutes have a look and see how it is getting on. It is better to slightly overcook puff pastry and get it really brown and crisp, than undercook it.

The secret of success in serving puff pastry is how little you actually put on the serving plate and how much you throw away. When the pastry is absolutely cooked, split it in two and if there are any layers of slightly greasy pastry, gently tear them off and discard. You will then be left with ethereal puff pastry.

Vol au Vents

I never make traditional vol au vents, but cut out fluted rounds and when cooked slice them across the middle. One circle is used as a base, the filling put on top of this *at the very last minute* (so many people combine the puff pastry and filling early on in the day, warm them through before serving, and wonder why the pastry has gone soggy!), and top off with the top of the pastry round. I then usually lightly paint the top with melted butter to add the finishing touch!

Stuff vol au vents with any of the pâtés at the beginning of the book, with Smoked Haddock in Cheese Sauce (see page 77), with kidneys cooked off as in the Victorian Breakfast (see page 182), or with Buttered Eggs, or a little smoked salmon.

Puff Pastry Cornets

These are so simple to prepare and, besides looking good, they are delicious to eat. The first requisite, naturally, is some actual cornet moulds which are available from most kitchen shops, but do beware of how you initially use them. With new cornet tin moulds first of all wipe them liberally with lard all over and then place them on a *cooling* tray and literally cook off at 450°F (230°C), Gas 8, for about 30 minutes. If you put them on to an ordinary baking tray you will find that the strip on which they actually rest is not

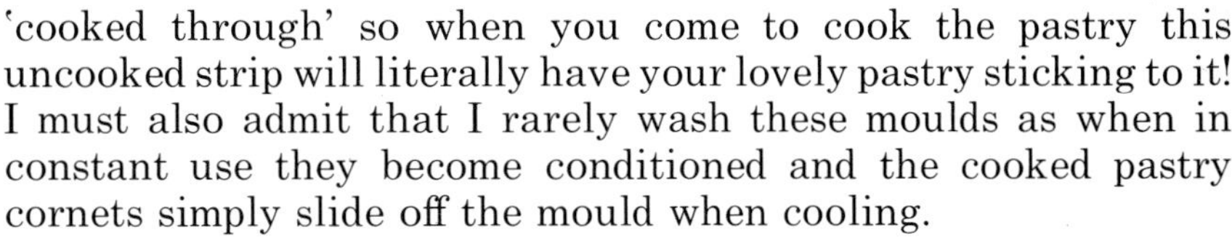

'cooked through' so when you come to cook the pastry this uncooked strip will literally have your lovely pastry sticking to it! I must also admit that I rarely wash these moulds as when in constant use they become conditioned and the cooked pastry cornets simply slide off the mould when cooling.

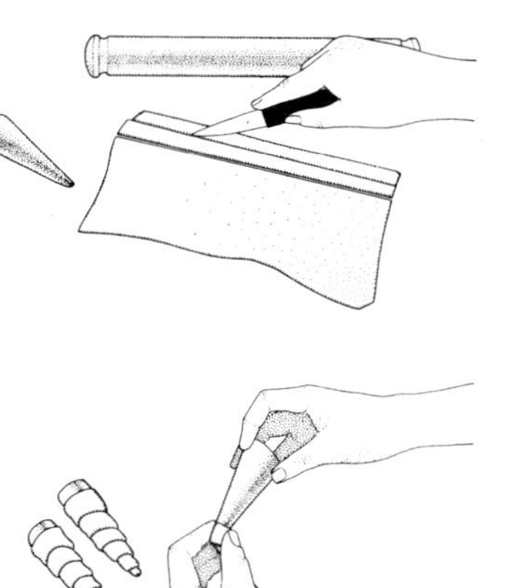

The puff pastry should be rolled out about $\frac{1}{8}$ in (3 mm) thick, and about 10 in (25.5 cm) in overall length, glazed with lightly beaten egg and water (equal quantities in a cup, bearing in mind an egg weighs approximately 2 oz or 50 g), and then using a sharp pointed knife cut into strips about $\frac{1}{2}$ in (1 cm) thick. Take the mould in your right hand, starting at the pointed end, use a little pressure at first to see the top end of the cut strip is firmly fixed in place and then slowly wind the mould round taking up the drooping length of pastry, naturally winding your way along the actual mould. Put in the fridge or freezer to chill and then when the oven is preheated to 450°F (230°C), Gas 8, and the cornets are well chilled, prick all over the pastry with the point of a sharp knife, glaze with egg and water and bake in the oven.

The length of cooking time will vary, depending solely on the way you have rolled them – with practice you will be able to make larger moulds as you will develop the knack of just lightly overlapping each twirl! Look at the pastry after 15 minutes and do remember that when you are satisfied with their colour (never take them too far if you are going to eventually serve them warm as they will then need a few more minutes to warm through), remove from the oven. When they have cooled (do not be impatient and attempt to remove from the moulds at once or you will crack them!), take off the moulds and place the cornets on a cooling rack.

Fill puff pastry cornets with any of the 3 basic pâtés (see pages 29–32). Serve cornets with Duck Liver Pâté or Cheese and Herb Pâté cold, but the Mushroom should preferably be warm. Do remember that with all puff pastry the actual filling is put in at the very last moment. In other words warm the cases separately from the filling and bring together at the last minute.

Milles Feuilles

I make milles feuilles from the basic puff pastry recipe, and cut them into $3\frac{1}{2}$-in (9-cm) rounds for starters and 2-in (5-cm) rounds for cocktails (much easier than attempting to slice neatly through a huge piece of puff pastry). Any filling can be used for milles feuilles – any leftover mince from a spaghetti sauce is good, as is any leftover cold Savoury Cream (see page 33). But for a very rich, superb starter to any meal the following takes a lot of beating.

Miller Howe Triple Pâté Milles Feuilles

The milles feuilles should be as crisp as possible. Slice the $3\frac{1}{2}$-in (9-cm) rounds through the middle and discard any soft pastry.

To bring the dish together, lay the first layer of cooked and cooled puff pastry on a pastry board and spoon on the Mushroom Pâté.

Then put the second layer of pastry on and pipe the Cheese and Herb Pâté on, smoothing it gently with a heated palette knife. Repeat with a third layer of pastry and with Duck Liver Pâté. Top off with puff pastry.

Decorate each portion with a twirl of cream cheese garnished with parsley and half a stuffed olive. Before transferring to the actual serving plate, place a blob of Cheese and Herb Pâté on the base of the plate to hold the pastry castle in place (you don't want it to topple!).

QUICHES AND SAVOURY TARTLETS

When you serve a quiche, you are applauded by gasps of delight from your guests and immediately rise in their estimation. But why, I wonder? Quiches are so easy to make and never go wrong provided you follow these basic steps.

When you serve a quiche, it should be on the way to cooling – the rich custard setting firm, the filling at the correct temperature for the flavour to blossom, and the pastry crispening. It is, in fact, the basic pastry recipe that makes or breaks your quiche but the following recipe for Savoury Pastry is so easy, particularly for those who tend to be heavy-handed, since there is no actual rubbing-in of fat to be done. Incidentally, I have tasted a similar recipe produced by a Magimix machine in one fell swoop – but the texture just isn't the same.

The Savoury Pastry

1 lb (450 g) plain flour

a pinch of salt

2 tablespoons icing sugar

10 oz (275 g) softened butter

2 eggs (at room temperature)

To make three 10-in (25-cm) quiches, or 16 individual 3-in (7.5-cm) quiches.

The only utensils required are a flat, clean mixing board, a palette knife and a polythene bag in which to store the end product.

Sieve the flour with the salt and icing sugar onto the board and make a well in the centre leaving the actual work surface exposed. Into this well put the butter – which should be soft enough to hold a deep thumb print. It is hopeless to try and make any pastry with butter straight from the fridge; not only would it take an age to soften but you would have such a job getting the egg worked into the butter that the sheer exhaustion would put you off making pastry for ever!

Break the eggs onto the butter and then, using the tips of your fingers, pat the egg into the butter. Personally, I think it is important to keep your fingertips at a 90° angle to the butter so that you are patting the eggs into the butter like a woodpecker attacking a tree; if you hold them at 45° (which so many people want to do) you *press* the eggs into the butter and get a heavier result. At this stage, you are aiming for a mixture resembling the fluffiest and lightest scrambled egg and it does not matter if you accidentally incorporate the odd bit of flour into the mixture. Tap, tap, tap away for about 8 minutes and you should be there – providing the butter was soft at first.

When you are satisfied that you have obtained the correct result, hold a large palette knife at right angles to the board and scoop the flour up from left to right, right to left, top to bottom, bottom to top, literally parcelling it over the butter mixture. Then swiftly cut through the mixture, always hitting the board with your palette knife at an angle of 90°. Remember that in the middle of your board you still have the wet, gooey egg-and-butter mixture, so, from time to time, scrape your knife along the board and turn the mixture over so that it all blends in. This sounds relatively simple but until you get used to it, it is a rather tiring task and your hand may ache a little – but persevere.

You will slowly see the mixture begin to form larger and larger crumbs. If your kitchen is warm, this will not take too long but, if it is cold, you could be at it for 20 minutes or more. For this pastry, the old wives' tale of cold hands, cold slab, cold heart etc. at this stage is a fallacy. The palette part of making this pastry is over when you begin to get a texture resembling a shortbread mixture. Now is the time to stop and divide the mixture into three equal parts. With the palms of your hands bring together each section to resemble a ball but do not, as so many cooks do, squeeze the pastry into perfect round balls. You have taken so much trouble and time getting as much air as possible into the pastry that it is madness to squeeze the very breath out of it in the final few seconds. Put the balls into a polythene bag, tie up and leave to chill overnight. It can be frozen without any ill effects.

Preparing the Case

When you want to make a quiche, remove the pastry from the fridge or freezer and, remembering its texture prior to chilling, wait until it comes back to this stage before you attempt to roll it. So many people are impatient and get annoyed when the pastry crumbles and cracks. It should really be like a large, soft ball of plasticine and, like this, it is easy to roll and coax into shape.

I favour loose-bottomed flan tins with simple fluted sides so that when the quiche eventually comes to the table it looks pretty and is simple to cut. Those smart porcelain dishes with recipes printed on their bases are not very good for cooking in and, in any case, when you put the pastry dough in, you can't see the filling recipe any more. And the poor guest who gets the first portion usually gets an unsightly heap of churned pastry and filling because it's so difficult to get a portion out! So, using a loose-bottomed tin, place the base on the work surface and flour lightly round the outside edge (do not flour the base itself). Place the ball of pastry in the centre of the base, then gently, oh so gently, press it down to start it on its way to flattening out. Holding a rolling pin at both ends, lightly work from the centre of the dough, easing the pastry towards the edge and then out over the base onto the floured board. Remember that the pastry you roll over the edge of the base is eventually going to form the walls of your flan so don't go too far with this. With a palette knife, carefully fold the outside rim back over the pastry, put the base into its ring and, using your thumbs, ease the turned-over pastry up the walls of the flan tin to form the sides of the flan. Lop off the excess and patch up any defects. I roll out little snakes from the surplus pastry and run these round inside the edge of the base in order to strengthen the case. Any cracking generally occurs in the base area so reinforcement at this stage helps to avoid this problem. Leave the case to chill – or even freeze – at this stage.

Baking the Case

When you want to cook the flan 'blind' set the oven at 325°F (170°C), Gas 3. Line the pastry inside the flan ring with kitchen foil, then add dried beans and bake the flan for 35 minutes. Turn off the oven, take out the foil and beans and leave the flan in for a further 15 minutes. It is rather important that the rim of the flan is covered with the foil for the blind baking, since the flan is to be baked again for a further 35 minutes with the filling in and if you haven't made sure that the rim is well covered at this stage, you will end up with a delightful quiche but a blackened rim! Remember, all this can be done prior to a dinner party and, since most of the fillings can be prepared in the morning too, I am sure you will agree that your performance will be better for a quiche on the playbill!

The Custard

2 eggs

1 egg yolk

a pinch of salt

a turn of freshly ground black pepper

a pinch of grated nutmeg

$\frac{1}{2}$ pt (300 ml) double cream

This basic custard recipe was given to me by my dear friend, Margaret Costa.

For each 10-in (25-cm) flan you need the ingredients opposite.

Now don't raise your eyebrows and say, 'So much cream?'. Just realize that you are getting *eight* portions from this, and your guests will adore the end result. Husbands, wives, lovers, friends, partners and prospective partners will think you very clever and the meal will be off to a simply splendid start. And while it is actually cooking (all quiches take 35 minutes at 375°F (190°C), Gas 5), you can happily relax with your guests, and not miss out on the pre-dinner drinks.

The Fillings

If you want your end product to look better and have the filling appear actually through the middle of the custard (as opposed to lying on the bottom), barely coat the bottom of the cooked flan with a layer of custard, bake that off for a few minutes, then put in your filling and add the remaining custard.

Onion

12 oz (350 g) chopped onions lightly sautéed in 1 oz (25 g) butter and a tablespoon of olive oil, then drained on kitchen paper. Put some custard in the flan first, bake off, then insert the onions and top with the remaining custard.

Mushroom

1 lb (450 g) sliced mushroom caps, sautéed in 1 oz (25 g) butter and a tablespoon of olive oil, and then drained well on kitchen paper. Place in the flan, then pour the custard over.

You can also fold 4 generous tablespoons of Mushroom Pâté (see page 30) into the custard mixture, and bake off as usual.

Prawn and Toasted Almond

1-lb (450-g) packet of frozen prawns and 3 tablespoons toasted, flaked almonds. This may sound extravagant but the net weight of defrosted prawns of a good quality is only about 12 oz (350 g). Place in the flan and pour the custard over.

Smoked Salmon

12 oz (350 g) diced salmon that has been soaked for 2 hours in ¼ pint (150 ml) cold milk. A variation on this is 8 oz (225 g) salmon and 4 oz (100 g) finely diced Jerusalem artichoke which provides an unusual contrast in textures. (You can substitute 2 tablespoons of clam juice for 2 tablespoons of the cream; this gives a delicious flavour.) Place in the flan and pour the custard over.

Smoked Haddock

12 oz (300 g) smoked haddock, mixed with ½ teaspoon English mustard and 1½ oz (40 g) finely grated Cheddar cheese. (See my note above about clam juice.) Place in the flan, and pour the custard over.

Piccalilli and Cauliflower

4 tablespoons of Piccalilli (see the recipe on page 201 and finely dice this), 8 oz (225 g) cauliflower florets with 1 oz (25 g) finely grated Cheddar cheese and 8 stoned black olives, one for each portion. Don't blanch the cauliflower first or else it will disintegrate. Just place everything in the flan case, and pour the custard over.

Spinach and Bacon

1-lb (450-g) packet of frozen spinach, cooked and minced, will give you about 12 oz (350 g) of spinach, or use 12 oz (300 g) fresh spinach leaves. Add 2½ oz (60 g) finely diced smoked bacon which has been de-rinded and cooked on a baking tray in the oven for 15 minutes at 350°F (180°C), Gas 4. (Save the fat as it is delicious poured over new potatoes.) Put everything into the flan case and pour the custard over.

Asparagus and Pine Kernel

8 sticks of cooked asparagus and 4 tablespoons of toasted pine kernels, in the flan case, with the custard poured over.

Crab

12 oz (350 g) frozen white crab meat, and substitute 2 tablespoons of dry sherry for 2 tablespoons of the cream in the original custard recipe. Fold the meat into the custard and put in the flan case.

Smoked Oysters with Celery and Pepper

A small tin of smoked oysters (about 4 oz (125 g) net weight), 4 oz (125 g) finely diced celery and 4 oz (125 g) finely diced red pepper. Place in the flan case and pour the custard over.

Leek and Walnut

10 oz (275 g) finely diced leeks, poached in $\frac{1}{2}$ pint (300 ml) white wine then drained and mixed with 4 tablespoons of chopped walnuts. Place in the flan case and pour the custard over.

Tomato and Cheese

About 8 oz (225 g) tomatoes skinned and diced (remove the pips), with 6 oz (175 g) finely grated Emmenthal cheese. If you like anchovies and black olives, strips of anchovy previously soaked in milk for at least half an hour then fanned out like bicycle spokes from the centre of the quiche, and a black olive for each portion, is a beautifully Italianate addition! After you've arranged your anchovies on top of the cheese and tomatoes, pour the custard on top.

Smoked Bacon

1 lb (450 g) smoked bacon, de-rinded, finely chopped, and baked at 350°F (180°C), Gas 4 for 15 minutes, will give you about 12 oz (350 g) bacon, which you put in the flan case. Pour the custard over.

Quiches are an ideal dish for using up leftovers and you would be surprised at what I have put in these to make supper dishes for friends. Finely chopped gherkins, bits of radish, *Moutarde au Meaux*, stoned olives, lots of chopped, fresh herbs, chopped bulb fennel, diced apple, diced kidney, black pudding from breakfast.... The more you put in, the more 'Solomon Grundy' the effect will be. My favourite garnish is a huge sprig of deep-fried parsley.

Cheese Savoury Tartlets

Using the Quiche Savoury Pastry recipe, make 16 × 3-in (7.5-cm) individual tartlets, and bake them off blind.

When cold, line the base of each tartlet with a teaspoon of Date Chutney (see page 201), and then pipe (with a $\frac{1}{2}$ in (1 cm) 6-point star nozzle) in enough Cheese and Herb Pâté (see page 29) to bring the filling just under the rim of the edge of the tartlet case. On top of this sprinkle very finely chopped crisp celery, and in the middle of each place a walnut.

To provide a complete contrast of texture and flavour use in addition the Cheesecake mixture (page 162) and, just as it is beginning to set, pipe the mixture in tiny star shapes around the edge of the tartlet case leaving the nut in the middle exposed! When completely set, garnish with slices of stuffed olive or shelled fresh peas (cook them lightly if you like) in summer. Serve with a salad made with apples, celery and walnuts.

This is an extremely tasty dish to make, even though it may appear messy to prepare. The end result is quite delicious as you have the mousse-like cheese topping, crisp celery and nut in the middle, and then the strong, firm Cheese and Herb Pâté sweetened with the chutney and, of course, the whole enclosed in the delicious crisp, buttery pastry!

As a substantial starter, you could serve 3 small tartlets for each person, one stuffed with Cheese and Herb Pâté, one with Mushroom Pâté and one with Duck Liver Pâté. A glorious combination of flavours.

CHOUX PASTRY

7½ fl oz (200 ml) water

2½ oz (65 g) butter

3¾ oz (scant 100 g) well-sieved *strong* plain flour

pinch of salt

3 eggs

Choux pastry is thought to be tricky – but believe me it isn't, provided you beware of the pitfalls I outline below. This mixing will give you 20-25 gougères, 30–40 éclairs, or profiteroles or 8 generous-sized swans.

Pre-set your oven at 400°F (200°C), Gas 6, and have some baking trays, a piping bag, and ¼-in (5-mm) plain nozzle ready.

1. Put the water and butter into a saucepan over *low* heat, and gently melt the butter. (If you put this over high heat and let the water come to the boil quickly to try and speed the operation up, you will get evaporation. Consequently, there won't be enough liquid for the flour to soak up when you add it, and the end product will be heavier.)

2. *Do* use strong flour for this recipe. (The high gluten content absorbs the water better and gives the final dough a much better expansion, thus your choux éclairs or puffs are larger and much lighter.) Sieve the flour twice with the salt.

3. When the butter is completely melted – literally lying on the top of the water – and you have the sieved flour ready, turn up the heat under the water. Put all the flour into the pan and, using a wooden spoon, bring the dough together and beat the living daylights out of it for 1 minute over reduced heat. (Try and use an old-fashioned wooden spoon, with a lovely rounded back. So many modern wooden kitchen spoons have straight backs and push the mixture against the side of the pan instead of crushing it.) Put this unattractive-looking dough into the very cold bowl of an electric mixer and wait until it is quite cold before continuing.

4. Have the lightly-beaten eggs ready and use a K-beater if you have one. With the machine on the slowest speed, put the egg mixture in *little by little,* never adding more until you are satisfied

that all has been thoroughly absorbed. (You *must* take time at this stage to see that all the egg is incorporated before adding more and also – whether beating by hand or machine – to make sure that the whole mixture is brought together. You may have to use a spatula to bring the dough into the middle of the bowl before adding more egg, especially if you are using an electric mixer.)

You will gradually see the mixture acquire a sheen and change to a pleasant gold colour. It will be of a strong batter consistency.

When all the egg has been added, beat vigorously for 1 minute before spooning the dough into the piping bag.

5. Always, *always*, well dampen the trays you are to use for cooking the choux pastry; when this is put into the pre-heated oven, the steam produced will give the pastry an initial boost to swell!

6. As you put the choux mixture into the oven, turn the temperature up *at once* to 425°F (220°C), Gas 7, and this surge of extra heat will also help the rising.

Choux pastry needs cooking for 10 to 20 minutes according to the size of what you are making, and the timings are given in the individual recipes. It can be used with savoury or sweet fillings. Here are the savouries; the sweet ones can be found in Act Three, on page 149.

Gougères

Gougères made from choux pastry are the Frenchman's answer to our British Yorkshire Pudding! They do look rather like those fluffy individual Yorkshire puddings (that I never seem able to make), but are quite crisp and make an excellent base for exotic or simple fillings.

Use a 9- or 12-portion tray (the ones you make cup cakes in), each portion being about $2\frac{1}{2}$ in (6 cm) diameter and 1 in (2.5 cm) deep. Use a $\frac{1}{4}$-in (5-mm) plain nozzle on a 10-in (25.5 cm) piping bag. If you don't have these particular-sized trays, individual tins may be used and the basic recipe for choux pastry will make you 12–15 individual gougères. Wet thoroughly any tins you are going to use and leave a few drops of water actually in each tin.

Start piping in the middle of each tin, move out towards the edge, and then do one top coating actually around the *outside* as if you were starting off a meringue nest! When you have finished piping, wet your work thumb well and by pressing this into the centre of the mixture in each tin, you gently force the mixture up the sides. (You are making individual tart cases with a thin lining of choux pastry on the bottom and the mixing as high as possible up the sides.) Now turn up the oven to 425°F (220°C), Gas 7, and bake the gougères for 20 minutes.

When they're baked, scoop out as much of the middle as possible, as the gougères cool, to leave you with a thin crisp cup case which can be either used immediately or put on one side until needed (when cold, store them in well secured polythene bags or put them in the freezer). Use a small sharp knife and cut round the risen top, then gently scoop and scrape out any dough from the inside with a teaspoon. There shouldn't be much soft dough, but it is far better to get rid of it at this stage.

When you wish to use the gougère cases they only need 2 or 3 minutes in a moderate oven at 350°F (180°C), Gas 4, to warm through. Just before taking to the table, insert the filling. At this stage, I keep some creamy mashed potato to hand in a piping bag and use this to secure the gougère well and truly to the plate, as they have a tendency to topple over as you set them in front of your guests!

Fillings

1. Use 1 lb (450 g) of Mushroom Pâté (see page 30) as a basis for a delicious kidney filling for gougères. Sauté 1 finely chopped medium-sized onion in 1 oz (25 g) butter and then add 8 finely diced kidneys. Sauté them gently with a crushed clove of garlic. When this is cooked, beat into the Mushroom Pâté which has reduced double cream and reduced Marsala wine added (see page 30). A nice final touch is a dash of port wine. Fill the gougères at the last minute.

2. Mix together 6 oz (175 g) of each of the following: chopped crisped bacon, chopped sautéed mushrooms, and sweetcorn kernels. As a substitute for any of these ingredients, you can dice some fennel bulb and poach it gently in ½ pint (300 ml) milk, and add it to the filling with some finely diced red pepper.

3. I also like to use about 1 lb (450 g) Liver Pâté (see page 31) which I warm through *very* gently (the butter tends to split if it gets too hot).

4. About 12 oz (350 g) Smoked Haddock with ½ pint (300 ml) cheese sauce (see page 77) is a delicious fishy filling.

5. Cook 6 oz (175 g) each of crab and prawns in ½ pint (300 ml) Pernod sauce (see page 50) – quite one of my favourites.

Savoury Cheese Éclairs with Pineapple and Bacon

choux pastry as above

12 oz (300 g) Cheese and Herb Pâté (see page 29)

3 tablespoons Bovril, melted

12 slices fresh pineapple

12 slices bacon

Using the basic choux recipe, pipe about 12 4-in (10-cm) éclairs with a ½-in (1-cm) nozzle onto dampened baking trays, and cook at 425°F (220°C), Gas 7, for approximately 20 minutes. Take them out of the oven, make a slit in the side through which you will later pipe the filling, and return to the oven to dry out for a few moments longer.

When you're ready to serve them, fill with Cheese and Herb Pâté, and brush the tops with melted Bovril. Place each on a circle of fresh pineapple and serve with a hot bacon roll (a 3-in (7.5-cm) piece of back bacon rolled to little-finger size, held with a cocktail stick and baked in the oven at 350°F (180°C), Gas 4, for 10 minutes).

This is a substantial starter, and very good and tasty as a supper dish.

Savoury Swans

choux pastry as above

1 lb (450 g) Cheese and Herb Pâté (see page 29)

Pipe 8 oval shapes onto a dampened baking tray, using a $\frac{1}{2}$-in (1-cm) plain nozzle. With a $\frac{1}{4}$-in (5-mm) plain nozzle, pipe 8 'S' shapes onto a separate dampened tray: these will be the necks and heads of the swan. The necks only take about 7 minutes to cook at 425°F (220°C), Gas 7, but the bodies will need 20 minutes.

When you take the bodies out, pierce one side of each with a sharp pointed knife and return to the hot oven for a few more minutes to dry out. When you want to serve the swans cut a slice off the top of each and then cut this into half to form the wings.

Before piping in the Cheese and Herb Pâté (or a flavoured cream, see page 209), make certain you have a hollow swan by using a teaspoon to remove any soft dough inside. Use a little cheese pâté as the anchor for attaching the neck and the wings.

You can serve your swans by themselves or on a bed of chopped lime, grapefruit and avocado jelly – which seems to be very popular with my guests, particularly those from North America.

Lime, Grapefruit and Avocado Jelly

Use a packet of commercial lime jelly. Arrange individual portions of overlapping grapefruit segments, avocado strips and lime slices (about 2 per person) on a rimmed plastic tray and, as the jelly is beginning to cool, pour it over the portions to completely cover the tray. I find it helpful to use a cocktail stick to keep the pieces of fruit together as when you pour the jelly over the portions they can float away into untidy shapes! When the jelly begins to set in the fridge, take out the sticks.

For choux pastry desserts, see page 149.

ROULADES

Roulades are relatively easy to prepare, simple to cook, a joy to serve, and a delight both to look at and to eat. Yet they rarely appear on menus and I've never really understood why. When served, they are invariably the cause of much comment from diners who have their own views on how they are made: three-quarters of them hair-raising and way off target! The colourful cartwheel effect of the finished dish, the different textures and combinations of flavours, make this dish a pleasure to serve.

The following recipes will each give you 6 generous-portion roulades.

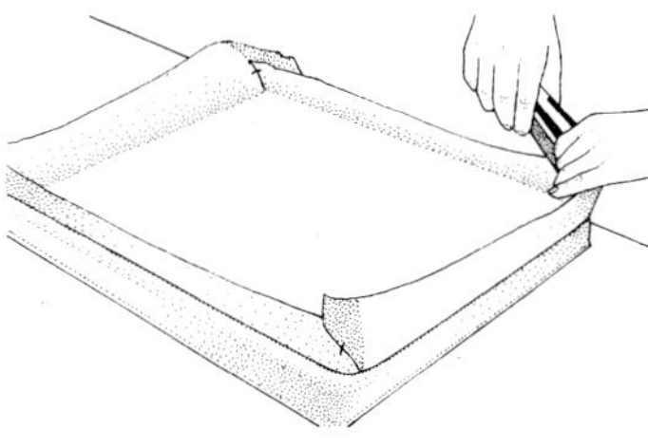

Beforehand
You need two trays measuring 12 × 8 in (30 × 20 cm) and $\frac{1}{2}$ in (1 cm) deep. First of all, the trays must be lined (sides and all) with a good quality silicone-treated greaseproof paper, making a tray within a tray. Staple the corners. For savoury roulades, paint this lightly with good olive oil, and for sweet ones, coat with melted butter. Do watch the quality of your greaseproof paper. Should you use an inferior type you will have a pantomime when trying to remove it from the roulade prior to serving. Dampening the paper in small circles in order to tear it off is not only painstakingly time-consuming but does nothing for the texture of the finished roulade.

The oven should be pre-heated to 360°F (180°C), Gas 4: in the case of a roulade a variation of 10 degrees in oven temperature is disastrous. *Double check* the temperature of your oven by using an old-fashioned oven thermometer. (Where, oh where, are those thermometers that used to show the correct oven temperature on the outside of the door?) By regularly using an oven thermometer you will occasionally be surprised to find a fluctuation between the actual temperature and the one set on the knob of the appliance due to low voltage of electricity or low gas pressure. Also a faulty thermostat – which I had recently – can be discovered before a dish is ruined.

For all roulades a copper bowl – cleaned out with a cut half lemon and salt – is ideal for beating up the egg whites to give a more solid, consistent and lighter end product. I also beat the egg yolks to a light, ribbony mousse texture (see page 160) when this method is required.

Method
There are two basic methods of making roulades. One is by beating the egg yolks separately in an electric mixer with sugar or salt and the other is by beating the egg yolks into the basic mixture. When using the first method I always lightly warm the mixer bowl and beater as well as the egg yolks, and I think the secret of a very light mixture is to add the sugar or salt a good 5 minutes after the beater has been happily working away and add it *little by little*. The whole process takes about 12 minutes.

I use eggs straight from the fridge which, I think, gives a better consistency for the egg white, but I always lightly warm the yolks, as I said, before incorporating them into the mixture.

When about to fold the first third of the stiffly beaten egg whites into the mixture, I turn the basic mixture out into a larger bowl so that the 'coming-together' can be more smooth. I also use a long-handled metal spoon which I hold so lightly in the hand that, by doing a figure-of-eight motion very, very gently, the egg whites disappear into the mixture. *Always* beat the remaining egg whites a little more before folding in the balance because while standing those few minutes, they could have become slightly moist and deflated.

Turn the mixture out onto the treated greaseproof paper and spread evenly by using a large palette knife which is, once again, held gently: the mixture should be *persuaded* into the corners, not pushed!

Set the timer and check at the end of the cooking period by gently opening the oven door and slowly bringing the tray half-way out. Insert a skewer in the middle and it should come out completely dry if the roulade is cooked.

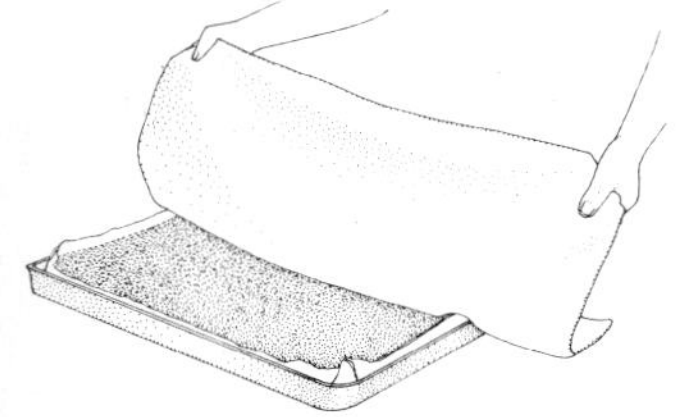

Turning Out
When turning out a roulade, first have a suitably-sized piece of aluminium foil on the table and then a sheet of good-quality greaseproof paper on top – this double thickness does help when you come to roll out.

The simplest method of turning out the roulade is to place a workboard that will cover the whole surface of the baking tray on top of the tray, and then invert the two. A more spectacular way – and relatively simple – is to have your greaseproof and aluminium sheets ready and then, with someone holding the tray at your side, open up the stapled corners, take a firm hold of the two corners furthest from you, lift quickly up into the air, and invert the roulade onto the prepared greaseproof paper.

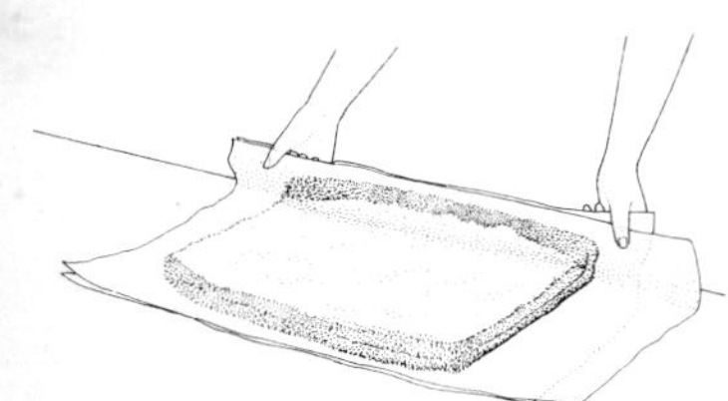

Rolling
When rolling the end product after it has been filled, I find the base of good silicone-treated greaseproof paper and foil gives strength to the rolling.

Starting at the end nearest you, take up the two front corners of the two sheets of paper and give the roulade a very gentle first turn away from you. By pushing away from you at a level running more or less parallel to the work surface, you should find the roulade rolls itself well. Then by opening out your hands and using your thumb and first finger as a circle shape, run along the outer surface until a roll shape is achieved.

It will take two of you to put the roulade back on to a serving platter; bring an appropriately-sized chopping board level to the work surface and just ease the roll on to it.

Please remember that the following recipes make *two* roulades.

Savoury Hazelnut Roulade Stuffed with Cheese and Herb Pâté

4 eggs, separated

2 egg whites

¼ teaspoon ginger

½ teaspoon onion salt

1 oz (25 g) soft brown sugar

6 oz (175 g) ground hazelnuts, sieved

In a warmed mixer bowl, beat the 4 egg yolks for several minutes and then very slowly add the ginger, salt and sugar, making certain you get a good ribbony mixture. This takes about 12 minutes.

Meanwhile, in a clean copper bowl, beat up the 6 egg whites until stiff.

Turn out the yolk mixture into a large plastic bowl and gently fold in one-third of the stiff egg whites. Beat up the egg whites again and incorporate the balance into the mixture; finally, gently fold in the sieved hazelnuts.

Turn out onto the prepared tray and bake in the pre-heated oven at 350°F (180°C), Gas 4, for approximately 12 to 15 minutes.

When cold, turn out as above and spread liberally with the Cheese and Herb Pâté (see page 29). Alternatively, line each roulade with 8 oz (225 g) plain cream cheese or a combination of cream cheese and Dolcelatte (4 oz (100 g) of each for each roulade).

The home-made Date Chutney on page 201 goes well with this.

Spinach and Mushroom Roulade

2 lb (1 kg) frozen chopped or leaf spinach (on no account use frozen *creamed* spinach)

½ oz (15 g) butter

½ nutmeg, grated

4 eggs, separated

¼ teaspoon salt

grated Parmesan cheese (to line)

For the sauce

1 pint (600 ml) rich white sauce (see page 205)

2 gills (250 ml) Marsala wine (reduced to 2 tablespoons)

1 lb (450 g) chopped mushrooms

1 oz (25 g) butter

Cook the spinach in boiling salted water, then leave to drain. To make certain all the water is out, put a handful of spinach at a time on a dinner plate, stack another dinner plate on top, and gently squeeze them together. Continue until all the spinach has been squeezed like this.

Mince the dried-out spinach on the medium blade of the electric mixer and dry out further in a saucepan in which you have melted the butter over low heat. Add the nutmeg.

Gently beat the 4 egg yolks, then beat them into the spinach. Stiffly beat the 4 egg whites with the salt and fold in one-third, and then two-thirds, of the beaten egg white into the spinach. Once again, I find a better result is obtained by turning the cooked spinach and egg yolk mixture out into a large plastic bowl so that when I fold in the beaten egg whites, the folding-in action is as light as possible.

Liberally sprinkle the greaseproof-lined tray with Parmesan cheese, turn out the mixture into it and spread evenly, using a large palette knife. Bake in the pre-heated oven at 360°F (180°C), Gas 4. for approximately 15 minutes. While baking, place a piece of aluminium foil on the work surface and a sheet of greaseproof paper on top of this. Lightly brush with oil and sprinkle with a little more Parmesan cheese.

Make the mushroom and marsala sauce by sautéing the mushrooms gently in the butter, draining them well on kitchen paper, then folding them with the reduced Marsala into the rich white sauce.

When you have checked that the roulade is cooked, remove it from the oven and turn out onto the prepared greaseproof paper. Immediately spread the mushroom mixture on top, even it out, and roll up.

An alternative filling for this roulade is the Mushroom Pâté on page 30.

1 lb (450 g) smoked salmon

1 fl oz (25 ml) clam juice (or dry sherry)

½ pint (300 ml) milk

3 eggs, separated

1 teaspoon onion salt

Smoked Salmon Roulade with Avocado Mousse

Clam juice makes a great difference to any fish roulade, but it seems virtually impossible to buy at the moment in this country, which is strange as it can be found in almost every food store in the States. Canned clams (which you *can* find) liquidized are *not* a good substitute. Use South African dry sherry instead.

Liquidize half of the smoked salmon with the clam juice or sherry and pass through a sieve. Soak the remainder of the salmon in the milk for about 2 hours. Beat up the 3 egg yolks to a ribbon consistency with the onion salt and transfer to a large plastic bowl. Combine with the sieved smoked salmon.

Beat three egg whites until stiff, and fold one-third, then two-thirds, into the mixture.

Line the prepared baking tin with the mixture and bake in the pre-heated oven at 360°F (180°C), Gas 4, for 15 to 20 minutes. When cooked, turn out and leave to cool. Take the smoked salmon out of the milk and liquidize it, then pass it through a sieve – use this as a thin coating over the cooked roulade.

4 avocado pears

1 teaspoon salt

½ pint (300 ml) good home-made mayonnaise (see page 132)

¼ pint (150 ml) double cream

1 level teaspoon gelatine mixed with ¼ pint (150 ml) dry white wine

Avocado Mousse

Peel the skins off the avocados, cut in half to remove the stones, and chop up the flesh. Combine in an electric mixer with the salt, mayonnaise and double cream, and slowly beat together to form a smooth paste.

Gently heat the gelatine mixture over low heat and, when ready, fold into the avocado pear mixture. (The use of gelatine is gone into in some detail in the Mousse section on page 159.) When it's about to set, spread onto the roulade over the sieved smoked salmon purée.

Roll and chill. Delicious.

1 lb (450 g) good smoked haddock

¾ pint (400 ml) milk

parsley stalks

6 black peppercorns

a few onion slices

½ teaspoon anchovy essence

½ oz (15 g) butter

6 eggs, separated

continued

Smoked Haddock Roulade with Prawns in Pernod

Poach the haddock slowly in the milk, with the parsley stalks, peppercorns and onion. When cooked, allow to cool. Remove the skin and bones, and liquidize or pass twice through a mincer, adding the anchovy essence.

Melt the butter in a saucepan over gentle heat and re-heat the haddock purée. Meanwhile, beat the egg yolks and beat into the haddock little by little.

Fold in first one-third, then two-thirds, of the 6 stiffly beaten egg whites, and cook in the pre-heated oven, 350°F (180°C), Gas 4, for 15 to 20 minutes.

$\frac{1}{2}$ pint (300 ml) thick white sauce (see page 205)

2 tablespoons Pernod

8 oz (225 g) chopped prawns

While the roulade is cooking, make the thick white sauce, flavour it with the Pernod and fold in the prawns. (If you are using frozen prawns, thaw out and then scatter the prawns on a baking tray and leave in the warming drawer for about 30 minutes – you'll be amazed at how much brine comes out.)

Spread the roulade with this mixture, roll and serve.

PANCAKES

1 lb (450 g) strong plain flour

a pinch of salt

1 tablespoon double cream

$2\frac{1}{2}$ oz (65 g) melted butter

4 eggs

4 eggs, separated

2 pints (generous 1 litre) milk

For frying

8 oz (225 g) melted butter

Sweet and savoury pancakes are enjoyed by most people – and not only on Shrove Tuesday! When I make them at home I like to do quite a lot as they freeze well, filled or unfilled, and so make a quick, handy standby for a starter or supper dish when someone turns up unexpectedly.

But although easy to serve at the last minute, they do take time and care to actually make. After trying every hint I could muster from all my friends, I find the following recipe and method the best.

This basic mixing will give you about 50 pancakes, so I will assume you are going to freeze quite a few!

Sieve the plain flour and salt into a large bowl and make a deep well in the centre. Lightly whip the double cream into the 4 eggs, add the 4 yolks from the separated eggs (leaving the 4 egg whites to one side), and pour this into the well in the flour. With a wooden spoon, slowly stir, gradually drawing in the flour from the edges. You will soon find that you need more liquid for the flour to absorb so add milk in the centre, little by little. Continue to stir, taking care not to beat the mixture, as you want a thick batter at this stage. (So many people wrongly assume that pancake batter should be beaten right from the start.) When you have incorporated all the flour and are satisfied that you have a lump-free mixing (remember to take the back of the spoon up against the sides of the bowl to knock out any small lumps), slowly add the rest of the milk, then beat in the melted butter. Cover with a tea towel and leave in a warm place for 4 hours. When about to cook, beat up the remaining 4 egg whites until very stiff and fold into the batter mixture.

If you are lucky enough to have 2 pancake pans, all the better. Have to hand the 8 oz (225 g) of melted butter for the frying and, having heated the pans through, add a little to each. Heat it, and swirl it around the base and sides of the pans, and then pour out any surplus. (Remember the butter is not really for *cooking* the pancake batter, but purely to stop the batter sticking to the base of the pan.)

Add a full tablespoon of the batter mixture to each pan and tip it from side to side so that the whole base is quickly covered. Cook until set and golden brown. Loosen the edges carefully with a pliable palette knife and, by picking up the edge furthest from you quickly with your fingers and using the palette knife underneath the pancake, you will find it easy to turn. I do *not* recommend the flamboyant tossing method!

Have a pastry board at the side with a clean tea towel spread out and as you start to stack the cooked pancakes (you will soon get the knack of cooking with 2 pans) bring the top half of the tea towel over the cooked pancakes to ensure that they are always covered.

It will take some time to do all these, so half-way through I suggest you eat a couple yourself, warm and sprinkled with orange juice (how about a little Grand Marnier?), and a little sugar. The sheer joy of sampling will recharge your batteries!

Fillings for Savoury Pancakes

1. Fill one pancake per person as a starter with about 3 oz (75 g) Mushroom and Marsala mixture (see page 30), and serve coated with about 2 oz (50 g) thick cheese sauce (see page 206).

2. Any of the other pâtés mentioned (pages 29–31) can be used for filling savoury pancakes.

3. Beat about 3 oz (75 g) Philadelphia cream cheese per person until soft and smooth, and then combine with diced apple, celery, red peppers and walnuts. Add some curry powder if you like.

4. Prepare at least 3 oz (75 g) thick white or cheese sauce (see pages 205 and 206) per person, and fold into it grated raw vegetables of your choice and any kind of nuts or raisins (minced dates are different and tempting too).

5. Any leftover meat can be minced finely and combined with fried onions, herbs, spices, grated cheese or a thick white sauce.

Before serving savoury filled pancakes, line them up on a well-buttered tin tray and cover with well-buttered greaseproof paper. Ten minutes in a medium oven is more than adequate to heat them through, but I invariably finish them off by coating them with white or cheese sauce, sprinkling them with plain or savoury breadcrumbs, and flashing them under a hot grill.

FRUIT

Miller Howe Utter Bliss

For 2

1 small melon

4 oz (100 g) strawberries or raspberries

1 tablespoon brandy

2 tablespoons icing sugar

1 half bottle sparkling white wine

2 tablespoons redcurrants

This is an excellent starter for a summer's evening – particularly if you can get hold of some fresh redcurrants. They seem to be more and more difficult to find each year.

This amount of wine will be sufficient for up to 8 portions.

Slightly top and tail the melon before cutting it in two 'around the equator'. This 'topping and tailing' will balance the portion better, but don't take huge slices off, otherwise the filling will run out. Remove the seeds.

Looking down into the well of the melon half, scoop out balls from all around the edge, with a medium-sized parisian scoop or melon baller. Return the balls to their 'home', bottoms up (it looks like a series of ball bearings on a piston ring!). Place your melon halves on a tray, cover well and leave until required.

Meanwhile, liquidize the strawberries with the brandy and icing sugar and leave to chill. Also place to chill the half bottle of sparkling white Burgundy, Asti Spumante or other wine of your choice and (if you've been lucky enough to find them) prepare your lovely fresh redcurrants by removing the stalks.

Cover the serving plates with doyleys and, if you live in the country, a large fern leaf for each guest. This goes over the doyley and underneath the melon portion – how about a few flowers too?

At the last minute, put the redcurrants into the well of the melon, lightly pour round the 'balled' rim the liquidized strawberries and fill the well to the brim with the sparkling wine. This really *is* Utter Bliss!

If you cannot find redcurrants, fresh, stoned cherries are delicious too.

Melon with Egg Flip Sauce

I am sure that you, like me, have occasionally discovered that you have bought a dud melon. The outside appearance and even the usual test of pressing in at the base have proved you wrong, and so what can one do? I discovered the following remedy for such a potentially expensive dilemma. In fact I like it so much that I have used the sauce with perfectly sound good melons!

Portion the melon into balls using a potato baller, and then you put them equally into individual serving glasses. Beat together a small can of condensed milk with 3 eggs and $\frac{1}{4}$ pint (150 ml) of cooking brandy until combined, and then fold into about $\frac{1}{2}$ pint (300 ml) of lightly whipped double cream.

Coat the melon balls with this and the start of your dinner party is a sure fire success!

Baked Banana with Bacon and Curry Mayonnaise

For 2

1 banana

$\frac{1}{2}$ oz (15 g) flour

1 egg, beaten

1 tablespoon savoury breadcrumbs (see below)

2 thin slices smoked back bacon

2 oz (50 g) Curry Mayonnaise (see page 132)

$\frac{1}{2}$ oz (15 g) desiccated coconut, toasted

An unusual dish to start off a dinner party, but one that is extremely popular and (I think) rather filling!

You need a fairly firm banana, and after skinning it you slice it through in half lengthwise.

Lightly flour and then egg wash each half and coat liberally with the flavoured breadcrumbs. Wind the thin slice of de-rinded bacon helter-skelter fashion round the coated banana and place on a well-greased baking tray.

When you wish to serve the dish, bake off the banana at 350°F (180°C), Gas 4, for 15 minutes and just before taking it to the table, coat the middle with a generous portion of Curry Mayonnaise and sprinkle the whole thing with the lightly toasted desiccated coconut.

Savoury Breadcrumbs

2 oz (50 g) onion, finely chopped

2 tablespoons parsley, finely chopped

1 clove of garlic, crushed to a paste with salt

8 oz (225 g) fine breadcrumbs

1 oz (25 g) strong Cheddar cheese, finely grated

I must admit that making breadcrumbs is very much easier if you are lucky enough to have one of those new machines which make short shrift of it. Stale dinner cobs, crusts from toast, any bread left over after making round croûtons etc. are best for making breadcrumbs, and much easier if rather crisp. At Miller Howe there is always a small roasting tray in the warming oven and any scraps of bread are automatically placed in this. With the heat from the basic warmer only, the bread is always hard and firm and easy to turn into breadcrumbs. It's also simpler to make your crumbs by hand on a sharp grater if the bread has been 'baked' first.

If you have a grating, grinding machine, simply add these ingredients in the following order: garlic, onion, bread, parsley, cheese, and everything will be done for you.

If you are doing it by hand, make sure the onions and parsley are chopped *very* finely. Crush the garlic to a smooth paste with the salt and grate the cheese very finely. Make the breadcrumbs on a grater, and combine all together in a mixing bowl.

After using the breadcrumbs on your bananas, fish, chicken or whatever, any leftovers can be stored in a screw-top jar in the fridge.

Baked Banana with Bacon in Puff Pastry with Curry Mayonnaise

For 2

1 banana

½ oz (15 g) melted butter

a few drops of fresh lemon juice

½ oz (15 g) desiccated coconut, toasted

½ oz (15 g) savoury breadcrumbs (see previous recipe)

2 thin slices smoked back bacon, de-rinded

1 oz (25 g) puff pastry (see page 34)

2 oz (50 g) Curry Mayonnaise (see page 132)

chopped fresh parsley to garnish

As the main course for a supper dish, use a whole banana per person, but for a starter a half banana is sufficient. Cut the ends off the peeled banana, cut it in half, and roll the pieces in the melted butter with a few drops of fresh lemon juice added. Coat the banana pieces liberally with a mixture of toasted desiccated coconut and breadcrumbs, then wrap the banana in the bacon.

Cut out squares of thin puff pastry and place your banana pieces across them from bottom left to top right, then bring over the open corners. Turn the finished portion over and place on a cooling tray and chill well. When ready to cook (and they take about 20–30 minutes at 475°F (240°C), Gas 9, according to size), place the cooling trays onto baking trays so as to catch the juice which may run out from the bacon and puff pastry. Following this method, you should have a banana served with crisp top pastry and an un-soggy base! Garnish the serving plates and top off with curry mayonnaise. You can sprinkle it with further toasted desiccated coconut or just plenty of chopped fresh parsley.

Miller Howe Savoury Cheese Peach

Per person

1 canned yellow cling peach half

½ oz (15 g) Cheese and Herb Pâté (see page 29)

1 oz (25 g) cheese topping for croûtons (see page 61)

This is my own personal favourite starter. My staff and I like to prepare (and eat) this particularly in winter when the hotel is closed, as it's so quick to do, relatively inexpensive, quite filling and very tasty.

Half fill the centre of each half peach with Cheese and Herb Pâté. Then make a ball of the cheese and egg croûton topping and flatten it out to cover the whole top of the half peach. When you wish to serve, warm the peaches through slightly in the oven at 325°F (170°C), Gas 3, and then put them under a very hot grill until the cheese, brandy and mustard paste on top begins to rise, sizzle and go brown. Serve as quickly as possible accompanied by a roll of grilled smoked bacon and an asparagus spear. The dish is easier to serve if you put the peach on a large plain cooked croûton, and a sprig of watercress with an orange twirl turns this into a feast! The sweet and sour tastes, the rough and smooth textures (if served on a croûton) do wonders for the taste buds.

Per person

1 fresh peach

1 oz (25 g) Cheese and Herb Pâté (see page 29)

2 oz (50 g) Curry Mayonnaise (see page 132)

$\frac{1}{2}$ oz (15 g) desiccated coconut, toasted

Savoury Cheese Peach with Curry Mayonnaise

Poach the peaches first for 5 minutes in a stock syrup (see page 211) with a couple of tablespoons of wine vinegar in it. Cut round the 'equator' of the peach and remove the stone. Fill the centres with Cheese and Herb Pâté and then stick the halves together again. Just before serving, coat liberally with Curry Mayonnaise, and sprinkle some toasted desiccated coconut on top.

Apple Hors d'Oeuvres

When I'm asked what I will take with me on Desert Island Discs (!) I will immediately reply, 'A crate of Granny Smith apples'. Apples have everything: nourishment, cheapness, flavour, availability, versatility – cooked or raw.

Apples are part of history, mythology and everyday life. They are supposed to have settled man's fate in the garden of Eden (although botanists tell us there were no apples there then), and they knocked scientific sense into Isaac Newton's head!

Apples should always be kept in a cool place away from severe temperature fluctuations. Never put whole, uncooked apples in a deep freezer. Always use a stainless-steel knife when preparing apples and never use copper or iron utensils when cooking them, as this will destroy the Vitamin C content of the apples. When cooking with apples, I suggest you prepare all the other ingredients first, and only peel and prepare the apples at the last minute as exposure to oxygen once again affects the vital Vitamin C.

A medium apple contains a great deal of water, traces of the vital Vitamins A, B and C, and is also a good source of roughage. It contains only about 45 calories, and has up to 3 times the filling power of the various expensive cellulose products sold today as slimming aids; so an apple eaten 10 minutes before a meal will help fill any gaps.

With hors d'oeuvres made from apples, ingenuity is the basic key, as practically any leftovers go well with diced raw apples to make effective and tasty starters.

Mix together cubed cheese, some chutney, sour cream, gherkins, olives, dates, banana, celery, tomato and serve them all on a bed of lettuce heart.

Diced apples go well with diced avocado pears, making an expensive fruit go further, and walnuts added too make this a most unusual combination.

A filling starter is a mixture of shredded apples, celery, nuts, raisins and finely shredded spring green cabbage. Coat the lot with cream and mustard.

Soak prunes overnight in French dressing then chop and mix them with diced apple, cream cheese and grated nutmeg.

Mix equal quantities of chopped apple with cold cooked peas and finely chopped red peppers, and fold into a rich mayonnaise.

Grated young root vegetables and thinly sliced apples made into individual-mould lime jellies look good and make a pleasant starter dish for a summer's supper – particularly if accompanied by softly poached cold eggs and Hollandaise Sauce.

Miller Howe Savoury Apple with Tarragon Cream

For 2

1 medium apple

1 oz (25 g) Cheese and Herb Pâté (see page 29)

$\frac{1}{2}$ oz (15 g) each of stoneless dates, bananas, walnuts

Tarragon Cream (see page 209)

Each winter my cooks and I travel around the globe presenting 'A Festival of British Country-House Cooking' in an attempt to wave the flag for our country and give us the opportunity to meet and to work with other people in the profession. This starter is always the most popular – I hope you have equal success.

The apples should be cut in half 'round their equators' and peeled. Remove the core with a parisian scoop. Fill the scooped-out centres with Cheese and Herb Pâté and also use the pâté to level off the top and bottom sections where the stalk and base have been removed. Mince together the dates, bananas and walnuts and put this mixture onto the flat cut side of each apple half. This will be the base of your dish and you want to place the apple onto the serving plate with the curved side upwards.

When ready to serve, pour over a generous portion of Tarragon Cream, and decorate with a sprig of fresh tarragon or a sprig of parsley, and the merest sprinkling of paprika.

Always use uncooked dessert apples as they are crisp to bite and much more refreshing as a starter to any meal. Cherries or grapes make a delightful garnish too!

Miller Howe Savoury Pear with Tarragon Cream

This is more or less the same as Savoury Apple with Tarragon Cream but I usually poach the pears in a stock syrup flavoured with a little vinegar (see page 211). First of all I peel the pears and remove the inside of the pear with a potato peeler. It is impossible to say how long to cook the pears as obviously this method depends entirely on how woody they are! But do not overcook, and keep on testing from time to time. I normally poach them in a saucepan on top of the stove cramping the pears in so that they stand up on their bottoms. Leave to cool on a cooling tray and then stuff each with about 1 oz (25 g) Cheese and Herb Pâté (see page 29). At the very last minute, when you have placed them on your lettuce leaf on the plate, coat generously with Tarragon Cream (see page 209). A couple of fresh mint leaves to substitute for the pear leaves coming from the remaining stem really makes this dish look marvellously dramatic.

Elderflower Sorbet

To serve 8

- **1 pint (600 ml) cold water**
- **juice and rind of 1 orange**
- **juice and rind of 2 lemons**
- **6 oz (175 g) cube or preserving sugar**
- **1 heaped tablespoon dried elderflowers**
- **1 egg white**

This is a marvellously refreshing starter or dish to serve between courses. Before you begin, make sure that your saucepan is spotlessly clean. I use half a lemon with some table salt to ascertain that every trace of grease is removed.

Put all the ingredients into the pan and bring the mixture to the boil. Turn down the heat and simmer gently for 12 minutes. Strain into an earthenware dish, cover with muslin and leave to cool. When cold, transfer to the freezer and leave overnight.

Bring out and leave in a warm kitchen for about 20 minutes and then beat well with a hand-held electric beater. At first this will be like a drilling operation but, surprisingly quickly, the centre hole will enlarge and you will soon have a smooth mush in the bowl. Beat the egg white stiffly and gently fold this into the beaten elderflower mixture. Return to the freezer until it sets again.

Serve in individual bowls garnished with fresh mint sprigs, redcurrants, a few fresh raspberries or gooseberries. You can also serve a tablespoon on top of fresh grapefruit, on fresh fruit salad, or inside a meringue nest.

Green Tea Sorbet

You can also make a sorbet with green or gunpowder tea, which replaces the heaped tablespoon of elderflowers. Otherwise the method is exactly the same.

Grapefruit and Mandarin with Elderflower Sorbet

Per Person

- **1 grapefruit**
- **1 mandarin orange (or tangerine)**
- **6 grapes**
- **6 strawberries or 6 cherries (if in season)**
- **elderflower sorbet**

You will need a whole grapefruit for each person dining and one mandarin orange (or tangerine, whatever is in season). Grapes, strawberries and cherries also make good seasonal touches.

To prepare the grapefruit you require a small, sharp-pointed kitchen knife. Fix in your mind a very definite line running round the equator of the grapefruit and insert the tip of the knife at a 45° angle to this line – half above and half below – and gently but firmly press the knife in. Remove the knife and then turn it through a 90° angle and repeat the process around the grapefruit and eventually you will have two zig-zag portions.

Take a curved grapefruit knife for the next step as you must remove the pith and grapefruit flesh from each section. Use the knife again to segment towards the core and as you cut through each side of each segment, so the actual fruit falls out and you are eventually left with a handful of pith!

When you put all the flesh back *into one half shell* you will be amazed at how *little* there is. The mandarin or tangerine, and grapes, strawberries or cherries more than amply fill up the shell.

Chill well and just before serving, place a generous scoop of Elderflower Sorbet (see opposite) on top. Served on plates decorated with doyleys, fern leaves and flowers, this makes a very pretty starter and is light and refreshing to the palate.

SCENE TWO
SOUPS

Visually there is little one can do here (although most recipes in this section give you some ideas on garnishing), but it is the part of the meal where the audience has to *think*. It's like a whodunnit, with all the guests trying to come up with the solution before the secret is revealed. (It leaves any Agatha Christie stone cold!) 'Yes, I can get tomato' (who wouldn't, looking at the colour?) 'but what is the other taste I should know?' 'No, it's red pepper, of course' (a real clever clog here). And *what* are they supping off their soup spoons? *Tomato, Apple and Celery*. 'Well, I never, I wouldn't have dreamed . . . but yes, of course, I can get the flavours now.'

They are always wiser after the event, but at least it has got everyone talking, and you have gone one up in their estimation with your clever juggling of vegetables or fruits to make a filling dish.

Cream of vegetable soups are such simple dishes to make and can give so much satisfaction, provided you use super stock, seasonal vegetables, and follow a basic recipe such as the one I give here. Soups are filling, not terribly expensive to make, easily stored in the fridge or freezer – and with a little imagination, can cleverly ring the changes in a part of the menu that can be dull. If good cooking is confidence, as I so firmly believe, this section will illustrate most clearly how, once the basics are mastered, you can go from imaginative strength to strength.

Stock

The first and most essential ingredient of a good soup is a good stock, and for cream soups, I use a chicken or turkey stock. Use the bones of a bird that you have already cooked, or the bones of a bird from which you have cut the suprêmes. The latter will obviously give you a stronger and clearer stock.

Use a 9-pint (5-litre) capacity pan. It should be fairly thick and spotlessly clean. Put the chicken or turkey bones in the pan, cover with cold water and then add celery heads and outer sticks, onion skins, parsley stalks, a few black peppercorns, a peeled clove of garlic, a couple of bay leaves, any leftover grilled tomatoes from breakfast, a teaspoon of salt, a couple of roughly chopped carrots (or the peelings alone would do). Bring gently to the boil and just simmer, simmer, simmer – for at least 4 hours. Skim, if necessary, and if you leave it overnight to cool, you can lift off any fat in the morning.

But you may want to keep the stock pot going, and you can keep topping up with water and other additions, such as the outer leaves of cauliflower, the tops and tails of French beans, mushroom skins etc. Almost *anything* can go into the stock pot (better there than in the waste disposal), as the richer bodied and flavoured the stock, the better the soup will be.

When ready to use the stock, pass through a very fine strainer and use as in the recipes below. You could also boil the stock to reduce it to an essence, when it can be frozen in those plastic ice-cube containers. Then you'll always have your own stock cubes to hand – infinitely better than the commercial variety which are pure monosodium glutamate and have no nutritional value whatsoever.

Croûtons

Croûtons must be crisp, crunchy and clean – a subtle temptation to the palate to counterbalance the velvety texture of the actual soup. I cut the bread into croûtons (dice) in the morning and leave them on a baking tray in a warm spot in the kitchen – or even in an unlit gas oven as there is usually sufficient heat from the pilot light to harden the croûtons. The staler the croûton, the less fat it will absorb in the cooking.

Smear the base of the frying pan lightly with a good oil and then, when really hot, add a generous knob of butter. Toss in the croûtons and cook off as quickly as possible. Always drain 2 or 3 times on kitchen paper before serving.

If you like, and it's appropriate to the soup, you can cut the croûtons slightly larger than usual and top them with delicious mixtures such as the following:

Cheese Topping for Croûtons

Break the egg into a small bowl, add the brandy, salt, pepper and mustard, and beat together. Grate the cheese into the mixture

1 egg

2 teaspoons cooking brandy

pinch of salt

freshly ground pepper

1 teaspoon *Moutarde de Meaux*

about 4 oz (100–125 g) strong Cheddar cheese

until the texture of the paste is fairly firm. Using a small palette knife, spread this paste onto each cooked and drained croûton and heat under the grill at the very last minute.

I also make larger croûtons still (bigger than a 10 pence coin), and dry them out in the normal way. Then I pipe a small blob of Cheese and Herb Pâté (see page 29) on the top and carefully cover this with Cheese Topping mixture before grilling. The guest is agreeably (I hope) surprised to find the different texture and flavour in the middle.

Other Soup Garnishes

Soup should not only taste good, but look good too. I think the actual visual effect of soup when placed in front of the guest is important.

Cream is often used as a garnish with good intentions, but bad results. If full fat cream is put straight into hot soup, it can split and look messy. I always put a generous portion of croûtons in the soup first and then, just before serving, pipe a simple twirl of cream on top of the croûtons. They help support the cream and allow it to be *seen* as a twirl.

Chopped parsley is often sprinkled on to a soup but why not try deep-fried sprigs of parsley as a garnish?

At the end of the recipes I give suggestions for garnishes. Most of them can be prepared beforehand, covered and stored in the fridge until needed – but if you do this, be sure to take them out in good time: a bowl of hot soup is not enhanced by a well-chilled garnish!

As a general rule, cream soups are most effectively garnished by the use of grated, chopped, fried or baked pieces of the main vegetable ingredient of the soup.

Basic Recipe for Cream Soups

To serve 10 generous portions

2 lb (1 kg) vegetables (see individual recipes)

4 oz (100 g) butter

8 oz (225 g) onions

$\frac{1}{4}$ pint (150 ml) dry sherry

$\frac{1}{2}$ teaspoon salt

freshly ground black pepper

2 pints (generous 1 litre) stock

1. Cut the vegetables into *even-sized* pieces.

2. Melt the butter in a saucepan.

3. Finely chop the onions, add to the pan and sauté slowly, until golden. Take care that they don't burn or 'catch'.

4. Add sherry with vegetables, salt and pepper and other seasonings (see individual recipes). Place a double thickness of greaseproof paper (which has been well dampened with cold water) over the ingredients and then place a lid on the saucepan. Simmer on a very low heat for the appropriate time (see individual recipes).

5. Add stock and liquidize (only half-filling the liquidizer each time), and then pass the mixture through a fine sieve into a clean pan.

6. Check the seasoning when reheating just before serving. Adjust it to your own taste, and remember that sugar counteracts a salty taste and vice versa.

The basic cream of vegetable soup recipe can be varied using vegetables, flavourings and seasonings as in the following recipes. *Remember always to use the butter, onions, dry sherry, salt, and freshly ground black pepper along with the 2 pints (generous 1 litre) of home-made stock.*

Apricot and Marrow

- 1 lb (450 g) apricots (soaked overnight in cold stock)
- 1 lb (450 g) marrow
- ½ teaspoon ground ginger
- 1 tablespoon castor sugar

Cook gently for 1 hour. Add the stock, liquidize, and then sieve. Garnish before serving with sprigs of fresh mint.

Broad Bean and Hazelnut

- 2 lb (1 kg) frozen broad beans
- 1 tablespoon castor sugar
- 4 oz (100 g) hazelnuts

Cook the beans and sugar with the basic ingredients for 40 minutes. Add the stock, and when liquidized and sieved, add the hazelnuts. Garnish with some extra broad beans. Cook them separately, slowly, and then remove the tough outer skin. Marinate them in a little lemon juice before adding them to the soup.

Brussels Sprouts and Chestnut

- 2 lb (1 kg) Brussels sprouts
- 6 oz (175 g) natural chestnut purée
- ¼ teaspoon ground nutmeg
- ½ tablespoon castor sugar

Cook gently for 40 minutes. Add stock, liquidize and sieve, and garnish with bacon bits that have been crisped in the oven and then drained well.

Carrot and Coriander

- 2 lb (1 kg) diced carrots
- 2 tablespoons dried coriander seeds
- 1 tablespoon castor sugar

Cook gently for 1 hour. Add stock, liquidize, and sieve. Garnish with croûtons, double cream and chopped parsley. An unusual addition is raw grated carrot.

Carrot and Leek

- 1 lb (450 g) diced carrots
- 1 lb (450 g) finely diced leeks
- 1 tablespoon castor sugar

Cook gently for 1 hour. Add stock, liquidize and sieve. Garnish with croûtons and cream.

Carrot and Orange

- 2 lb (1 kg) diced carrots
- 1 tablespoon castor sugar
- 1 pint (600 ml) fresh orange juice

Cook gently for 1 hour. Add the fresh orange juice to the stock, and pour into the carrots. Liquidize and sieve. Garnish with a scored slice of fresh orange with a whirl of cream piped on top and sprinkled with finely grated raw carrot.

Cauliflower Cheese

- 2 lb (1 kg) cauliflower (remove the thick stalk)
- ½ teaspoon nutmeg
- ¾ teaspoon dry English mustard powder
- ½ tablespoon castor sugar
- 4 oz (100 g) grated Cheddar cheese

Cook gently for 45 minutes, add stock, then liquidize and sieve the soup. When reheating, add 4 oz (100 g) finely grated Cheddar cheese. Garnish with small sprigs of cauliflower that have been lightly fried in oil, then drained well. Sprinkle very finely grated cheese on each bowl just as it is being served. Large sprigs of deep-fried parsley also look good – and taste super!

Courgette and Fennel

- 1 lb (450 g) courgettes
- 1 lb (450 g) outer leaves of bulb fennel
- ½ tablespoon castor sugar

Add stock, then liquidize and sieve. Garnish with very thin slices of courgette which have been egg washed, floured and fried off, then drained well.

Curried Apple

- 2 lb (1 kg) unpeeled apples
- curry powder to taste (see below)

If you are using cooking apples you will have to add about 4 tablespoons sugar. Cook the apples gently for 1 hour. Then add the stock, liquidize and sieve.

I usually experiment with this soup to get the correct taste at the end when it has been cooked and liquidized. I put about ¼ pint (150 ml) stock into a liquidizer and then add pinches of cinnamon, garlic, cumin, celery seed, turmeric, chilli, mustard seed, coriander, elderflower etc, and blend. Pass through a fine sieve and then add little by little to the soup, tasting after each addition until you have reached the desired strength. This way no two curried soups ever taste the same.

Curried Marrow
Follow the recipe for Curried Apple.

Curried Pumpkin
Follow the recipe for Curried Apple.

Leek and Mustard

- 2 lb (1 kg) finely diced leeks
- 4 tablespoons dry English mustard powder
- ½ tablespoon castor sugar

Cook gently for 45 minutes. Add stock, liquidize and sieve. Garnish with heads of mustard and cress.

Mushroom

- 2 lb (1 kg) fresh mushrooms, including the stalks
- ¼ teaspoon cumin powder

Cook for 1 hour, add the stock, then liquidize and sieve. Garnish with two turned mushroom heads that have been fried in butter and then drained well on kitchen paper, along with a large sprig of fresh parsley.

Mushroom and Mustard

Use 2 lb (1 kg) mushrooms as for the Mushroom soup above, but cook off with 4 dessertspoons of *Moutarde de Meaux*. Add stock, liquidize and sieve. Garnish with sprigs of watercress.

Pea, Lemon and Mint

- 2 lb (1 kg) frozen peas
- 1 lemon cut into six wedges
- 6 large sprigs of fresh mint or 2 tablespoons dried mint
- 2 tablespoons castor sugar

Cook gently for 40 minutes. Add stock, then liquidize and sieve. Garnish with a handful of reserved cooked peas which have been marinated in the juice of half a lemon.

Pea, Pear and Watercress

- 1 lb (450 g) frozen peas
- 1 lb (450 g) peeled and cored pears
- ¼ teaspoon ground mace
- 2 bunches watercress

Cook the peas, pears and mace together gently for 35 minutes and then add the watercress and continue cooking for a further 15 minutes. Add stock, liquidize and sieve. Garnish with croûtons, thin slices of fresh pear fried in a little butter, with cream and a sprig of fresh watercress.

Spinach and Apple

- 1½ lb (675 g) leaf spinach
- 8 oz (225 g) apples, quartered
- ¼ teaspoon nutmeg
- 1 tablespoon castor sugar

Cook gently for 45 minutes. Add stock, liquidize and sieve. Garnish with lemon slices and finely diced apple.

Spinach and Whiting

- $1\frac{1}{2}$ lb (675g) leaf spinach
- 12 oz (300 g) fresh whiting
- $\frac{1}{2}$ nutmeg, finely grated
- 1 tablespoon castor sugar
- 1 teaspoon anchovy essence

Cook gently for 45 minutes. Add stock, liquidize and sieve. Garnish before serving with a few warmed prawns and toasted almonds.

Sweetcorn and Curry

- 2 lb (1 kg) frozen sweetcorn kernels
- 2 teaspoons medium-hot Indian curry powder

You can experiment with this soup as described in the recipe for Curried Apple soup.

Cook gently for 40 minutes, add stock, then liquidize and sieve. Garnish with sprigs of parsley.

Sweetcorn and Peanut

- $1\frac{1}{2}$ lb (675 g) frozen sweetcorn kernels
- $\frac{1}{2}$ lb (225 g) salted peanuts
- $\frac{1}{4}$ teaspoon ground ginger
- $\frac{1}{2}$ tablespoon castor sugar

Cook gently for 45 minutes; add stock, liquidize and sieve. Garnish with toasted salted peanuts, and I rather like this served with 'soldiers' of hot toast spread with peanut butter!

Tomato, Apple and Celery

Use just over 10 oz (275 g) of each of these three items. Add the tomatoes whole (the stalks too). Simply wipe and cut the apples into 4, leaving the core on each section. Use the head ends of celery stalks preferably. And add a $\frac{1}{4}$ teaspoon of nutmeg with a tiny pinch of ground ginger. Cook gently for 1 hour, then add the stock. Liquidize and sieve and garnish with an apple slice and chopped fresh chives.

Tomato and Tarragon

- 2 lb (1 kg) ripe tomatoes (with stalks)
- 2 tablespoons dried tarragon or 4 tablespoons fresh tarragon
- 1 tablespoon castor sugar

Cook gently for 40 minutes, then add stock. Liquidize, sieve and garnish with the fresh green ends of tarragon sprigs. This soup is particularly nice if served chilled.

Turnip and Dill

- 2 lb (1 kg) diced turnip
- 1 tablespoon dried dill
- $\frac{1}{4}$ tablespoon castor sugar

Cook gently for 1 hour. After adding the stock, liquidize, sieve and garnish with croûtons, cream and chopped parsley.

Smoked Haddock

2 lb (1 kg) smoked haddock

In this recipe you use the butter, onions, sherry, salt and pepper of the basic cream of vegetable soup, but you substitute 2 pints (generous 1 litre) of *milk* for the stock. Cook gently for 45 minutes, then add milk, liquidize and sieve. Garnish with croûtons, cream and then red lumpfish roe.

SCENE THREE
FISH

This is the course when I like to see – and usually do – my guests sink back into their chairs and really start to relax. An audience will sit enraptured for three hours through a good theatrical production and so do guests at my dinner parties. But it is important to see that apart from a pretty 'set' for the play, the furniture is practical and comfortable. The artists have to act the harder if you are watching from a wooden bench in the gallery – so remember when choosing dining-room furniture that what you sit on is as important as what is placed in front of you. Personally, I like carver chairs with comfortable arms, which we can settle down into as the evening progresses.

Most plots have sections where you digest what has gone before and think ahead to what might happen next, and the fish course is one that could help here. None of my fish recipes is difficult and the deliberate stark simplicity provides a complete contrast to the rest of the meal.

I have, as I said, selected the simplest of fish dishes for you to prepare, cook and serve, and these are some of the most popular at Miller Howe. Fresh fish should, of course, be used and these recipes can all be prepared in the morning, popped into the oven just prior to dinner, and served with style. Where butter is called for, be generous, and do endeavour to time the cooking so that the fish, when cooked, goes more or less immediately to the table.

HALIBUT

As this is a particularly meaty, filling fish, there is no reason why it should not be used as a main course, but with a main course you have to take more care with your choice of vegetables. But as a fish course – or a first course – I hope you will agree that I have tried to create interesting textures and flavours.

You are the only person to determine how much you are going to give each guest, but 3 oz (75 g) is sufficient (off the bone!) for a fish portion and 6 oz (175 g) generous for a main course. Wash the fish well under a slow-running cold tap. Place the portions of halibut on a well-buttered baking tray which has been lightly seasoned with salt and freshly ground black pepper. Do not pack the fish onto the dish but leave a good inch (2.5 cm) clear round each portion. Pat the fish dry with kitchen paper and lightly season.

Baked Halibut with Yoghurt, Fennel and Cheese

Per Person

3 oz (75 g) halibut

2 tablespoons natural yoghurt

1 tablespoon finely chopped fennel bulb

1 tablespoon strong Cheddar cheese, grated

The use of yoghurt with the halibut in the following recipes complements the fish and certainly makes it a joy to eat – and it is not so rich as using cream.

Coat each piece of fish liberally with the yoghurt. Place the chopped fennel on the top of each portion. Cover the whole dish with transparent cling film and put it in the fridge until required.

Remove the film and bake in a preheated oven at 350°F (180°C), Gas 4, for 30 minutes. Light the grill and grate the strong Cheddar cheese very finely. Sprinkle the cheese generously over each portion and then put the fish under the hot grill for a few minutes until the cheese begins to bubble and turn slightly brown in patches. Use a fish slice to turn out each portion onto a hot plate and serve immediately.

To ring the changes, you can add finely chopped apple or celery, or use them instead of the fennel.

Halibut Baked with Yoghurt, Lime and Fresh Ginger

Per Person

3 oz (75 g) halibut

2 tablespoons natural yoghurt

juice and rind of fresh lime

about $\frac{1}{4}$ teaspoon of grated root ginger

Place the portions of halibut onto the well-buttered baking tray. Grate the rind of the lime and as much ginger as you want into the yoghurt. Squeeze the juice from the lime over the portions of fish before coating them with the yoghurt mixture. Bake in the preheated oven at 350°F (180°C), Gas 4, for 30 minutes.

How much fresh ginger you use depends very much on personal taste, so when you first prepare this dish be rather sparing with your grating. I find the combination of lime and ginger is a clean refreshing flavour, and I use it often.

Halibut with Five Fresh Herbs in Yoghurt

Per Person

3 oz (75 g) halibut

2 tablespoons natural yoghurt

a mixture (about ½ tablespoon) of chopped fresh herbs: tarragon, basil, parsley, marjoram, thyme (be sparing) or mint

Liberally coat each portion of halibut on the well-buttered baking tray with the yoghurt. Sprinkle the chopped herbs on the top of each portion.

Bake in the preheated oven at 350°F (180°C), Gas 4, for 30 minutes. When ready to serve, garnish with some sprigs of the fresh herbs. (See my notes on *Herbs* on page 216.)

Baked Halibut with Apple, Walnut and Celery

Per Person

3 oz (75 g) halibut

1 tablespoon melted butter

freshly ground black pepper

¼ Granny Smith apple

¼ stick celery

1 tablespoon lemon juice

1 tablespoon chopped walnuts

Place the portions of halibut on the well-buttered tray (remembering to leave the space around), and pour the melted butter over each portion. Sprinkle with freshly-ground black pepper. Chop the apple (unpeeled) with the celery stick (being as generous or as mean as you like with the celery) and toss in the fresh lemon juice. Spoon this mixture over the fish.

Bake in a preheated oven at 350°F (180°C), Gas 4, for 30 minutes. Then have the grill ready and sprinkle on finely chopped walnuts (remember they are slightly bitter when cooked, so don't go mad).

Baked Halibut with Smoked Salmon, Avocado and Hollandaise Sauce

Per Person

3 oz (75 g) halibut

about 1 oz (25 g) smoked salmon

¼ avocado pear

1 tablespoon lemon juice

½ oz (15 g) melted butter

1 oz (25 g) Hollandaise Sauce (see page 207)

Put the portions of halibut onto the well-buttered baking tray. Slice the smoked salmon (which has been soaked in cold milk for 2 hours) so that it more or less covers the top of each portion. Cut the avocado quarter two-thirds of the way down in order to make a fan (see the photograph of a fan gherkin between pages 208 and 209 for method), and put this on top of the smoked salmon. Sprinkle with the fresh lemon juice. Coat liberally with melted butter and bake the fish in the preheated oven at 350°F (180°C), Gas 4, for 30 minutes. Just as you are about to serve it, coat liberally with the Hollandaise Sauce.

There is no reason, after you have cooked halibut in the basic way outlined in the recipes above, why you should not start experimenting with your own variations on the theme. Tomato and cucumber with grated horseradish combined with the yoghurt is summery; peanuts liquidized with garlic and soya sauce is filling but quite palatable, and I have liquidized some leftover tuna fish with olive oil and garlic and combined this with yoghurt.

Try some of your own ideas. But I am sure you will find the basic method easy to do and fun to serve.

SOLE

Somebody suggested to me one evening in the restaurant that I shouldn't serve sole as it was such a 'common' dish. To which I replied that so was Eliza Doolittle, but she gave a lot of pleasure to a great many people in *My Fair Lady*. And so it is with sole.

Sole cooked simply with garlic and cheese-flavoured butter, sole creamed exotically with Hollandaise, sole with watercress and orange – they're all so succulent and tempting.

Again, as with halibut, you have to decide how much to give each guest, but 4-oz (100–125-g) fillets make a good-sized fish course portion, and 6 oz (175 g) is a meal in itself for a main course. Wash the sole well under a slow-running cold tap, skin, and dry well on kitchen paper. Liberally butter the baking dish or tray you are going to use, and sprinkle with salt and freshly-ground black pepper.

All these sole dishes look so elegantly simple when served, which is probably their main appeal.

Baked Savoury Sole

Per Person

4 oz (100–125 g) fillet of sole

2 tablespoons Savoury Breadcrumbs (see page 54)

1 oz (25 g) melted butter

Make the breadcrumbs (you will find full instructions on page 54), and then pour the melted butter into this dry mixture to bind it to a 'sticking' consistency. You want the fillets of sole well coated with the breadcrumb mixture, and you want the coating to stay on! Lift the coated fillets onto the well-buttered baking tray, cover and leave them until you want to cook.

Pre-heat the oven and bake at 350°F (180°C), Gas 4, for 20 minutes. Just before serving, flash the fish under a hot grill so that the little pieces of cheese begin to brown and bubble. The only garnish you need is a generous wedge of fresh lemon and a sprig of fresh parsley.

Variations on Baked Sole

As you will have learned on basic principles by now, I shall just outline a few variations on my basic theme rather than spell them out.

1. A piece of smoked salmon and an avocado wedge, as in the halibut recipe (see opposite) are good with sole.

2. Add 1 teaspoon desiccated coconut per portion to the breadcrumbs, and bake off a couple of buttered slices of banana as an accompaniment to each fillet of sole.

3. Add 1 teaspoon ground hazelnuts to the breadcrumbs, and serve the cooked sole garnished with orange slices.

4. Add a generous sprinkling (about 1 teaspoon) of ground almonds to the breadcrumbs. Finely dice about ½ teaspoon each of red pepper

and bulb fennel and place them on top of each fillet before it goes into the oven (don't flash *this* dish under the grill as the peppers will burn).

5. Add the grated rind of a fresh lime or lemon to the breadcrumbs and serve the cooked fish with piped butter flavoured with the lime or lemon juice (see page 78).

Rolled Baked Sole

Per Person

4 oz (100–125 g) fillet of sole

1 oz (25 g) filling of your choice (see below)

2 oz (50 g) white wine sauce for serving (see page 206)

This is a slightly more complicated way of serving sole, but well worth the effort.

Wash the fillets as before under a slow-running cold tap, skin and dry them well on kitchen paper. Place the fillets *skinned side up* on your work surface and coat them with the filling of your choice.

Roll each fillet up in the shape of a small Swiss roll, and wrap each up in a well-buttered and seasoned double-thickness of greaseproof paper. Hold together with a small elastic band or tie with thin string. Tightly pack the portions on a wire cooling tray placed inside the roasting tray.

When about to cook, pour enough boiling water into the bottom of the roasting tray just to come up to the base of the cooling tray and bake in a preheated oven at 350°F (180°C), Gas 4, for 30 to 40 minutes. (Instead of water, I sometimes boil up and use white wine.)

Carefully remove the greaseproof paper and serve coated with the full-bodied white wine sauce.

Fillings

1. Mushroom Pâté (see page 30). You could use Noilly Prat instead of the reduction of white wine for the sauce, and garnish each fillet with half a teaspoon of red lumpfish roe and a sprig of parsley.

2. Cheese and Herb Pâté (see page 29), thickened with 1 tablespoon fresh breadcrumbs per portion.

3. Mashed banana with a touch of curry powder, thickened with 1 tablespoon breadcrumbs or ground almonds.

4. Liquidize 1 oz (25 g) shrimps or prawns per portion with just a little butter.

5. Soak some sultanas in brandy overnight. Lightly fry 1–2 tablespoons finely chopped onion in a little butter and mix into a thick paste with ground almonds before adding the soaked and drained sultanas.

6. If you're feeling extravagant, liquidize together ½ oz (15 g) each of avocado pear and smoked salmon.

SALMON

A good fresh salmon is simplicity itself to cook and in no way can frozen salmon come anywhere near in either appearance or taste. Living where I do, I find salmon at its best between April and mid-July. This is when the healthy fat fish, oily and succulent, are starting to wend their way up the rivers to their spawning grounds. Hang the price: buy them then and, for salmon at its best, cook it the following way.

A fish kettle is a must and you can improvise by using a deep roasting dish. The whole salmon must be completely immersed in the water when being cooked, so make sure your dish is large enough. To prevent the fish touching the bottom of the dish, spread thick balls of crumpled greaseproof paper over the base.

Poached Salmon

For the fish stock

2 tablespoons olive oil

1 teaspoon wine vinegar

4 peppercorns

6 stalks fresh parsley

1 teaspoon salt

a few onion rings

1 chopped carrot

The exact amount of fish stock will depend on the size of your fish, and these quantities are *per each pint (600 ml) of water.*

Bring the stock to the boil and simmer for about 5 minutes and then immerse the salmon in it. When brought back to the boil, simmer for purely and simply *one minute per pound (450 g) gutted weight* – yes, one minute a pound.

Salmon cooked whole are best, but if you are only cooking a piece, do be sure to grease the exposed ends well, and cover them with a double thickness of greaseproof paper taken actually over the body of the fish and held in place with an elastic band. If you don't do this I find that these large areas of exposed flesh are over-cooked even at one minute per pound (with the whole fish, the flesh is protected from the liquid by the head and tail). Even when cooking a whole salmon I tend to replace the guts with well-greased greaseproof paper so that the inside of the fish doesn't get overcooked.

Leave the fish in the liquid until it is quite cold and remove just prior to serving.

People tend to frown when I say that salmon only needs one minute per pound, and I'm sure they inflict a 4-minute poaching on their fish. Those extra 3 minutes are doing an incredible amount of damage, so do please believe me and do it my way.

When serving, be very generous with the mayonnaise (use a *very good* olive oil). Accompanied by minted new potatoes and a few peas, you have the best possible summer meal I can think of.

Salmon Stuffed with Mushroom

When salmon is coming to the end of the season I occasionally gut one and stuff it with Mushroom Pâté (see page 30) and poach it in the way mentioned above. Serve cold with a sauce of finely chopped cucumber and yoghurt, flavoured with the rind and juice of a fresh lime.

Baked Salmon Steaks

Per Person

1 salmon steak (approximately 8 oz or 225 g)

1 0z (25 g) melted butter

2 tablespoons white wine

a little salt

freshly ground black pepper

a few parsley stalks

Hollandaise Sauce (see page 207)

This is another delicious dish to be served during the peak months of the salmon season.

Butter the baking tray well and place the steaks meat-side down on it. Coat the steaks generously with the melted butter, pour over the white wine, sprinkle lightly with salt and freshly ground black pepper, and put a few parsley stalks on top.

Bake them in a pre-heated oven at 375°F (190°C), Gas 5. This size of steak needs a bare 8 minutes at this temperature to be ready for the table.

Serve with the Hollandaise Sauce, and what easier dish could you have?

Salmon au Gratin

If you have any salmon left over, flake the flesh and arrange in any dish suitable to the amount of fish you have – a ramekin, scallop shell, steak and kidney pie dish even – and put in a bain marie. Make the white wine sauce (see page 206) and keep it warm in a double saucepan. Warm the salmon through in a low oven set at 300°F (150°C), Gas 2, for about 10 minutes, remove and coat with the sauce, sprinkle with breadcrumbs, chopped parsley and a little Cheddar cheese. Finish off under a hot grill, and serve immediately.

TROUT

Now that there are so many trout farms springing up around the country, lovely fresh trout are available the whole year through. If they have been well fed (particularly in the weeks prior to their catch!) they are a deep good-looking pink and taste marvellous. Best of all, they are very easy to serve at a dinner party.

Before serving, however, try and find out the source of your trout, and try them on the family first. Farm trout take up to 2 years to breed fully and during this time are fed on commercial pellets. Just prior to being caught, they may be given better-quality foodstuffs to improve their flavour and colour, but I have eaten farm trout that tasted high and very strong. (The same thing happens, of course, to those yellow battery chickens: the poor creatures have been fed the cheapest fishmeal available and nothing seems to remove its flavour from their bodies. I remember years ago, when I worked in Central Africa as a Junior Cadet Officer, religiously mixing sherry with the meal for a doomed free-range chicken as I had been told by the delightful old African cooks that it would make the bird tipsy, therefore not so tense or tough – and tasty!)

Fresh farm trout are slimy to the touch and have bright eyes. (If they have been frozen first and cunningly defrosted before being put out on the fishmonger's slab, beware!) Lay the trout down on your work surface with one eye *facing* you and one eye down on the board, cut off the head and tail, and run your knife from tail to head through the middle where the main bone lies. Discard this bone along with the guts and rinse lightly under a slow-running cold tap and then pat dry. Have to hand a well-buttered metal tray or two, large enough to take the fish.

As with the other fish recipes, the quantity you serve depends on whether you want the trout for a fish course or a main course. As a general rule, one half fish is a generous portion for a fish course.

Simple Baked Trout

Nothing could be easier as you just lay the filleted trout on the buttered trays, skin side down, and liberally baste them with further melted butter and leave until you wish to pop them into the oven. Bake them at 350°F (180°C), Gas 4, for 20 minutes.

Baked Farm Trout with Lemon or Lime Butter

Per person

½ trout fillet

juice and rind of ½ lemon or lime

1 oz (25 g) butter

halved olives and sprigs of parsley to garnish

Squeeze the lemon or lime juice over the trout fillet and then sprinkle with the grated rind (do remember to grate the rind before squeezing the juice!). Top with the butter.

Bake them at 350°F (180°C), for 20 minutes.

As a garnish, make up some lemon or lime butter (see page 78), and pipe it onto the whole slices of lemon or lime. Top each with a half olive and a sprig of parsley and put these onto the fish just before serving.

Baked Trout with Hazelnuts and Grapefruit

Per person

½ trout fillet

1 oz (25 g) butter, melted

1 oz (25 g) ground hazelnuts

2 grapefruit segments

Wash the trout and pat dry. Lay skin down on the buttered tray and coat generously with the butter. Cover the buttered fillets liberally and evenly with the ground hazelnuts. Bake them at 350°F (180°C), Gas 4, for 20 minutes, and then, just before serving, place 2 segments of fresh grapefruit in the middle with a sprig of parsley. You will be agreeably surprised by such a delightful contrast of flavours.

Baked Trout with Hazelnuts and Orange

Exactly the same as above – the orange, naturally, being for those with a sweeter tooth.

Per person

$\frac{1}{2}$ trout fillet

1 oz (25 g) Cheese and Herb Pâté (see page 29)

Fillet of Farm Trout Baked in Cheese and Herb Pâté

Simply place fillets of farm trout on buttered baking trays and liberally coat with the pâté and then bake at 350°F (180°C), Gas 4, for about 30 minutes. This is very nice garnished generously with toasted almonds. The pâté itself can also be served – piped on to a whole lemon slice – with most grilled fish.

SCAMPI

I don't usually like to work with frozen products, but I think there is room for frozen scampi (provided you buy the jumbo size of a well-known brand). So many bags or packets of frozen scampi seem to consist of more frozen liquid than scampi! Find a reputable brand and stick to it, and you will find that scampi in your freezer is a good standby.

Scampi take about 4 hours at room temperature to thaw completely. Help them on their way by removing from the bag or packet after about 2 hours and spreading them evenly on a cooling tray (inside a roasting tray so that the defrosting liquid won't run all over the place).

Cook scampi in a double steamer. When the water in the base starts to simmer swiftly, the scampi need only 4 minutes in the top steamer with a lid on and they are cooked! They can be served hot or cold.

For 2

8 oz (225 g) defrosted scampi

$\frac{1}{4}$ teaspoon fresh grated ginger

juice and grated rind of $\frac{1}{2}$ lime

Scampi with Ginger and Lime

If you like the flavours of ginger and lime – and they go so well with so many dishes, including scampi – simply sprinkle the fresh grated ginger and the grated rind and juice of the lime over the scampi and steam as I described above.

Cold Scampi

Serve cold scampi with Hollandaise Sauce (see page 207) or the rich mayonnaise (see page 132). Scampi are not cheap so the individual dishes can be augmented by serving on a bed of rice, or a bed of celery and apple strips marinated in good French dressing to provide a contrast in texture. Hard-boiled eggs with mayonnaise also help to 'pad out' a scampi dish and, of course, I always serve slices of buttered wholemeal bread (see page 185).

Larger quantities of scampi can be cooked by placing the defrosted scampi on a cooling tray inside a roasting tray full up to the base of the cooling tray with salted boiling water. Bring back to the boil on the top of the stove and then immediately cover with a metal tray or foil and steam for 4 minutes only. The scampi will be just cooked – moist, tender and succulent. If marinated beforehand in the grated rind of a fresh lime and juice with a little grated fresh ginger, they will taste even better. Try them set in aspic flavoured with plenty of chopped fresh tarragon and fennel – they are out of this world!

FINNAN HADDOCK

This is my very favourite party dish, but do be careful when buying finnan haddock. So much 'smoked' haddock these days is purely and simply dyed, and when you cook it in milk the fish gets paler and paler, and the milk more and more orange! Always try to buy it on the bone as I have nearly always found this to be the genuine article.

On the bone allow 6 oz (175 g) each for a fish course portion and 8 oz (225 g) for a main course.

Smoked Haddock in Cheese Sauce

For 4–6

2 lb (1 kg) smoked finnan haddock

$1\frac{1}{2}$ pints (900 ml) milk

a few fresh parsley stalks

a couple of onion rings

8 peppercorns

Place the haddock in a baking dish that will take the fish in one layer and add enough milk to cover. Add the parsley, a couple of onion rings (no more), and the peppercorns.

Bake slowly in the oven at 300°F (150°C), Gas 2, for about 45 minutes. Remove the fish from the milk (retaining the milk) and flake the flesh off the bone into a bowl.

Pass the milk through a strainer and use it for making a Cheese Sauce (to each pint (600 ml) of milk for the basic white sauce, add 4 oz (100 g) finely grated Cheddar cheese, but see also the recipe on page 206). Fold the haddock into the finished sauce and cover with a butter wrapping (never throw away butter wrappings as they are ideal for putting, inside down, on top of the sauces, and can be used for storing pastry and cooked root vegetables).

To warm through, place the bowl of haddock and sauce into a bain marie with boiling water, and place in a medium oven at 350°F (180°C), Gas 4, for about 30 minutes. You can also warm it through in a double saucepan which takes about 30 minutes. Then portion it out onto plates piped with mashed potato to make a 'nest' for the fish, or just put into ramekins which can be topped off with a little mashed potato and flashed under a hot grill.

You can also use smoked haddock and cheese sauce with puff pastry rounds, with pancakes or gougères, or simply serve it by itself in ramekins with soldier strips of hot buttered toast. If you feel extravagant, you can add a couple of tablespoons of cooking brandy to the sauce, and I occasionally fold in some sultanas that have been soaked overnight in brandy. But always, always, fill your pastry *at the last minute.*

Lemon, Lime or Orange Butters to accompany Fish

A Kenwood is handy for making this, and the end product can be stored for a long time in a freezer or for up to a week in the fridge.

Before you start, make certain that your butter is relatively soft, as you don't want to strain your Kenwood, and that your grater is sharp. I find at Miller Howe the ordinary stainless steel graters only last one full season so do bear in mind that this piece of equipment in your kitchen will not last for ever if constantly in use.

For each 1 lb (450 g) of soft butter you will require the juice and fine rind of 2 lemons to make the lemon butter, the juice and rind of 3 average limes for lime butter, and rind and juice of 2 oranges for the orange butter. The K-beater quickly blends all this together and then you simply store the end product in a plastic container, or spoon out like a sausage on to a piece of greaseproof paper which you then roll up to look like a stick of old-fashioned seaside rock. This latter method makes for ease of serving as you simply cut off slices as thick or thin as you want. I personally prefer to pipe the butter into shapes either directly on to the fish or onto slices of lemon, lime or orange. In turn, these shapes can be decorated with parsley, olives, fan gherkins or anything that takes your fancy and then chilled to set in the fridge!

Do remember that finely chopped fresh herbs are tasty when combined with butter, and if you are a lover of garlic this, crushed, makes a good garnishing butter as well.

MENU

MENU 1

A simple 3-course meal

Tomato, Apple and Celery Soup with Cream and Croûtons (see page 66)

Lamb Cutlets with Orange and Ginger (page 93)

Winter Root Vegetables (page 125)

Creamed Potatoes (page 121)

Lemon Ice Box Pudding (page 166)

Home-made Wholemeal Bread (page 185)

A light simple Beaujolais, slightly chilled, would go well with the main course.

The order of preparation for this simple 3-course meal allows you an easy build-up to the night in question.

Two Days Before

Prepare the Lemon Ice Box Pudding and the Wholemeal Bread.

The Day Before

Prepare the soup, the root vegetables, and trim, flour and seal the cutlets themselves. Peel the potatoes and leave in cold water.

Arrange the flowers.

Morning

Double-check your shopping, and set the table. Put the serving dishes and plates into the warming drawer, the plates for the pudding into the fridge, and prepare the coffee tray, hiding it discreetly away.

Check that:
all lamps are working, and have bulbs
the heating is OK
the spare bedroom for coats and the cloakroom are organized
tapes or records are selected for your background music
the flowers are watered (I so often forget to top them up on the actual day, and they can get very droopy)

Cook and cream the potatoes, and leave them in a buttered double saucepan.

Prepare the Garnishes

For the soup, a peeled and cored apple ring (sprinkled with lemon) per serving, a celery twirl, and some chopped parsley. Fry off the croûtons and leave to drain on absorbent paper.

For the main course, prepare a scored orange twirl for each serving (you could put them on a well-greased tray sprinkled with a little demerara sugar, and then they can be served warm), and of course some finely chopped parsley.

For the Ice Box Pudding, prepare some lemon twirls.

Evening

About 2 hours before you want to serve your main course, put your prepared cutlets into the pre-set low oven with the orange juice and ginger (work it out so that you allow time for your guests to drink the soup first). With a casserole, however, the odd 10 to 15 minutes will not matter (provided this extra cooking time is *not* at the end when the lid is removed and you are browning the cutlets!).

Have ready the tray for the Winter Root Vegetables, wrapped in foil.

Cut and butter the bread and leave it on the serving plate under a damp tea towel. Make sure the soup ladle is close to the soup pan and that you have the double cream whipped and in a piping bag. The soup only takes about 20 minutes to warm through – gently stir occasionally – and don't forget to double-check the seasoning at this stage. When the guests are seated, portion out the soup into the warmed dishes, garnish, and serve along with the Wholemeal Bread slices.

Take the lid off the casserole now, and put the root vegetables in their foil parcels into the oven to warm through (the oven is now set at high, remember, so be careful not to overdo things).

The creamed potatoes in the buttered double saucepan should start heating through now as well.

When the soup is finished, clear away efficiently. Open out the foil parcels of vegetables, take the casserole out, set out the warm main course plates, and serve. Garnish each plate, and serve the wine.

The Ice Box Pudding is served on the chilled plates with whipped cream and the lemon twirls. At this point remember to start the coffee, so that this will be ready when the pudding has been eaten – but do allow your guests a second helping. I'm sure they'll say 'Yes, please'.

MENU 2

A 3-course meal with a choice of desserts

Pea, Pear and Watercress Soup
with Cream and Croûtons (page 65)

Breast of Chicken with Marsala Sauce
and Toasted Almonds (pages 100 and 209)

Purée of Parsnips with Toasted Pine Kernels (page 120)

Grated Zucchini in Fresh Lime (page 117)

Small New Potatoes

Calvados Apple Chocolate Crunchies (pages 153 and 211)

or

Orange Mousse with Shortbread (pages 159 and 194)

Home-made Wholemeal Bread (page 185)

An inexpensive but pleasant dry white Burgundy would
go well with this, or if you prefer a sweeter wine
find one of the Alsace variety

This 3-course menu, with a choice of sweets, is still simple, when organized and prepared carefully.

Two Days Before

You can make the Wholemeal Bread and the Shortbread well in advance.

You can also prepare the breasts of chicken (with your own personal choice of stuffing – Mushroom Pâté or Cheese and Herb Pâté are excellent). Leave them in the fridge, wrapped in their individual foil parcels.

Make stock for the soup with the chicken carcases.

The Day Before

Make the soup with the chicken stock.

Cook and purée the parsnips before storing them in the fridge.

Make the bases for the Apple Crunchies. Prepare the Calvados Apple Purée and leave in the fridge.

Arrange the flowers.

Morning

Check your shopping and set the table. Prepare the coffee tray and put the plates and dishes in the warming drawer.

Check:
the lamps
the heating
the room for the coats and the cloakroom
the tapes or records
the flowers

If needed, scrape the potatoes and leave them in a pan of cold water. Otherwise wipe them clean. Grate the courgettes and leave them to marinate in the rind and juice of the limes.

Reduce the cream and the Marsala for the chicken sauce. Leave to cool in a double saucepan.

Make the Orange Mousse (it *can* be prepared the day before, but I find it much better if made on the day).

Prepare the Garnishes

For the soup, put a few small slices of pear sprinkled with lemon juice on a well-buttered tray, so that they can be warmed through just prior to the meal. Put ready some sprigs of watercress, a handful of cooked petits pois, the whipped double cream and croûtons to serve with the soup.

For the main course, chopped fresh parsley looks good over the sauce on the chicken, and with the potatoes. Toast the pine kernels and almonds in the oven (don't forget about them!).

For the mousse, you will want some orange quarter slices along with a small tin of drained lychees. Have ready doyleys on plates and fern leaves for presenting the mousse. If you have any fresh mint, this looks nice on the Chocolate Crunchies.

Quarter, core and slice the apples at the last minute and soak in white wine. Fill the Crunchies with the apple mixture just before serving, and garnish the Orange Mousse.

Evening

Put on the soup to heat gently for about 20 minutes, and put ready the prepared garnishes.

Set out the warmed soup plates and have the soup ladle handy.

Cut and butter the bread and leave on the serving plate under a damp towel.

Put the purée of parsnip in the double saucepan, and have the frying pan close by with oil and butter ready for the last-minute frying off of the drained, grated zucchini.

Have ready the roasting and cooling trays and the water boiling just before cooking starts. Pre-set the oven just before your guests are expected to arrive, and 35–40 minutes before you will want to eat them, put the chicken breasts in (allowing time for pre-dinner drinks, then soup).

As you start to serve the soup, begin to warm up the parsnip purée, the zucchini, the sauce for the chicken, and put the potatoes on to boil.

Fill the Crunchies with the apple mixture and garnish with the drained apple slices just before serving, and garnish the Orange Mousse.

ACT
TWO

ACT TWO

SCENE ONE
MAIN COURSES

SCENE TWO
VEGETABLES

SCENE THREE
SALADS AND SALAD DRESSINGS

You – the producer, director, stage manager and artist are the star here, and so much depends on your script, your choice of menu. The only theatrical point I would make, though, is that you shouldn't give your all here, as you have a further act to sustain. A bad third act will ruin the reactions to your first two, so leave a bit of energy, wit and cunning for Act Three.

The dishes in this section can all be prepared well in advance and without much sweat and toil involved during the performance. Don't worry if everything doesn't come 100 per cent up to scratch (it is *very* difficult being all the aforementioned people rolled up into one, *and* audience as well: it is far easier being a cook in a commercial operation where you spend all your time watching what you are doing).

At home, things tend occasionally to go haywire, but if I haven't rubbed off some of the old pro feeling on to you by now, it will be difficult to shrug off over-cooked carrots or slightly scorched turnips. During this course, tell your own witty tales and divert attention from your mistakes (if any) by actually commenting on them. 'Such a pity I over-cooked the carrots', will *immediately* bring shouts of contradiction (the right line at the right time is so important). And you will have got them eating out of your hand – purely in a metaphorical sense!

SCENE ONE
MAIN COURSES

The main course, obviously, is just that. The central attraction of the meal – or the *star* of the evening.

Having plumped for your main dish you must consider whether it is dry or wet, sweet or sour, chewy or tender, powerful or bland, and decide what goes with it. I don't mean just the vegetables, although they are very important (I outline throughout what goes with what). You must also consider the remainder of the meal, and work it out so that every dish complements every other. If the main course is going to be dominant, like Roast Leg of Lamb with a tomato and garlic sauce, you must seek a 'delicate' soup to precede it – a simple purée of a root vegetable without any added herbs or spices. Then you can use something really forceful to open the evening – one of the Cheese and Herb Pâté dishes, maybe, or a Duck Liver Pâté variation,

Never follow sweet spicy dishes with similar ones, and never have a creamy fish dish such as Haddock in Cheese Sauce followed by Breast of Chicken in a wine sauce. A good contrast to the smooth texture of the haddock, for instance, would be Roast Chicken stuffed with herbs or Roast Duck cooked so that the skin is as crisp as toffee apple.

BEEF

It used to be said that we were a nation of beef eaters, but with the price of beef now, I think that delightful saying is a trifle out of date. I serve Roast Sirloin of Aberdeen Angus Beef on alternate Sundays at the hotel, and I must admit I always like to be firmly on duty on those occasions, for there is little that can challenge the sensual aromas of roast beef as the oven door is opened for basting. Beef is nostalgic for me, too, as it reminds me of my mean, cunning, old Yorkshire Great-Grandfather who used to sit proudly at the head of the table each Sunday surrounded by his family – his two sons, their offspring, and then us great-grandchildren. After the inevitable bowl of steaming soup in would come two enormous Yorkshire puddings and Great-Grandfather would always in his rascally way say: 'Now come on all of ye; those who eat most pud get most of Mary's roast beef.' Always eager to take up the challenge, we youngsters would stuff ourselves with Yorkshire pud and gravy and leave no room at all for the thin slices of succulent beef that the old man carved later!

Simple Roast Beef

A 6-lb ($2\frac{3}{4}$-kg) sirloin of beef *on the bone* will serve 8 guests. First of all, I wipe the meat with a dry kitchen cloth and then liberally coat both sides with salt and freshly ground black pepper. In the base of an appropriately sized roasting tray I scatter onion skins and carrot peelings (if there are any to hand), along with a few parsley stalks. And then, when the joint has been placed in the roasting tray with the fat side up (the bones form a natural rack for good distribution of heat) I liberally sprinkle the seasoned fat side with 2 tablespoons of curry powder. When cooked, there is no trace of this powder but cooked without it, oh, there is a subtle difference in the taste.

The oven should be preheated to 475°F (250°C), Gas 9, and the beef left for the first 30 minutes. Turn the oven down to 350°F (180°C), Gas 4, and continue to cook for a further 2 hours, basting about every 20 minutes. Your joint should then be medium rare (which is how *I* like it).

Never carve the joint immediately the cooking time is finished but remove it from the oven, cover with foil, and leave in a warm, completely damp-free area (a shelf on top of the stove if you are fortunate enough to have such a thing). Carve it about 10 to 15 minutes after the joint is out of the oven.

Serve with Blackcurrant and Beetroot Jelly for a change, instead of the inevitable mustard and horseradish!

Blackcurrant and Beetroot Jelly

This is quickly made by using those jars of baby beetroots which are the ideal size and shape, along with a packet of commercial blackcurrant jelly. Simply make up ½ pint (300 ml) of the jelly if you are serving 6 to 8 guests and put about 20 beetroot balls in a suitably sized dish. Top up with the prepared jelly and leave to set. These two flavours are different and very tasty with the roast beef. I often put a generous blob of creamed horseradish on the top too, and garnish with chopped chives. They all add to the success of the occasion.

Beef in Guinness with Orange

These quantities will serve 4 to 6 people.

- **2 lb (1 kg) rump steak cut into 2-in (5-cm) cubes**
- **seasoned flour**
- **2 oz (50 g) butter**
- **4 oz (100 g) finely chopped onions**
- **2 crushed cloves of garlic**
- **4 oz (100 g) sliced carrots**
- **2 oz (50 g) diced turnips**
- **2 oz (50 g) diced celery**
- **pinch each of fresh nutmeg and allspice**
- **2 bottles of Guinness**
- **salt and freshly ground black pepper**
- **juice and rind of 2 oranges**
- **2 tablespoons freshly chopped parsley**

Dip the steak pieces into the seasoned flour, taking care not to be over-generous at this stage. Melt the butter and sauté off the onions. When they have turned golden, turn the heat up and drop in the meat cubes to seal. Remove the meat and onions from the frying pan and transfer to a casserole dish. Quickly seal the vegetables (the garlic first) in the remaining fat and cover the meat with this.

Stir the nutmeg and allspice into the Guinness and pour on to the ingredients in the casserole. Season with salt and pepper. Cook at 250°F (130°C), Gas ½, for 6 hours and then add the juice and rind of the oranges. At this stage I prefer to leave the casserole overnight and then the following day cook through at 300°F (150°C), Gas 2, for about 45 minutes. Serve with finely chopped parsley sprinkled over.

Wolfgang's Austrian Steak

4 × 8-oz (225-g) rump steaks, about $\frac{1}{2}$ in (1 cm) thick

3 tablespoons plain flour seasoned with salt and freshly ground black pepper

2 oz (50 g) butter

6 oz (175 g) finely chopped bacon

1 medium-sized onion, finely chopped

2 small carrots, finely chopped

1 pint (600 ml) beef stock

$\frac{1}{2}$ teaspoon allspice

$\frac{1}{2}$ teaspoon thyme

3 tablespoons wine vinegar

juice and rind of 1 lemon

2 oz (50 g) plain flour

$\frac{1}{4}$ pint (150 ml) Marsala wine

$\frac{1}{2}$ pint (300 ml) double cream

Coat the rump steaks with seasoned flour (not too much at this stage) and then seal them in the melted butter in a frying pan. Transfer the steaks to drain on kitchen paper, then fry off the bacon until well done, and remove it from the pan. In the combined residue of original butter and bacon fat, lightly fry the chopped onion and carrot. Meanwhile mix together the beef stock, the allspice, thyme, wine vinegar and lemon juice and rind. Sprinkle the 2 oz (50 g) flour over the vegetables in the pan and stir vigorously to make a well-mixed smooth roux, add the seasoned beef stock to the pan and stir again.

Put the steaks in a suitably sized flameproof casserole, pour the sauce over, and then sprinkle the bacon evenly over the 4 steaks. Cook in the oven at 325°F (170°C), Gas 3, for $1\frac{1}{2}$ hours.

Remove the steaks from the casserole and put them back in the oven on a tray or ovenproof plate. Place your casserole on top of the stove, and add the cream and Marsala to the vegetable broth. Cook, stirring continuously, until thick and well reduced, and then serve with the cooked steaks.

LAMB

Living in the English Lake District has many advantages, one of them being the local lamb. It appears on the menus at Miller Howe as regularly as clockwork as I buy 3 whole lambs on the hoof each week at the auction in Kendal. It is interesting to see, throughout the year, how the taste and texture changes, but it is a main course that is utterly reliable (provided it is well hung). In the spring, it is tender and juicy; in the summer it tastes delicious, and in late autumn it is a little tougher and much more fatty, but still tasty.

The sheep farmer's skill comes to the fore in his actual selection of sheep to be sent for slaughtering. The best commercial weight is about 80 lb (36 kg). The farmer feels the back of the animal and decides when the backbone and loins are reasonably well covered with meat – fatty lamb is not looked on too kindly by butchers! As in all walks of life, it is the greedy ones that go first (I have always said I don't mind meeting my Maker 3 or 4 years sooner as long as I can eat and drink my fill twice a day, rather than go 3 or 4 years later by watching every morsel and drop that goes down my gullet), and by this very fact most sheep farmers pan out their slaughtering.

Roast Leg of Lakeland Lamb

This size of leg will serve 8 people

a 6–7-lb (3-kg) leg of lamb

4 oz (100 g) softened butter

sea salt

freshly ground black pepper

onion skins

carrot peelings

parsley stalks

One of the luxuries of living in the Lakes is the joy of being able to eat local lamb throughout the year, and one of my personal perks when carving the legs is to keep the juicy, tasty end knuckle for myself!

Wipe the leg dry with a kitchen cloth and then coat liberally with the butter (I normally do this by simply rubbing the butter all over the joint by hand) and then season liberally with sea salt and pepper. Have on the base of the roasting tray some onion skins, carrot peelings and parsley stalks if available and place the leg, skin side up, on top of these. I tend to roast at 450°F (230°C), Gas 8, for 2 hours, basting every 30 minutes. An average leg should come out 'medium' done like this.

To ring the changes, various herbs may be incorporated into the butter according to the time of year. Mint is an obvious choice, and I like rosemary as well, but for me a selection of basil, tarragon, a little sage, parsley, rosemary, mint and possibly marjoram all tend to improve the flavour of the roast.

Leg of Lakeland Lamb baked in Hay with Herb Butter

a 6–7 lb (3-kg) leg of lamb

4 oz (100 g) softened butter

chopped herbs of choice

sea salt

freshly ground black pepper

clean hay

Follow the instructions for the above, but in the base of your roasting tray lay some clean hay and on this place the leg of lamb that has been daubed with the herb butter. Cover again with clean hay. Cover the whole tray with aluminium foil (otherwise the hay will catch fire), and bake at 475°F (240°C), Gas 9, for 3 hours. No need to baste. No need to look at the meat. You will gasp when you eventually remove the dish from the oven and take off the foil, as the aroma is glorious.

Easterledge Pudding

1 lb (450 g) easterledge

1 medium-sized onion, finely chopped

1 cup (about 8 oz or 225 g) pearl barley

a little salt

2 oz (50 g) butter

3 eggs, lightly beaten

An old-time custom introduced to me by my Grandmother was the serving of easterledge pudding with lamb in mid spring. The easterledge stalks should be removed and then the leaves coarsely chopped (young green fresh nettles are quite delicious too!) and combined with the finely chopped onion, the pearl barley and some salt. Put all this into a muslin bag and tie well and then gently poach for $1\frac{1}{2}$ hours.

Drain the easterledge and barley well and take a saucepan with its base liberally covered with melted butter. Put in the drained easterledge and barley mixture with the 3 lightly beaten eggs which you have seasoned (3 eggs for each 1 lb (450 g) of easterledge), and stir until the eggs scramble. Serve at once as a vegetable with your lamb.

Loin of Lamb

A whole saddle will give you 14 cutlets and approximately 14 slices of loin, and a coöperative butcher will, I feel sure, prepare exactly what you need. For 6 people I just use a half saddle, rolling and tying the lower part and trimming the cutlets well to reveal a fair amount of bone. When roasting this, do remember to cover each protruding cutlet with foil, or else you may well have charred bone ends when it comes out of the oven. I prefer to roast the loin at 475°F (240°C), Gas 9, for about 35 minutes as I like my meat to be moist and slightly pink. The meat should be placed on a bed of sliced carrots and onions (and parsley stalks if available), and adding finely chopped mixed fresh herbs makes a beautifully aromatic dish.

I don't like gravy with loin of lamb, so I serve it with the following accompaniments:

- 6 sprigs of fresh mint
- 1 tablespoon castor sugar
- $\frac{1}{2}$ gill (75 ml) wine vinegar
- 1 gill (150 ml) water
- 1 Granny Smith apple

Mint Sauce and Apple

Take the fresh mint off the stalk and finely chop with the castor sugar. Make it into a sauce with the water and vinegar, and then add the very finely chopped apple.

Onion Purée

Two recipes for this may be found on page 119. When the cutlets and loin are portioned, you coat each piece with a spoonful of Onion Purée – very delicious indeed!

Port and Stilton Cream

When you are at the end of a Stilton, scrape out as much as you possibly can and beat into it a little port to give you a creamy mixture. This, piped onto the individual cutlets and portions of loin, is tasty too.

Lamb Cutlets in Orange and Ginger

- **12 lamb cutlets, very well-trimmed**
- **flour, seasoned with salt and pepper**
- **olive oil**
- **1 $6\frac{1}{4}$-fl-oz (178-ml) can concentrated frozen orange juice**
- **6 pieces of preserved ginger, very finely chopped**
- **2 oranges**

This is a good casserole dish that I often serve for dinner. It also freezes well. The cutlets are trimmed of fat, otherwise the sauce will be too rich, and these quantities are for 6 people.

Dry the trimmed cutlets well on kitchen paper. Coat with seasoned flour.

Heat a thin layer of good olive oil in a frying pan and seal each and every cutlet well, but do not overcook at this stage. The meat will be ready when the blood starts to show through. Do remember that a cutlet has a side and two ends and these, too, need to be sealed.

Remove onto clean kitchen paper and dry well.

Most cans of concentrated frozen orange juice give strict instructions on how to dilute, but for this dish you need quite a strong flavour of orange so only dilute the frozen orange juice with *half* the stipulated amount of water. Pour this into an ovenproof casserole and put in the dried cutlets. Sprinkle on the finely diced preserved ginger. Put the lid on the casserole, place in the preheated oven at 225°F (110°C), Gas $\frac{1}{4}$, and cook for 2 hours. Then remove the lid and turn up the temperature to 400°F (200°C), Gas 6, for 20 minutes.

Serve garnished with fried orange circles or scored twirls, and plenty of chopped parsley or watercress. Any leftover gravy is lovely when used in any variation of carrot or turnip soups!

Lancashire Hot Pot

2 lb (900 g) fatty chump chops

a teaspoon of salt

freshly ground black pepper

6 medium-sized potatoes, peeled and cut crosswise into $\frac{1}{4}$-in (5-mm) slices

6 lambs' kidneys with membranes removed and cut into $\frac{1}{4}$-in (5-mm) slices

2 oz (50 g) butter

approximately 1 lb (450 g) onions, coarsely sliced

2 peeled and finely chopped carrots

$\frac{1}{2}$ pint (300 ml) lamb stock (after simmering for about $\frac{1}{2}$ hour)

Ooh, I do love a Lancashire Hot Pot, particularly when made from very fatty lamb chops and using lamb's kidneys too! I know this traditional dish has been updated considerably by fine establishments and occasionally sports oysters and mushrooms but, for me, my Nan's recipe can't be beaten. These quantities serve 6 people.

I like to use really fatty chump chops for this recipe, but if fat isn't to your liking, *you* don't need to (but oh, what a waste!).

The lovely brown pottery casserole dishes are ideal for this although obviously not essential. But do bear in mind that the dish is cooked in 5 layers – potatoes, chops and kidneys, potatoes, chops and kidneys, and finished off with potatoes, so the size of your casserole is quite important.

Paint the base of the casserole with melted butter (the sides too) and sprinkle generously with salt and freshly ground black pepper. Spread evenly on the base of this about one third of the prepared potatoes, on top of this place 3 lamb chops side by side. Now put in half the kidneys and sprinkle these with further salt and pepper. Dot over 1 oz (25 g) of the butter at this stage. Sprinkle on half the onions, and then do another layer of potatoes; repeat the meat-and-kidney layer, add the other ingredients and dot with butter before topping off with the balance of the potatoes. Pour over the reduced lamb stock. Bake at 325°F (170°C), Gas 3, for 2 hours and serve with lots of freshly chopped parsley and some good pickled onions (see page 200).

For 6

6 good-sized mutton chops

2 tablespoons wine vinegar

2 tablespoons olive oil

2 tablespoons rum

1 teaspoon salt

1 teaspoon brown sugar

1 clove garlic, crushed

1 teaspoon black pepper

1 teaspoon marjoram or thyme (whichever you prefer)

1 medium onion, finely chopped

butter and oil for frying (see recipe)

Mutton Chops in Winter Marinade

For the marinade, simply mix together all the above ingredients – except for the onion and the chops! Fold in the chopped onion.

Pour the marinade on to a baking tray just big enough to take the 6 mutton chops. Place the chops on the marinade and, after 12 hours, turn them and leave them for a further 12 hours.

When you're ready to cook the chops, remove them from the marinade (which you discard), and fry them in about 2 oz (50 g) butter with 3 tablespoons of oil in a frying pan. Cook for 4–6 minutes on each side (remembering to seal the ends too). The exact length of cooking time depends on how well you like your mutton cooked. I cook mine for barely 4 minutes as I prefer the inside slightly pink!

PORK

The old wives' tale that you should 'never eat pork unless there is an R in the month', is still looked upon as Gospel by many people, but with all the modern methods encountered these days in pork farming, rearing and producing, I find the quality varies little throughout the year. It is a tight-grained meat, so it takes longer to cook than most meats – and few people enjoy a rare pork joint.

When you purchase your pork look for the purest of white fat, the palest of pink flesh and the thinnest and smoothest rind. You shouldn't go far wrong then.

Loin of Pork with Dijon Mustard and Rosemary

Half a loin will be generous for 8 guests.

Have your butcher take the loin off the bone, and when you get home, lay the joint out on a table. Coat it all over with a layer of Dijon mustard about $\frac{1}{4}$ in (5 mm) in depth, then scatter liberally with fresh sprigs of rosemary removed from the stalk. Roll up the joint and tie, and then put further mustard on the fat top and more rosemary. Bake at 375°F (190°C), Gas 5, for $1\frac{1}{2}$ hours.

When you come to slice the loin you will be surprised at how delicate the otherwise strong mustard has become. The oil in it will have eased through the meat and it will have a pleasant texture and a most enjoyable taste.

6 pork cutlets trimmed – about 1 in (2.5 cm) is ideal

salt

freshly ground black pepper

1 bottle of dry white wine

2 oz (50 g) butter

3 tablespoons oil

6 leaves of fresh sage

For the sauce (see page 209)

1 pint (600 ml) double cream

$\frac{1}{4}$ teaspoon salt

1 tablespoon dry English mustard

2 tablespoons tomato purée

6 gherkins

Pork Cutlet in Tomato, Mustard and Cream Sauce

This is such an easy dish to do, I often feel guilty when contented diners say how much they have enjoyed it. Should you decide to serve it, do bear in mind that it is quite rich so you should take care with what you serve before it (how about grapefruit segments with tangerines served with Elderflower Sorbet?) and what comes after (Apple and Orange Farmhouse Pie, perhaps). The secret of the lusciousness of the pork is in the length of time you leave it in its marinade. Don't go to town on an expensive white wine for this (I have also marinated it in cider and been well pleased with the result). And for goodness' sake don't be mingy with the double cream when you cook the sauce as it is this cleverness that simply makes the dish.

Place the pork cutlets on the base of a casserole and sprinkle liberally on both sides with salt and freshly ground black pepper. Pour over the bottle of dry white wine, cover with lid, and leave for 2 days in the fridge. You can turn the cutlets occasionally, but this isn't essential.

Preheat the oven to 325°F (170°C), Gas 3, and allow yourself 2 hours for the cooking time. Take the cutlets out of the marinade, dry them off, and seal in the hot butter and oil. Put them back in the wine in the casserole, and add the sage. Put the casserole in the oven, double checking the oven temperature, and baste frequently.

For serving, all you do is remove the sage from the dish, put the chops on to the plates, coat generously with the thick shiny sauce (see page 209), and garnish with a gherkin fan. Food for the gods! Don't, whatever you do, throw away the juices remaining in the casserole – they will enhance any soup you may subsequently make.

HAM

Ham was very much part of the Christmas scene in my Grandmother's house, and I can vividly remember the sweet cured hams hanging up in the wash-house. Some time prior to Christmas the boiler would be lit, hay and bay twigs placed in the base and the hams would be boiled. The baked hams used to be coated in flour paste and baked in the oven at the side of the fire in the sitting-room, and the fragrant perfume of cloves would pervade the house with their warm atmosphere. They were prepared for the neighbours, friends and family, and brought in a source of revenue to be spent immediately on gifts for my Nan's own family. Even now at Miller Howe it is traditional (I don't know why) for us to purchase a couple of local farm, sweet cured hams for Easter and Christmas; it's good to know that there are always emergency

Tomato, apple and celery soup, and cauliflower soup, garnished with almonds

From top, clockwise: **Baked trout with hazelnuts and grapefruit; baked halibut with yoghurt, fennel, celery, apple and cheese; rolled baked sole with white wine sauce; Finnan haddock and cheese sauce in a gougère**

Wolfgang's Austrian steak and Parisian potatoes

Lamb cutlets in orange and ginger, and potatoes baked with cream and cheese

supplies for packed luncheons, late-night snacks, afternoon-tea sandwiches and high tea – and for when I'm feeling a little peckish myself!

Boiled Ham

I seldom follow the soaking instructions on commercial hams as I feel they are far too short. I always soak my hams for a couple of days in cold water, and I change the water at least twice a day. Then I put the soaked ham into a saucepan, completely cover it with fresh cold water and, after bringing to the boil, simmer for about 20 minutes. I then remove the ham from the saucepan, wash it again, and start the whole process of bringing to the boil and simmering again.

Approximate cooking times at this stage are:

10–12-lb (5-kg) hams 12–14-lb (6–6.5-kg) hams	3–3½ hours
15–16-lb (7-kg) hams	4 hours

Test your ham by stabbing a skewer right into the middle. If it comes out with apparent ease the cooking is over.

Baked Ham

As I said earlier, hams used to be encased in flour paste and then baked, but nowadays aluminium foil is easier to use. The ham should be soaked for 2 days – as for boiled ham – and if, before you start the cooking, you think the skin is still rather 'tacky', take a clean nailbrush and scrub it well. Then wrap carefully in foil.

Preheat the oven to 350°F (180°C), Gas 4, and bake for 15 minutes per 1 lb (450 g) without removing the foil. Remove from the oven, throw away the foil, and take off the skin (easily done if you use a small, sharp knife). Then in the lovely loose fat make long, even, criss-cross scores (in other words you get an overall effect and pattern of diamonds) and in the centre of each diamond insert a clove, point downwards. Coat liberally with soft brown or demerara sugar (if you are feeling generous, a bottle of sweet Guinness or strong cider poured over before you add the sugar improves the taste even further), and return to the oven which you have increased to 375°F (190°C), Gas 5, and bake for 30 minutes more.

Ham Steaks Braised in Cider

Ham steaks became very much the *in* thing to serve with slices of baked pineapple in the 'fifties, but I think this method of serving ham has literally been done to death.

Look up the recipe for Pork Cutlets opposite; the actual cooking and preparation times are identical, *but* use cider instead of wine and liberally coat each ham steak with mixed English mustard before marinating. If you wish to be slightly extravagant, for each steak soak a tablespoon of sultanas in a tablespoon of cooking brandy and add them halfway through cooking.

Fresh raw apple slices (Granny Smith's with skins left on) makes a nice topping for these as you bring them to the table.

VEAL

There is frequently a great anti-veal attack in the media, which for a short time has a positive effect on its popularity. But these outbursts seem soon to be forgotten and people start eating it again after a week or two.

When you buy fresh veal it should be the faintest, most delicate pink in colour, with practically no fat.

Loin of Veal Baked in Yoghurt with Fresh Herbs

4-lb (1.8-kg) loin of veal

2 pints (1 litre) yoghurt

8 tablespoons chopped mixed herbs

This size of loin will serve 8 guests. Be generous with the amount of yoghurt you use for this marinade – I usually use 2 pints (1 litre) – and into this I fold the freshly chopped herbs. Leave the veal in the marinade for up to 36 hours, turning it from time to time.

Spread out a large piece of aluminium foil and place the piece of veal on this. Start to turn up all the corners and sides of the foil so you will not lose any of the yoghurt marinade which you now pour over. Fasten the foil loosely round the loin and simply bake in the oven at 375°F (190°C), Gas 5, for 1¾ hours.

A variation on this theme is to use the popular green peppercorns (about 2 tablespoons) instead of the herbs.

Escalopes of Veal with Flavoured Cream

6 escalopes

2 oz (50 g) butter

1 gill (150 ml) cream

1 gill (150 ml) Marsala wine

salt

freshly ground black pepper

a few sprigs of marjoram

Quite often these days, it is very tricky to purchase (even from a reputable butcher) the genuine escalopes cut from the small area of leg called the 'noix'. The following recipe, however, has never failed me at home, when I have cooked escalopes whose exact origins were doubtful.

The escalopes should be extremely thin and are easily flattened further by placing each one on a piece of transparent cling film. Cover them with another piece of cling wrap and bash them flat with a rolling pin or, better still if you have one, a meat cleaver.

Melt the butter in the frying pan and take care not to over-heat, as the escalopes are to be merely touched with brown when cooked. When the escalopes are adequately sealed, remove them to a tray lined with kitchen paper and keep hot. If you have a surplus of butter in the pan, pour this off and put in the cream and Marsala with the marjoram leaves. Simmer this for about 5 minutes and then serve poured over the escalopes.

CHICKEN

You often see 'Fresh Farm Chickens' advertised for sale, which after cooking with eager anticipation, are slightly disappointing. They are usually 'fresh' out of a chicken battery! I must admit that they are better than their frozen counterparts but, for me, there is just nothing to compare with the flavour of the *free-range* fresh farm chickens, that have been ambling around the farmyard picking up grit and grass, nibbling weeds and herbs, eating lovely home-grown corn as opposed to fishmeal concentrates. When shopping, please seek out those free-range chickens, as they are *so* much better.

Roast Chicken

A 2½–3½ lb (1–1½ kg) bird should serve 4 people.

2½–3½ lb (1–1½ kg) roasting chicken

½ peeled onion

1 peeled carrot

1 sprig fresh parsley

4 oz (100 g) butter

salt

freshly ground black pepper.

Using a tea towel, dry the inside and outside of the bird and then place half a peeled onion and a peeled carrot inside along with some fresh parsley. Smear the bird liberally with butter and then sprinkle salt and freshly ground pepper over it.

Place it breast down in a small roasting tin and put it in a preheated oven at 375°F (190°C), Gas 5, and cook for just over 15 minutes. Remove from the oven and turn onto its left side and baste well. Return to the oven and after a further cooking period of just over 15 minutes, remove the tin again and put the bird on to its right-hand side after basting. Return to the oven for a further 15 minutes, and when you take it out for the third time, place it breast up and baste well. Turn the oven up to 400°F (200°C), Gas 6, and cook for a further 15 minutes.

The detailed diagrams below will, I hope, help you carve and portion the bird neatly.

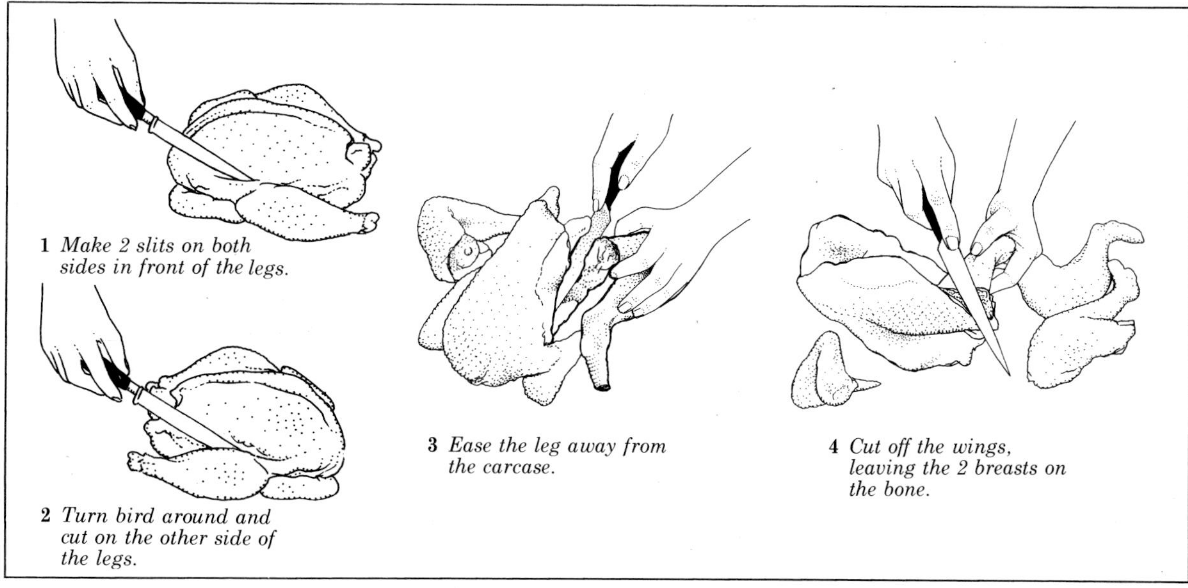

1 *Make 2 slits on both sides in front of the legs.*

2 *Turn bird around and cut on the other side of the legs.*

3 *Ease the leg away from the carcase.*

4 *Cut off the wings, leaving the 2 breasts on the bone.*

Roast Chicken with Fresh Herbs

Fresh herbs enhance any dish, and chicken is no exception to the rule. Any available fresh herbs should be chopped very finely, and a bird weighing $2\frac{1}{2}$–$3\frac{1}{2}$ lb (1–$1\frac{1}{2}$ kg) will need 2 tablespoons of herbs made into a paste with 4 oz (100 g) soft butter. The secret of this dish is to get the butter between the skin and the flesh, which is really very easy.

Place the bird, breast up, with the legs away from you, and gently ease the skin off the top part of the bird. Using your first, second and third fingers held out flat you ease your way down each breast and then round over the hump of each leg. By liberally coating your fingers with the herbed butter you will be able to place this all over the bird. Roast as described above.

Roast Chicken with Cheese and Herb Pâté

Using about 6 oz (175 g) of the Cheese and Herb Pâté (see page 29), insert it as above and follow the instructions for Roast Chicken.

Braised Chicken

If I want to serve cold chicken as a supper dish, and as moist and buttery as possible, I prepare the chicken in either of the above 2 ways, but put it into a casserole half-filled with good chicken stock and lots of diced fresh vegetables. Turn it 4 times during the cooking period which is at 300°F (150°C), Gas 2, for 2 hours.

Leave the chicken to cool in the stock and remove just prior to serving. I am sure you will be surprised by its moistness and flavour.

Sliced Braised Chicken with Hollandaise

The Hollandaise Sauce (see page 207) can be served with this, but is no good for a picnic as the butter content of the sauce hardens when it cools!

Sliced Braised Chicken with Curry Mayonnaise

This dish was, of course, made famous by the Cordon Bleu Cookery School who served it at the Coronation of Queen Elizabeth II. Serve a similar dish by using the Curry Mayonnaise given on page 132.

Breast of Chicken

It is best to buy the suprêmes on the bone as it is much more economical. It is essentially an easy operation to remove the breasts from the chicken, and with the leftover carcase, you can make a superb stock.

One suprême (a chicken breast) will serve 1 person. For ease of service, individual portions of breast of chicken can be cooked in foil (see below), or the breasts can be braised on the bone – *my* favourite way, although it does entail more work just before serving.

Breast of Chicken Cooked in Foil

Per person
1 chicken breast
2 tablespoons white wine
1 tablespoon melted butter, plus
$\frac{1}{2}$-oz (15-g) knob of butter
salt
freshly ground black pepper

Cut out squares of foil big enough to enfold the breast comfortably, and lay them on the work surface. Coat the foil liberally with melted butter and then place the prepared breast of chicken crosswise, breast up, running from the bottom left-hand corner to the top right corner. Fold up the sides of the aluminium foil, as you now want to sprinkle the breast with white wine (and without this folding-up operation some of the wine will overflow!). Put a generous knob of butter on top of each breast and then season with salt and freshly ground black pepper. Bring together the top left and bottom right corner and fold over the edges, forming a shape resembling the Sydney Harbour Bridge (or a Cornish pasty), making certain it is all well sealed. Place the foil packets on a cooling rack in a roasting tray and, just as you are to start cooking, pour enough boiling water to cover the base of the roasting tray. Cook at 350°F (180°C), Gas 4, for 35–40 minutes.

When serving, pour the liquid from the cooking (the juices, wine and butter) over the chicken breast on the plate, and then you should coat with a sauce of your choice.

Breast of Chicken Poached on the Bone

I normally put a small scrubbed carrot and half a peeled onion inside the ribcage of the chicken and do the suprêmes (each chicken giving you 2 portions) similarly to Braised Chicken by cooking them, breast down in the stock, at 300°F (150°C), Gas 2, for 1 hour (see opposite). A pair of rubber gloves makes for ease of portioning, but the meat will literally fall off the bones and, likewise, the skin peels off like the wrapper off a sweet.

Stuffings for Breast of Chicken

Either Mushroom Pâté (see page 30) or Cheese and Herb Pâté (see page 29) make delicious stuffings, but here are a few further variations.

1. For each breast you need roughly 2 dried apricots and 2 teaspoons ground almonds. Soak the apricots in brandy or white wine until nice and plump (preferably overnight), then roughly chop them and make into a paste with the ground almonds.

2. For each breast you need roughly 2 chopped walnuts, 1 teaspoon finely diced peppers and 1 oz (25 g) butter. Chop the walnuts and the red peppers and combine them with the butter. (If you're preparing a much larger quantity of this stuffing, as I'm sure you are, you can pipe the walnut butter, with a large nozzle, into strings, and freeze it. Then, just before cooking, you take the butter out of the freezer, cut off the right length, and place it in the breast.)

3. For each breast you need roughly $\frac{1}{2}$ oz (15 g) avocado, and $\frac{1}{2}$ oz (15 g)

smoked salmon (yes, smoked salmon and chicken *do* go together!). Having soaked the sliced smoked salmon in milk to remove some of the salt, liquidize it, then fold in the finely chopped avocado to which a little lemon juice has been added. A Pernod Sauce (see page 51) goes very well with this.

4. For each breast you need roughly 1 teaspoon each of very finely diced apple, walnut and celery, and 1 oz (25 g) cream cheese. Incorporate the apple, walnut and celery into the cream cheese. A little paprika makes a spicy addition.

5. For each breast you need roughly 1 oz (25 g) belly pork, $\frac{1}{4}$ teaspoon grated fresh root ginger and the juice and rind of lime. Mince the belly pork very finely and grate the root ginger and lime rind. Leave it to marinate in the lime juice for 24 hours before cooking.

6. For each breast you need roughly 1 oz (25 g) Cheese Topping for croûtons (see page 61) and 1 oz (25 g) dried stale wholemeal breadcrumbs, mixed together.

Hollandaise Sauce (see page 207) and any of its variations, as well as Béarnaise Sauce (see page 208) go very well with the breast of chicken recipes.

Baked Breast of Chicken with Fresh Lime Served with Smoked Bacon and Hollandaise Sauce

For 4

4 chicken breasts

juice and rind of 2 limes

4 tablespoons seasoned flour for coating

1 egg, beaten

4 tablespoons Savoury Breadcrumbs (see page 54)

4 middle cut rashers smoked bacon

Hollandaise Sauce (see page 207)

Marinate the chicken breasts in fresh lime juice, allowing half a lime to each portion – in other words, one whole lime does two whole chicken breasts! When marinating for 24 hours, sprinkle the grated rind over as well.

After the meat has absorbed all the liquid, coat each breast first with seasoned flour, then dip in beaten egg. Roll in the savoury breadcrumbs and place the chicken suprêmes on a baking tray and bake at 350°F (180°C), Gas 4, for 35–40 minutes.

On a separate tray have ready a middle rasher of smoked bacon for each suprême and bake these for about 12 minutes.

When serving, drape the bacon slice over the chicken suprême using the curled-up belly part of the rasher as a container, and into this spoon the Hollandaise Sauce.

This is a lovely dish, as you have the chewy breadcrumbs first, then the very juicy soft flesh of the chicken, with the smoked bacon and the Hollandaise providing a rich accompaniment.

Impromptu Stuffings

When cooking poultry I usually put on the menu 'Rich Old-Fashioned Stuffing', and then just make up the recipe as I go along, depending on what I have to hand. The livers of the bird are a must

To fill a 1-lb (450-g) loaf tin

1 medium onion, finely chopped

2 oz (50 g) butter

4 oz (100 g) breadcrumbs

4 oz (100 g) chicken livers

2 oz (50 g) sausagemeat

1–2 tablespoons chopped fresh herbs

and they are enriched if marinated overnight in brandy or Marsala wine, and the stuffing is the better if you are able to buy a few extra livers.

Some people stuff the actual birds, but I don't do this – I just use the carrots and onions and herbs for the insides when roasting, as explained earlier.

Fry off the finely chopped onion in the butter until golden brown and then add the finely chopped liver. Bring the mixture together to a fairly firm texture with the sausagemeat, some breadcrumbs and fresh herbs (tarragon, fennel fronds, and parsley are all extremely good, but marjoram has a delicious flavour in a stuffing). Ground almonds can be used, and a few sultanas marinated overnight in brandy add a further richness to the stuffing. Garlic can be used if you are a garlic fan, and so can diced apples. Grated cheese can add an unusual flavour to your end product, and pine kernels and most nuts are interesting if added to stuffings. Occasionally I have also combined a little leftover purée of spinach with the stuffing and this makes it very tasty.

When you are happy with the taste and texture of the stuffing all you do is put it in a 1-lb (450-g) loaf tin and then when you want it, heat it through in the oven with the chicken or duck for 30–40 minutes.

Be bold and experiment – you will be surprised at what delightful combinations you can come up with. *Improvise* with your stuffings!

POUSSIN

Boned poussins are available nowadays and make a relatively easy main course, provided you spend time earlier stuffing the bird. And this is a bird I *would* serve with the stuffing inside. Normally they are large enough, when stuffed, to be literally cut down the middle from head to tail to give you 2 portions – not forgetting, of course, that the stuffing itself is a filler!

This is my favourite way of stuffing boned poussin. Put a full slice of de-rinded smoked middle-cut bacon flat on your work surface and then either coat this liberally with grated farmhouse Cheddar cheese or, better still, a thin slice of the cheese itself. Then put a generous tablespoon of your chosen stuffing in the middle and roll the bacon up to resemble a thick sausage. This you literally push into the boned poussin to plump it out. Roast the poussins in a pre-set oven at 350°F (180°C), Gas 4, for 30–40 minutes. When cooked and cut down the middle you get the skin, flesh, bacon, cheese and then stuffing.

Use the recipes on the previous pages for stuffing Breast of Chicken, but multiply the quantities by three.

DUCK

A delicious dish but one that simply must be cooked for the exact moment of serving. I vividly recall, with horror, the now infamous TV programme where an equally infamous Cookery Expert showed us how one of the larger establishments cooked duck for a banquet. It was brought in fresh from the market in the early morning, cooked mid-morning, portioned at lunchtime, neatly arrayed on silver trays immediately and left to rest in steam ovens all afternoon. Eventually, I suppose, it was 'flashed' under the grill at the last moment before being ceremoniously served in the flashy restaurant. Heaven forbid!

Only fresh ducks should be served. The frozen variety, although they can be very tasty, never seem to develop the correct crispness of skin, as the pores are broken down in the freezing and defrosting process.

With a clean cloth, thoroughly clean the inside of the duck and then persistently stroke the outside skin with a dry cloth in order to dry the bird as much as possible. For even better results, hang the bird in an airy part of the kitchen (not in a hot place, mind you) for 24 hours, with newspapers or a tray placed underneath to catch the odd drops of blood.

Place a carrot and half a peeled onion inside the rib cage, along with a sprig of parsley and, if in season, a little thyme, together with a generous sprinkling of sea salt and freshly ground black pepper. Remembering that most birds will give 4 portions, provided they weigh 3 lb (about $1\frac{1}{2}$ kg) and over, take a roasting tray that will fit the bird or birds and cover the base and sides with kitchen aluminium foil (which makes for easier cleaning). Place a cooling tray inside the roasting tray, and then put the bird on that, breast up.

Pre-heat the oven to 475°F (240°C), Gas 9, and I neither prick the bird with a fork nor sprinkle it with seasonings as so many recipes say. I simply put the duck into the oven (and if you are doing 2 or more in the same tray, do for goodness' sake see that there is plenty of room *around* them so the heat will get at every single inch possible), and then cook them for $1\frac{3}{4}$ hours.

The secret of getting a duck to the table with skin as crisp as an old-fashioned toffee apple and meat a little on the dry side is that every single 15 minutes the tray is taken out of the oven (closing the door behind you *immediately* as you do not want any fall in temperature) and any fat is drained off into a container. Beware of using plastic bowls for this, as towards the end of the cooking the fat is extremely hot and I have known plastic bowls suddenly to wilt visibly, leaving a glorious greasy puddle on the work surface or floor. If you think about it, cooking a duck this way means that it is almost continually in a dry hot atmosphere. Just leaving it in the oven for the full period would mean that eventually you would have practically *half a pint* or *300 ml* of fat *per bird* lying in the base of the roasting tray turning a crisp roast into a pot roast, and never giving your bird a dry, crisp skin. Of course, the first couple of times the bird is taken out there is relatively little fat in the base of the roasting tray, but as the cooking time goes on you will be amazed, I'm sure, at what an amount of delicious fat you get.

The fat from the duck has many uses – my Nan used to make soap from it – but potatoes roasted in duck fat and Parisian potato balls fried in duck fat are delicious and I also love, for supper, potato trimmings done in this fat. Scrub large potatoes thoroughly clean first and then, with a peeler, start peeling off the skin, endeavouring to go as far as you can without breaking the flow (rather like the old-fashioned children's game when you threw the various lengths of apple skin over your shoulder to see what letter it would resemble and thus reveal your future lover!). These are then fried off in a saucepan of boiling duck fat, drained and sprinkled well with salt. Quite something!

All this means, however, that you should know more or less when your guests are going to sit down, and how long they are going to take with their first courses. Ten minutes either way isn't terribly important, and after the cooking time is past you need only turn the oven off, leaving the ducks in it if your party is running late.

Cooked this way the duck is also delicious served cold and should you be cooking and serving duck for the first time, try to get a trial run on the carving (carving being the wrong word really as you literally cut the bird into 4)! It is far better to serve it cold for the family so you can practise at leisure literally chopping the bird in two lengthwise and then separating the leg from the breast portion. Naturally, you discard the ribcage bones and I often pull out the bottom leg base too.

Although I have a sweet tooth, I am not one for serving cherries, blackcurrants, or orange sauces with my duck. Plain wedges or slices of orange, grapefruit (perhaps sprinkled with Grand Marnier?) or, better still, fresh lime. But I also love Calvados Apple Sauce (see page 211) as an accompaniment, and a rich stuffing made from the duck livers (see page 102).

ROAST LOCAL FARM TURKEY

This is the simplest possible way of cooking turkey. When the bird is in the oven, I baste it only once during the cooking time. I learned the method from Katie Stewart and it never fails: the skin is always absolutely crisp, the flesh slightly nutty with the constant soaking of butter, and the whole bird very moist. The only

1 turkey, weighing about 12 lb (6 kg)

double thickness of butter muslin 30 × 30 in (77 × 77 cm)

$1\frac{1}{2}$ lb (675 g) salted butter

2 large carrots

1 large onion

1 apple, quartered

parsley stalks

thing that is unusual is the use of the butter muslin, which you must have in double thickness of the size specified.

Scrape the carrots and peel the onion, then put the carrot peelings and onion skin in the bottom of your roasting tray. Put the carrots, onion and quartered apple inside the rib cage of the bird along with $\frac{1}{2}$ lb (225 g) of the butter. Chop the parsley stalks roughly and combine these with the remaining 1 lb (450 g) butter, which you then smear liberally over the breast and legs of the bird.

Put the turkey – breast upwards – in the centre of the doubled muslin, and then draw up the muslin over the breast (top left corner to bottom right corner and then bottom left corner to top right), securing it finally with cocktail sticks. Put the muslined turkey into the roasting tray, and put into the pre-heated oven at 350°F (180°C), Gas 4, and leave for 4 hours.

As the butter melts and the juices begin to run, the butter muslin absorbs them and keeps them circulating around the bird. By this time you may well be thinking that it will end up like a pot roast – wet and flabby. Well, it doesn't! As the heat builds up, so the salt tends to come out of the butter and cling to the skin. Baste the bird half-way through the cooking time with the juices from the roasting pan – over the muslin.

When the cooking time has expired, you simply take the bird out, peel off the muslin, and start to carve.

Serve with Cranberry Sauce and Chipolata Sausages (which you simply bake on a tray in the oven alongside the turkey for 30 minutes, before browning-off under the grill). Accompany it with Rich Old-Fashioned Stuffing using the livers (see page 102).

Cranberry Sauce

1 lb (450 g) frozen or fresh cranberries

1 pint (600 ml) red wine

rind and juice of 2 oranges

arrowroot to thicken

If the cranberries are frozen, see that they are defrosted before starting to make the sauce. Scatter the cranberries on a baking tray and warm through in the oven at 350°F (180°C), Gas 4, for about 16 minutes. *Don't* cook them. Reduce the wine and the orange juice, and thicken with the arrowroot. Just before serving, fold the cranberries into the reduced wine and orange juice.

SCENE TWO
VEGETABLES

Vegetables play a tremendous part in my food scene as I can never have enough of them. At Miller Howe I serve *six* fresh vegetables with my main meat course. One well-known cookery writer once firmly told me that all she wanted to do was savour the taste of the main dish, and that the varying flavours of accompanying vegetables distracted her. All *I* can say is that cooking is a very personal matter. I love vegetables above all and I like to cook and serve lots!

Vegetables are very versatile and often a disappointment when dining out as they are frequently overcooked and underseasoned. When last-minute-cooked vegetables like French beans, courgettes and mangetout are obtainable most of the year from good greengrocers, they certainly add to a dinner party. But I would like to give you ideas for cooking the more mundane vegetables that will make them a talking point at your party! We all know that fresh vegetables are the better for being cooked as late as possible and served as soon as possible but, when entertaining at home, this isn't always feasible.

Nowadays, due to the miracles of transportation, almost anything that you could wish to buy in the vegetable line is available. I have actually seen Kenyan French beans being picked at 4 o'clock in the afternoon, carefully sorted and packed at the main agricultural station, rushed out to Nairobi Airport, being given VIP treatment in the cargo holds of British Airways' overnight flights and in the hands of Covent Garden suppliers the next day! So get to know your local, good greengrocer and encourage him!

One of the plagues of vegetable buying these days is the plastic and polythene bags in which so many come ready wrapped. If you do buy them this way, check the date if you can (and the quality: I've had many a difference of opinion with a large chain store when I've tried to feel if a carrot was sweating). As soon as you get your plastic-wrapped vegetables home, take them out and let them breathe. Store in a cool, airy place or in the salad drawer of your fridge.

As far as preparation prior to cooking is concerned, I would always rather wipe than wash, and scrub rather than peel in the case of root vegetables. I would always suffer a little earth for the sake of taste and succulence: there is *so* much flavour in the skins of new potatoes, carrots or new season's parsnips after the initial preparation.

The art of cooking vegetables is the *under*cooking of them. It's not a case of how *long* they have to cook, but how *short* a time you, personally, consider they need. Give me undercooked, crisp vegetables any day, even if I do have to chew a little, as the flavour and food value won't have disappeared into the cooking water! Quite often people in the restaurant tell me that the carrots weren't cooked. I just smile and try to explain that chewy is better than soggy, and a bit of roughage won't do them any harm. On the contrary, in fact!

Another aspect of the art is, of course, cooking fresh vegetables as near as possible to when you want to serve them. With many recipes, this is a case of stir-frying at the last minute, which is time you must allow for in your schedule. Although some people think it sacrilege, I firmly believe that it is quite possible for you to serve four or five fresh vegetables at your dinner party, without too much extra work – if you follow my instructions. . . .

When entertaining, you want to have most things done before the arrival of your guests – this is one of the main themes of my approach to entertaining – and even with vegetables this is possible. Obviously, the basic cleaning and preparation can be done in the morning, after which I put them into dampened plastic bags and return them to the salad drawer of the fridge. But you can also par-cook (*under*cook) your vegetables before your guests arrive and merely warm them up again just before serving.

After par-cooking, strain and drain them, toss in butter and wrap up in aluminium foil. Put the foil parcels on a cooking tray in a roasting pan of warm water and leave in a warm oven. Under-cooked vegetables, well tossed in butter, will come to no harm for up to 1 hour stored like this, but always, *always*, see that you have literally red-hot serving plates to use for the main course. Hot plates will ensure that the temperature of the food is retained or even enhanced. Why serve on to cold plates and do endless damage to your food?

If you have an electrically heated trolley – which I find indispensible – you're lucky, as the par-cooked vegetables will happily keep up to 1 hour.

Another way of preparing your vegetables in advance is to purée them (an ideal dish, according to the *Good Food Guide for Toothless 80-Year-Olds*!). As well as saving you time in the evening (they can be cooked and puréed in the morning and then warmed through in a double saucepan in the evening), they are very *in* (think of the new French cuisine).

When cooking vegetables for a dinner party, always be generous in your calculations. Not because there might be a greedy gourmand in the party, but because cold vegetables used in other ways the next day are super. I like to mix any leftover vegetables together like bubble and squeak (sometimes folding in a little French dressing as well) and then pan fry them in butter and onions to which a little mustard has been added. When well-fried and browned, serve with chopped fresh herbs and a fried egg, and you have a feast! If I have only a small surplus of cooked vegetables from the night before, I make a smaller 'bubble and squeak' and serve it with lots of freshly grated raw root vegetables in a good French dressing.

Leftovers can also be liquidized and thinned down with stock and made into either a cream or vegetable soup, or, with herbs and spices added, made into a curried vegetable soup. They also make nice fritters if coated in breadcrumbs and toasted ground hazelnuts, and served with rashers of fried bacon – pour the bacon fat over just as you take them to the table. Or else you can mince the vegetables together with what is left of the fowl or joint and make a sort of cottage pie. Served with home-made chutney it is a delicious luncheon, supper or high-tea dish.

In the summer (when we *have* a summer!) I go for days at home eating vegetables with barbecues, but I never cook the vegetables. So delicious and so good for you. Raw cauliflower florets with curry mayonnaise (some people blanch them off first), French beans with lots of freshly ground black pepper, raw mangetout dressed with fresh lemon or lime juice, grated carrots with a little caraway and lemon, shelled young peas and broad beans in walnut oil, grated courgettes left in a good French dressing, grated raw beetroot with horseradish – the combinations and concoctions are endless. And then there are always celery, tomatoes, radishes and spring onions! . . .

ASPARAGUS

I don't care what the French or Floridans say, there is no asparagus in the world to compare with the British, especially that from Suffolk. So there! And although the season is relatively short, British asparagus is a magnificent herald of the approaching summer. As soon as my supplier phones to say the first beds are ready for picking, I immediately order 20 bunches and a few days later start the weekly supply. Alas, the weeks rush by, and once the Suffolk season is over, tempt me not with the thick Christmas asparagus flown in from far-away places, and for which the very finest Hollandaise does nothing!

I always serve asparagus within 36 hours of it being picked, while it is still at its prime. After 48 hours it is still edible, but add a further 24, and I think it acquires an unappealing earthy flavour. Asparagus needs careful handling and even more careful cooking. Remember, it is a dish that will not wait for your guests – but they won't mind waiting for it to cook to just the correct texture. I only give four stalks at the most for a starter in a four- or five-course meal, but as a solitary main course I have been known to eat a whole bunch myself with lashings of Hollandaise and well-buttered wholemeal bread. With a bottle of well-chilled Sancerre, it's a feast fit for a king!

An asparagus pan, although an item of kitchen equipment used for a relatively short time of the year (like a fish kettle), is a good investment for me, but *you* can improvise. Remove the bases from the asparagus sticks, trying to get them all more or less the same size, and then lightly scrape the white part of each stick with a sharp stainless steel knife. Lightly tie up your bundles first close to the base and then just below the green flowery tips (making certain that your bundle or bundles will fit into your cooking receptacle, of course) and then, if you're not going to cook it straight away, leave to stand in very cold, lightly salted water. An asparagus pan is ideal – but if you haven't one, improvise with a coffee pot, or something similar, with lightly crumpled foil in the base and pushed round the sides of the bundle. Take care that the flowery ends never come into contact with the water throughout the cooking, as the heads should only be steamed.

Remove from the soaking water, and change the water in the pan. Add a tablespoon of olive oil, some stalks of parsley and a couple of black peppercorns and bring the fresh water back to the boil. Remember where the height of the water was when you soaked the asparagus first, as when you plunge the bundles into the boiling seasoned water you do not want the water to come up as far as the base of the flowery tips. Leave them to simmer. The cooking time naturally varies according to the thickness of the asparagus, but generally allow between 8–15 minutes. Remove from the pan, cut the string, spread the asparagus out on to a tray lined with kitchen paper and serve immediately with Hollandaise (see the easy recipe on page 207).

BEAN SPROUTS

These seem to be more readily available these days, and are the simplest of vegetables to serve as they need no preparation. Simply toss them off in a heated mixture of oil and butter and serve straight from the pan. Add them, cold and crisp, to a boiling hot consommé or serve raw with grated fresh ginger and red and green peppers as a salad. Tossed in a salad they are nice, and with mushrooms in an omelette they make a pleasant and unusual combination of textures.

BEETROOT

This certainly doesn't seem the most popular of root vegetables (my own aversion to it is due to the dye getting everywhere). It is, however, available most of the year and is seldom expensive.

Top and tail the beetroot and wash in cold water. Be careful here because if you pierce the skin it will 'bleed' on cooking and lose much of its flavour. Cook in boiling, salted water. Small-to-medium-size beetroot take about three-quarters of an hour to cook, but larger ones will take about $1\frac{1}{2}$ hours. They are cooked when the skin slips off easily when pressed gently with your fingers. Don't prod them with knives or they'll bleed.

Leave to cool, then dice them and serve in a white sauce, or simply by themselves. I think thyme is a pleasant herb to serve with beetroot.

BROAD BEANS

I like these best early on in the season (about June) when they are so small and sweet. I know they are a bore to prepare – the large pods seem to produce far too few actual beans, and the shelling bowl fills up painstakingly slowly! But make the following dish once – as a starter or salad – and you'll be longing for June to come round again.

Broad Bean and Spinach Salad with Crispy Bacon

Don't wash or cook the spinach. Simply wipe the leaves clean with a slightly damp cloth, tear into thin shreds and divide between 6 ramekins (one for each guest).

For 6

1 lb (450 g) spinach

$\frac{1}{2}$ lb (225 g) new broad beans

6 oz (175 g) chopped, de-rinded, smoked bacon

Shell the beans and drop them into boiling salted water. Cook for 2 minutes only after the water comes back to the boil. Take off the heat immediately and strain.

Now for the 'difficult' bit! Take each individual bean and hold it in your working hand at its base between thumb and first finger. With the other hand peel off a corner of the bean's skin, give a squeeze at its base, and out will pop the inner kernel! The skin left in your hand (which you discard) is rather tough and firm, whereas the inner bean (which you use) is soft and pulse-like.

Put the beans on top of the spinach and leave them to cool. When you wish to serve them, put the chopped bacon on to a baking tray in a high oven at 425°F (220°C), Gas 7, and bake for about 6 minutes. Spoon the bacon fat over the beans and spinach and top with the baked crispy bits of bacon. Be generous with freshly ground black pepper and serve with thickly-buttered slices of wholemeal bread.

BRUSSELS SPROUTS

I love fresh small Brussels sprouts and serve them a lot. But come mid-February, I think they are on the way out, as they tend to develop a slightly bitter flavour and their outer leaves turn a bit yellow. Serve them simply with butter or bacon fat as below, or in a purée.

Fried Brussels Sprouts with Chestnuts

For 4–6

1 lb (450 g) Brussels sprouts

$\frac{1}{2}$ lb (225 g) fresh chestnuts

4 tablespoons bacon fat

Remove any wilting outer leaves, slice off their bases, and cut a small criss-cross on their bottoms with a sharp stainless-steel knife. Add them to boiling, salted water, bring back to the boil and simmer for 3–6 minutes according to their size – but *do not* overcook. When you want to serve them, have some bacon fat melted in a small frying pan and toss the sprouts off in the hot fat until they are browned on the outside.

Meanwhile, place the chestnuts in a bowl and cover them with boiling water. Remove two at a time and using a small sharp knife, remove the outer shell and the inner skin. It's quite a simple process, really, provided you work quickly and don't let the water go cold (otherwise you have to throw out the water and repeat the process).

Chop the chestnuts and mix them in with the browned sprouts and bacon fat. Serve as quickly as possible.

Pork cutlets marinaded in white wine, baked cabbage with garlic and juniper, and purée of parsnips with toasted pine kernels

A breast of chicken taken off the bone, stuffed
with cheese and herb pâté, ready for baking

Winter root vegetables cut to equal size and ready for their foil 'parcels'

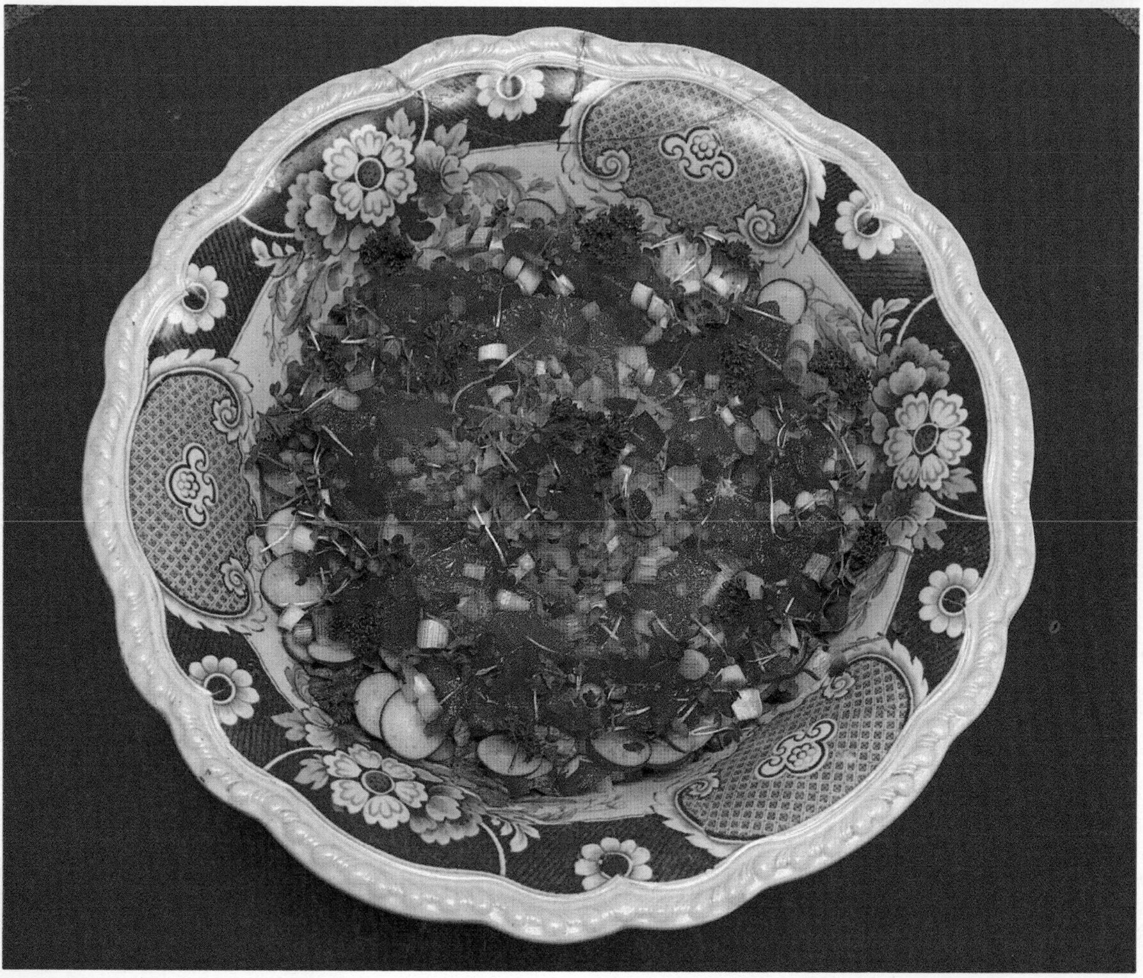

Preparing tomato and orange salad
A 'Solomon Grundy' mixed salad

Purée of Sprouts with Bacon

For 4–6

1 lb (450 g) Brussels sprouts

1 oz (25 g) butter

$\frac{1}{4}$ pint (150 ml) single cream

4 oz (100–125 g) chopped, de-rinded, smoked bacon

Remove any wilting outer leaves, slice off their bases and cut a criss-cross on their bottoms with a sharp knife. Add them to boiling salted water, and simmer until they are very tender. Drain well, then return to the dried pan with a generous knob of butter and dry out over a low heat. Liquidize with single cream and pass through a fine hair sieve into the buttered top of a double saucepan and reheat when needed. When reheating, lightly fry off small pieces of smoked bacon, dry these on kitchen paper and sprinkle over the purée. A lemon twirl not only looks nice on top of this but the taste of the juice is interesting.

CABBAGE

A delicious vegetable, both cooked and raw, far from the connotations of school dinners and the literary cliché of its smell. This recipe is one of my favourites, and it appears often on the Miller Howe menus.

Baked Cabbage with Garlic and Juniper

For 4–6

2 lb (1 kg) cabbage

8 juniper berries

2 large cloves garlic, peeled

$\frac{1}{2}$ teaspoon sea salt

2 tablespoons olive oil

A firm green cabbage, 2 lb or 1 kg in size, will give you quite a generous serving, and this dish is delicious warmed through the next day and served with some French dressing.

Remove the outer leaves and cut the cabbage into four. Cut out the firm, hard stalk from each quarter and slice the cabbage very finely with a sharp stainless-steel knife. In a pestle and mortar (or liquidizer) pound (or blend) the berries with the garlic and sea salt, until you get a smooth paste.

Just cover the bottom of a 9-pint (5-litre) saucepan with the olive oil and heat through. Put in the juniper–garlic mixture and stir sharply with a wooden spoon. Add the finely grated cabbage and stir-fry for several minutes until the cabbage is well coated with oil, then bake in the preheated oven at 425°F (220°C), Gas 7, for about 15 minutes. If you like very crisp vegetables, just stir-fry in the saucepan for about 3 minutes – the flavour is by then imparted to the cabbage and as the vegetable is so finely chopped, it will have heated through.

Red Cabbage Spiced with Apples and Orange

Red cabbage is a much-maligned vegetable, particularly in the North of England where, in my young days, it was only served pickled with the inevitable (but delicious) hot-pot. Despite this, whenever it is in season, I serve the following casserole dish, but

2 lb (1 kg) firm red cabbage

4 oz (100 g) butter

1 lb (450 g) Granny Smith apples

½ lb (225 g) onions

2 cloves garlic *with* ¼ teaspoon each of powdered nutmeg, allspice, cinnamon, thyme and caraway seed *liquidized with* ½ pint (300 ml) red wine *and* 2 tablespoons wine vinegar

freshly ground black pepper

juice and finely grated rind of 2 oranges

2 tablespoons brown sugar

enjoy it even better the following day served cold with a French dressing. In fact, I do believe I cook it to serve at a dinner party purely and simply because I wish to enjoy the leftovers the following day!

Shred the cabbage finely, taking particular care to remove the inside middle stalk, and toss off in the melted butter, making sure all the leaves are coated evenly. Put a ½-in (1-cm) layer of the cabbage into the base of a casserole pot (which will eventually in layers take all the cabbage, so do make sure your casserole is the right size before you commence the next, tedious but necessary, process). Then sprinkle on some of the peeled, cored and sliced apples, and a generous sprinkling of the finely chopped onions. Give this layer a generous coating of freshly ground black pepper and a sprinkling of the orange rind.

Repeat this process over and over until you have reached the top of the casserole and you have nothing left. Pour the liquidized garlic, spices and wine over the top of the dish incorporating the orange juice and sugar, too. Bake in the oven at 375°F (190°C), Gas 5, for 30 minutes.

CARROTS

Carrots are available most of the year, and add colour to any dish. If you're lucky enough to find some of those little finger-sized new season's carrots, cook them plainly and deliciously and serve simply with butter, but when the carrots aren't so sweet – in autumn and winter – try the following recipe:

Purée of Carrots

For 6

1 lb (450 g) carrots

¼ pint (150 ml) single cream

Carrots are delicious when puréed (as are the other winter root vegetables, turnip and parsnip) and extremely rich and satisfying. They're good for invalids in the winter during the inevitable bout of colds as they are no effort to devour (in fact, they titillate the palate), and are very reminiscent of nursery food.

Cut the carrots into fairly even shapes and cook until tender, strain, and put back in the saucepan over a low heat to dry out and then liquidize with the cream.

To add a special flavour, mix in 1 tablespoon of powdered coriander.

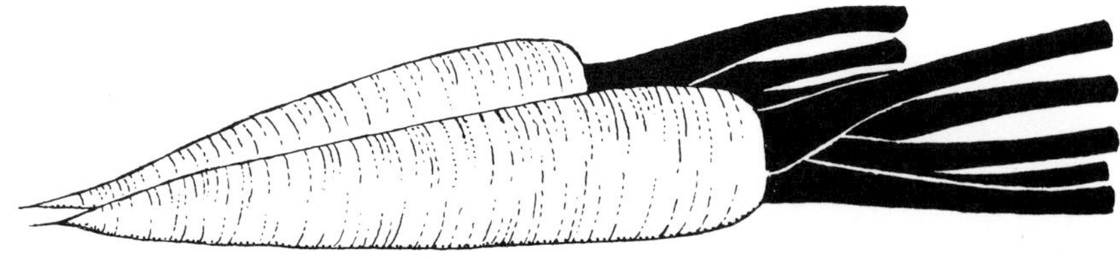

Glazed Carrots with Caraway and Lemon

For 6

1 lb (450 g) carrots

1 teaspoon sea salt

2 oz (50 g) butter

1 teaspoon caraway seed, finely ground in pestle and mortar

juice and rind of a small lemon

The preparation of the actual carrot is important as after peeling these should (in fact, *must*) be cut into equally-sized pieces (see the photograph of root vegetables). Add the sea salt to a pan of cold water and when boiling, add the carrots. When the water comes back to the boil, cook for only *4 minutes*! Strain and dowse under running cold water. After wiping out the saucepan melt the butter and reheat the carrots in this, scattering over the ground caraway seed and juice and rind of the lemon. This literally only takes a few minutes.

CAULIFLOWER

Cauliflower is relatively simple to cook, and it can be delicious provided you take a little time and care in the actual preparation. Remove all but the very smallest of leaves from round the base and, using a sharp-pointed, stainless-steel knife, try to scoop out as much of the middle of the stem as you possibly can. Leave it to soak in cold, salted water for about 15 minutes.

The easiest way to cook cauliflower is to put it in the pan head down (this stops any scum turning the 'flowers' dark) in boiling salted water. It is impossible to tell you how long to cook the cauliflower, for so much depends on size and age, but after the water has come back to the boil, simmer for 10 minutes and then test the stalk with a sharp-pointed knife. Always remember to under-cook it so your cauliflower is nice and crisp (you must *never* let it go soft and mushy).

When serving straightforward boiled cauliflower, melted butter with chopped herbs adds to the flavour, but I like a few toasted almonds scattered over the top.

Fried Cauliflower Florets

Take as many florets as you require and blanch in boiling salted water, remove and leave to drain. Lightly beat an egg and dip the florets into this before coating liberally with savoury breadcrumbs (see page 54). Then simply fry in a mixture of oil and butter. If you like crisp vegetables, fry for a couple of minutes only.

CELERY

This stalk vegetable used to be available only during the winter, and was never bought until it had had a frost on it. The Celery Man used to stand in the Barrow Outside Market surrounded by heads of the stuff, all white on top with pale green leaves showing and then clarted up at its base.

Celery and nutmegs were my pet aversions when out shopping with my Nan. She would immediately reject what to me was good celery, stoutly saying 'Manky inside'; likewise with nutmegs which were sold at so much for four. Size she did not care for, but weight was very important. Some of the biggest nutmegs were riddled with worms, she claimed, and gave you nothing like the same quantity as their firm, solid, smaller neighbours! Each nutmeg would be held and weighed in the palm of her hand and either purchased or rejected with a smile of scorn.

But back to celery. This was always served with high tea or with the cheese and teacakes at supper. It would be added to stews and casseroles but never served as a vegetable.

Now that it is available most of the year, I serve it as the base for cocktail titbits, cut and curled as a garnish for salads, invariably with cheese, sometimes chopped up finely in cream soups or salads. Large tomatoes with their bottoms sliced and insides removed, then filled with diced celery and mayonnaise, are pleasant with a summer salad. Finely chop celery and mix with chopped cucumber, and serve with natural yoghurt. (I also tell you to use celery with halibut and yoghurt in another section of the book.) The outside leaves can be used in the stock pot (but take care, as it has a dominant flavour) and they can also be used to form the base of vegetables for a roast.

COURGETTES
(OR ZUCCHINI)

This is a vegetable that is now available most of the year, as it is imported from Kenya, Morocco and Spain. The only thing to watch for when buying is that they should not be longer than 6 in (15 cm); if they're bigger than this, I find the skins tough and the insides rather pippy. I like them simply fried in butter; to do this I wipe them clean with a damp cloth, cut off each end, score them lengthwise and then blanch off in boiling salted water for a minute or two. I then remove them from the saucepan and dry well, and then fry off in butter with a liberal sprinkling of sea salt and lots of freshly ground black pepper. Remember to under-cook them so that you get a lovely crisp vegetable full of vitamins and flavour.

If your courgettes are on the large side, wipe them first, score them and then cut into thin slices and leave for a few hours spread out sprinkled with salt. This will draw out some of the extra moisture and you will have to dry them on kitchen paper. Simply dust them then with seasoned flour and deep fry – the only drawback is they do tend to make the oil rather dirty! Fried courgettes are delicious when served with Tomato and Garlic Sauce (see page 211), or have you ever served them with a tablespoon of natural yoghurt?

Grated Zucchini (Courgettes) with Fresh Lime

For 4–6

- **1 lb (450 g) courgettes**
- **2 limes or 1 lemon**
- **2 oz (50 g) butter**

An unusual method of serving for a dinner party. Wipe the courgettes, top and tail them, and then grate them finely on a grater or in the Magimix. Mix with the grated rind of fresh limes or lemon and the juice, and leave for most of the day. When you wish to sérve them, all you do is toss the grated courgettes off in heated butter for about 4 minutes.

Courgettes in Cheese Custard

For 4–6

- **1 lb (450 g) courgettes**
- **1–2 tablespoons olive oil**
- **1 medium onion, finely chopped**
- **1 clove garlic, crushed**
- **½ pint (300 ml) double cream**
- **2 eggs and 1 egg yolk**
- **4 oz (125 g) grated Cheddar cheese**
- **fresh parsley, marjoram, basil or tarragon**
- **salt and freshly ground black pepper**
- **1 oz (25 g) butter**

I also like to bake courgettes in a cheese custard for a supper dish which goes extremely well with cold meat or, better still, grilled Cumberland sausages.

Wipe the courgettes, top and tail them, slice them thickly, and fry off in the olive oil. Remove and drain well on kitchen paper whilst frying off the onion with the garlic in a little extra oil. Drain these, too. Make the custard by beating the eggs and egg yolk into the cream, before adding the cheese, seasonings and herbs to taste.

Butter a medium-sized ovenproof casserole and line with about half an inch of the custard. Bake this off at 350°F (180°C), Gas 4, for about 8 minutes. Then arrange the onions and courgettes on top, and put in the rest of the custard. Cook at the same temperature for a further 20–30 minutes, until set.

FRENCH BEANS

These days, in so many ways, we have so much to be thankful for, and I think the superb Kenyan French beans available throughout the year come into this category. Having lived in Africa for many years and still a frequent visitor to that continent, I have seen how well organized the farming – and marketing – is in Kenya.

These Kenyan beans are definitely the best ones to buy for a dinner party, but the following method may be used for any home-produced French beans. They are commonly called runner beans and although very delicious indeed, it does take time, care, love and patience to string and cut them ready for cooking!

French beans I literally and simply blanch for 2 minutes in boiling sea-salted water, and then immediately drain and dowse them in cold running water. When I want to eat them I put a couple of tablespoons of good oil in a frying pan, and when heated add a similar amount of butter and toss the beans off in this, being very liberal with freshly ground black pepper.

LEEKS

Leeks seem to be a much-neglected vegetable, and I can't think why. In my younger days I seem to recall we only used to have leeks during the winter; they never seemed to deteriorate as March came round, like so many winter vegetables, but just suddenly were not available any more.

Their main drawback is that they are messy to prepare, as their layers of skin hoard tiny particles of dirt which have to be sought out and thoroughly washed away. Cut off most of their tops leaving about 3 in (7.5 cm) of the basic stem and from this remove the outer skin until you come to the fairly clean white leek. I often find it better to slit each leek lengthwise in half and then you can see quite clearly if there is any further dirt to remove. Wash well in cold water with added salt. I usually cook them by putting them into a saucepan and covering with boiling water. Bring the water back to the boil and continue to cook the leeks *uncovered* for about 8 minutes. If the leeks are dirty you will have to wash them leaf by leaf and then chop the leaves, so the cooking time will be shorter. But if you have clean whole leeks the cooking time will, naturally, be longer. But, once again, *do not* over-cook.

Al dente leeks are delicious served with a plain white sauce or a cheese sauce. This latter makes a nice supper dish, which you finish off under the grill with toasted breadcrumbs and more grated cheese on top, letting the dish bubble away for a few minutes.

If you want a more substantial dish you can wrap each cooked whole leek with some leftover cooked ham and coat with a thick cheese sauce, and finish off under the grill as above with breadcrumbs and cheese.

I often serve leeks garnished with soured cream or savoury yoghurt. For the latter, simply add tomato purée, a little crushed garlic and a touch of curry powder to the yoghurt, and then stir in finely shredded carrot. Served on a bed of lettuce with some watercress and an orange twirl, you have a filling starter.

If you want to be extravagant, braise diced cleaned leeks in white wine and serve with toasted almonds sprinkled on at the last moment.

ONIONS

My Nan used to say, 'A house without onions is a house without a soul', and I can vividly remember the string that always hung on the door of the wash-house. She used to buy them regularly from the onion man who came round on a bicycle – then there was the watercress man and, yes, I can remember a muffin man – where have all these characters vanished to . . .?

Most savoury and main courses need, or are enhanced by, onions. Soups are definitely lacking without them, and their skins add colour to a stockpot.

Fried, finely chopped onions add flavour to Savoy cabbage, baked potatoes, Brussels sprouts coming to the end of their season, beetroot, glazed carrots, buttered leaf spinach or diced turnip. Half a peeled onion should always be placed inside any bird you are going to cook and, of course, most roasts are the better for being placed on a bed of roughly chopped onions, complete with skins.

Purée of Onion

For 4–6

1 lb (450 g) onions

about 1 pint (600 ml) milk

2 tablespoons Crème de Cassis

This is delicious served with lamb. Pop your peeled whole onions into an ovenproof casserole, cover with milk and cook in the oven at 350°F (180°C), Gas 4, until the onions are about to fall apart – about 45 minutes.

Remove the onions, cut up fairly small and then put into the liquidizer with a little of the milk. Purée well and strain through a plastic sieve. Add Crème de Cassis to taste.

Another way of making an onion purée is to use one medium onion for each couple you are going to serve. Cut up coarsely and put in a saucepan with the merest drop of water and a sprinkling of demerara sugar. Leave over a low heat for at least an hour, stirring from time to time. The onions will begin to shrivel and colour, and will reduce quite considerably, leaving you with a mixture resembling marmalade. Sprinkle some sherry vinegar on to this as if you were spiking your fish and chips! Liquidize and then add Crème de Cassis to taste. You could also try Crème de Menthe.

Savoury Supper Onions

Per person

1 medium-sized onion

chicken stock (see method)

2 oz (50 g) Mushroom Pâté (see page 30)

1 oz (25 g) grated strong Cheddar cheese

Make certain each onion is more or less the same size, top and tail and remove the outer skin. Poach off in a good chicken stock (to come half-way up the onions) in a covered flameproof casserole on top of the cooker, taking care to keep on testing to see that they are *just* cooked. Remove from the heat, leave to cool and then take out the centres (do not throw away!) with a grapefruit knife. Fill the onions with Mushroom Pâté (see page 30) and liquidize the centres with a little of the stock. When ready to serve your meal, simply warm the onions through in the oven, take out and sprinkle generously with grated strong cheese and finish off under the grill. Serve with the onion purée.

PARSNIPS

Parsnips, once they have had a frost on them, are a tasty vegetable and served as a purée are not only delicious but easy to do early in the day when you are entertaining. See also under *Winter Root Vegetables* for another method of serving parsnips.

Purée of Parsnips with Toasted Pine Kernels

For 4–6

1 lb (450 g) parsnips

1 oz (25 g) butter

¼ pint (150 ml) single cream

2 tablespoons toasted pine kernels

Peel the parsnips, cut them into even-sized pieces and simmer in salted water until tender. Drain well and put back over a low heat and toss in the butter. Liquidize with single cream. (You will need a little more cream if you use a liquidizer rather than a Magimix.) See you really liquidize them well and to make an even smoother purée, pass through a very fine plastic sieve into a double saucepan that has been brushed inside with butter. All you have to do, when needed, is to reheat it in the double saucepan and top the dished-up purée with toasted pine kernels.

If you don't like pine kernels, you can simply liquidize some fennel herb with the parsnips, and add a last-minute touch of grated nutmeg.

GARDEN PEAS

I must admit defeat and say that this is one vegetable that is invariably best bought frozen. The combine harvesters that you see on the TV adverts *do* seem to be able to pick out the smallest and sweetest, for most frozen petits pois are just that. I have spent hours laboriously shelling peas for 60 guests at Miller Howe, left them in cold water, gently cooked them in simmering sweetened water liberally strewn with shredded lettuce, an onion ring, perhaps a pinch of salt and a hearty sprinkling of castor sugar, a little melted butter and a squeeze of lemon. I have steamed them, casseroled them, refreshed them half-way through cooking – and I invariably end up with bullets. New, mid- and end-of-season pickings have all gone through the same rigmarole. I have beamed at guests and said, 'The peas are fresh,' to be met with complete disbelief. So French Petits Pois à la Freezer for me. Yes, do add a little bit of fresh mint or lettuce or onion or butter or oil, but throw away your strong opinions on frozen foods with this particular vegetable.

MANGETOUT

The crispiest, crunchiest and sweetest vegetable you can imagine, and available for most of the year now that they are imported from Kenya, Morocco and Spain and seem to be grown in increasing quantities in this country. Occasionally they are a bit dirty, so they need washing in very cold water. Top and tail them and remove the strings. Put them in a large flat container, cover with ice cubes and leave until the last minute to cook them. Then take out of the container, pat dry and simply stir-fry quickly in a mixture of heated oil and butter. One minute and no more if you want them hot and crunchy. Serve as quickly as possible. They are quite nice served simply chilled as an accompanying salad with a good French dressing, but quickly stir-fried is my favourite method.

POTATOES

Potatoes are not my favourite food as I can get fat on other richer and more tempting things – but they can be so good. Baked on a bed of sea salt and served with Cheese and Herb Pâté or a flavoured butter, potatoes are filling and fattening, but fun. What is more delicious than freshly picked new potatoes simply wiped with a cloth and then gently simmered with lots of fresh mint? But for me potatoes done with lots of cream and cheese or glazed with lots of butter and brown sugar typify my whole approach to life: if you are going to indulge, well, go the whole hog!

Creamed Potatoes

For 6–8

2 lb (900 g) potatoes, peeled and evenly cut

pinch of sea salt

1 egg

4 tablespoons double cream

2 oz (50 g) butter

half a grated nutmeg

Creamy mashed spuds are good at a dinner party as they come to no harm reheating in the top of a double saucepan.

Cover the potatoes with cold water and add the sea salt. When the water comes to the boil, reduce the heat and allow to simmer until the potatoes are cooked (in other words test by gently jabbing the end of a sharp pointed knife into the potatoes after about 15 minutes). Strain well, wipe out the saucepan, return potatoes to the pan and dry them out over a low heat, tossing the pan from side to side (this takes only a few minutes). The potatoes can be put through a mincer or any sort of electrical gadget, but I personally prefer to use a good old-fashioned hand potato masher, which is so satisfying to use. When you have a relatively smooth texture add the lightly beaten egg, the double cream and rest of the butter and beat until creamy and light.

As I said earlier, when the potatoes have reached this stage, they can be kept warm in a double saucepan, but do see the base and sides of the pan are well buttered before you add the spuds.

When serving, sprinkle over some grated nutmeg, and if you want to ring the changes, surprise your guests by adding half a tablespoon of creamed horseradish or a teaspoon of mushroom ketchup.

Duchesse Potatoes

For 6–8

Use the basic creamed potatoes but do not use any butter (only the egg and cream). Pipe large walnut twirls on to a well-greased tray and then, with the end of a wooden spoon, make an indentation at the top of the twirl and into this place a teaspoon of Tomato and Garlic Sauce (see page 211).

When you wish to serve them, you simply reheat and brown under a hot grill.

Baked Potatoes

The best-sized potatoes are between 8 and 10 oz (225–275 g) and these should be scrubbed well with a nail brush (for goodness sake wash any soap off the bristles if you don't have a nailbrush for use in the kitchen only!). Dry the potatoes well and make a small cross with a sharp pointed knife on the top of each. Your small roasting tray should be completely covered about ¾ in (2 cm) deep with good sea salt and the potatoes bedded down in this. The oven should be pre-set at 425°F (220°C), Gas 7, and the potatoes are cooked for at least 2 hours at this temperature. All you do then is remove the potatoes from the tray (you may have to use brute force to remove the salt encrusted round the base of the potatoes), and, pushing in up towards the centre of each potato, open up the cut across. Pipe some Cheese and Herb Pâté (see page 29) or flavoured butter into this.

I fully appreciate that apart from being filling, these are fattening, but be warned, guests seldom refuse a second helping!

Potatoes Baked with Cream and Cheese

These are scrumptious and sinful but relatively easy for a dinner party as they are just left to cook in the oven while you are entertaining your guests.

The potatoes should be about 2½ in (6.5 cm) in length and more or less evenly shaped (do take care when peeling, and if you have the time and patience, turn the actual potato to make it look like a rugby ball). Cover them with cold water and a pinch of sea salt and bring to the boil. Simmer for 5 minutes only. Drain well and place in a casserole dish. Pour double cream half way up the potatoes and then cover the whole dish with grated Cheddar cheese. Bake at 375°F (190°C), Gas 5, for approximately 1 hour. Remove from the oven and sprinkle liberally with chopped parsley.

Parisian Potatoes

These may appear wasteful at first but what is left of the potato after you have scooped out the balls can be used for creamed potatoes. First peel the potatoes, then, using a 'baller', make those lovely round shapes resembling grapes.

Heat a mixture of oil and butter (or better still, duck fat, and you will be amazed at the difference!) and fry the potatoes over a low heat. I prefer to cook them slowly and when they are ready, whatever you do, *don't* put them in anything covered to keep hot or else they will become soggy. I tend just to leave them in the frying pan at the side of the stove until I want to serve them (they take about 40 minutes to cook) and they gradually become more brown, crisp and buttery!

Before serving, drain on kitchen paper and sprinkle liberally with salt.

PEPPERS

I used to think that red and green peppers came from two different plants as the red pepper is so much sweeter than the green. Now that I know the red pepper is only the green one much riper, it's logical that it will be sweeter, having soaked up the sun for longer.

I am not too keen on cooked peppers, but they are quite pleasant when added to casseroles and I never bother to skin them. I find this a very tedious job, putting them under a hot grill until the skin begins to blister and burn. And I seldom seem to get all the skin off when I rub it under a running tap! It just doesn't seem worth the effort.

Throughout the book I give many ideas on how to use peppers – stuffed with pâtés, as garnishes, etc – but do be sure to remove not only all the seeds but also the white pith as this is rather bitter. I like them best served raw in salad, and if finely diced and mixed raw with vegetable purées or added as a last-minute garnish to soup, the texture makes an interesting contrast.

TOMATOES

Available throughout the year nowadays, tomatoes vary very much in quality, so in August – the month of the *very best* tomatoes – do everything you possibly can with the glut of cheap local tomatoes available. Make soup, chutney, purée, sauce and juice.

A few doors away from my Nan lived the Lambs who had an

allotment. Each summer Mrs Lamb would sell home-grown tomatoes and I used to pop round most evenings for a pound. They had just been plucked with their stalks left on, and Mrs Lamb used to pick out all the very small, firm, ripe tomatoes for me. Perhaps it was then that I discovered how *sensuous* food was, as plucking the stalk from those small vegetable fruit and sniffing was a sheer joy. As for eating them, nowadays the tomatoes from the local farm are often as sweet, but nothing can recapture those early memories.

There are very few dishes which will not be improved with the addition of tomatoes, and I have even made a tomato ice-cream (not one of my more successful efforts, mind you). They make marvellously filling dishes when stuffed, raw or cooked, served hot or cold, and you can get rid of endless leftovers this way! Large tomatoes can also be filled with many goodies – such as some of my pâtés (see pages 29–32) – but buttered eggs are nice, well-seasoned and liberally scattered with chopped fresh herbs. Savoury rice can also be used as a filling.

The best herb to use with tomatoes is basil (difficult to buy and even more difficult to grow) but I love tarragon too. Tomato and Tarragon Soup served hot or cold is one of my favourites (see page 66).

When grilling tomatoes I warm them through slightly first in the oven and, out of season, a sprinkling of castor sugar does seem to bring out the flavour. Don't be too faddy about skinning tomatoes for salads but, due to an unfortunate experience early in my hotel training, I always skin tomatoes for sandwiches. I was at Browns in the days of Captain McCallum who, one afternoon, came storming into the stillroom going purple in the face, demanding to know who had made the sandwiches on the tea trolley. I was the culprit and got a good dressing-down: 'My boy, one never serves skins or seeds of tomatoes as many gentlemen have dentures and they play havoc with the gums.' One ticking-off was enough for the day, I thought, but five minutes later he was in again, as I had served raspberry jam with the scones, and I hate to think what *their* pips did to his unfortunate guests!

Tomato Purée

This is a good thing to make when there is a glut of tomatoes (sauce too, see page 210), as you can freeze it. Use any amount of fresh, ripe tomatoes (I normally make purée in 5 lb ($2\frac{1}{2}$ kg) batches). Liquidize them, pass through a fine sieve into a saucepan and cook until thick. Occasionally you may find the pips of the tomatoes have made the mixture rather bitter, so add a little sugar to counteract the bitterness. This method is much quicker than skinning and removing the pips first.

TURNIPS

I find turnips very useful – for purées, and for the foil parcels in *Winter Root Vegetables* – and we serve them a lot at Miller Howe.

Diced Turnips with Honey

For 4–6

1 lb (450 g) turnips

2 tablespoons clear honey, at least

Peel your turnips and then cut into neat-sized cubes. Cook in salted water until tender and then drain well and put back in the saucepan over a low heat for a few minutes to dry out. Then add runny clear honey according to your personal taste.

Purée of Turnips

Purée 1 lb (450 g) of turnips as described under Carrots (page 114) and add ½ tablespoon of dill.

WINTER ROOT VEGETABLES

Carrots, turnips and parsnips can all be pre-cooked prior to the arrival of your guests and then be kept warm.

First of all, prepare them by cutting into as even-sized pieces as possible; it is no use whatsoever having some pieces as large as walnuts and others as small as peas, as it stands to reason that by the time the walnut-sized pieces are cooked the pea-sized pieces will be mushy. Put the chopped vegetables into separate pans of boiling, salted water, bring back to the boil and simmer for 3 minutes. Strain the water off and immediately refill the saucepans with cold water, add a little salt and finish off the cooking. It is impossible to say exactly how long they should take because it depends entirely on how big your pieces are, but keep constantly prodding them with the point of a sharp knife and, when cooked to your liking, remove and strain well.

But don't *over*cook them as, if you are going to serve these vegetables *later*, it is at this stage that you have to decide how underdone to leave them in order to serve them at the right texture later on. There again, personal taste comes into it. As I have said, I like my vegetables always to be slightly crunchy. Not only do they taste better as the flavour has not been boiled away, they are more satisfying to the palate and still full of vitamins. Put each root vegetable (after par-cooking, draining and drying out as above) onto a well-buttered piece of foil, bring each corner up to the middle and seal well. Stand the packets on a cooling tray in an appropriately-sized roasting tin full of hot water. Leave in an oven set at 200°F (100°C), Gas Low, and the vegetables will be quite tasty served an hour and a half later *provided* you haven't hopelessly overcooked them to begin with.

Before you seal the foil packets you can add lemon juice to the carrots, a little bacon fat to the turnips, and butter to the parsnips.

SCENE THREE
SALADS AND SALAD DRESSINGS

With salads, you can let your imagination run riot. Although no salad is expensive to make, some are time-consuming – all that shredding, chopping and grating! Although some salads need to be marinated in oil or French dressing, it is better if most salads are put together as late as possible before serving. Savoury salads can be prepared earlier in the day as described in the section on Garnishings (see page 215), as can the actual preparation and some of the chopping, as long as vegetables are wrapped in transparent cling film and stored separately in the fridge or larder. It's absolutely no use dressing your salads earlier, as the result will be rather like limp, soggy cotton wool. Always dress a salad *at the very last minute.*

In my youth, salads used to be served in the summer only, and at other times were looked upon as a sheer extravagance such as you might have for a high tea on Boxing Day. Lettuce then was such a price, and tomatoes were hardly heard of in the depths of winter. Nowadays, of course, salads are available throughout the year, but need different approaches with the varying seasons. We all know that soft-skinned winter tomatoes need a touch of castor sugar to give a sweeter taste to their mushy flesh, and that there is nothing, but nothing, to compare with a freshly-picked lettuce out of your own garden in the summer.

The basis of most salads is lettuce, and I like mine simply wiped with a damp cloth rather than washed (and thus softened). I then whirl it dry in one of those lettuce shakers. If I am using lettuce out of my own garden I always discard the outer leaves – not that I am a maniacal insecticide dispenser during the growing time, but I have noticed the liking my neighbour's cat has for my lettuce bed (perhaps that's why they grow so well)!

Cos lettuces are my favourite – the inner leaves are so tender and sweet – but the cabbage types which keep so well are a must for any fridge during the summer. Chinese cabbage lettuce seem to be appearing on the market these days in more abundant quantities, and I tear up the green leaves and then chop the white tasty stem finely and scatter this over the leaves.

Personally, I like to make individual salads for each of my guests, preferably in wooden salad bowls which have been first well rubbed with a cut clove of garlic. I tear the lettuce up into small pieces, and then add everything else finely chopped. By everything, I really *do* mean everything. Tomato, cucumber, spring onion, radish, grated cheese, endive, watercress, parsley, apple (tossed in fresh lemon juice), peach, mango, walnuts, cherries, sultanas, carrot, celery, hard-boiled egg, red and green peppers, French beans, and why not add a few whole grapes (pipped of course), and that good old standby, mustard and cress? I serve the dressing separately at the table and let each of my guests take as much or as little as he or she likes.

Apple, Walnut and Celery

For 4

2 Granny Smith apples

12 large lettuce leaves

2 oz (50 g) chopped or halved walnuts

4 sticks of celery, trimmed

French dressing

Peel and core the apples (an apple corer makes a hole right through the middle of the apple, removing the stalk and most of the pips) and then cut them into thin slices with a stainless steel knife (or use a mandoline grater, which is ideal for this purpose).

The dressing used for this salad should contain at least one-third of the best walnut oil as the flavour is quite distinct. Leave the apple slices in the dressing as long as possible. Tear up the lettuce leaves, then finely chop the celery, reserving a few pieces to make twirls.

When you want to serve the salad, put the apple slices on top of the prepared lettuce, cover with chopped or halved walnuts and then top off with either celery twirls or finely diced celery. The combination of textures and flavours is delicious.

French Bean Salad

For 4

1 lb (450 g) French beans

French dressing

This is one of my favourite salads (available most of the year if you use imported fresh French beans from Kenya). Simply top and tail the beans and then blanch for several minutes in boiling, salted water. Drain well. Toss liberally in a good French dressing and be generous with a sprinkling of freshly-ground black pepper. Very munchy, tasty and delicious.

Grated Carrot with Caraway and Lemon

For 4

1 lb (450 g) carrots

1 teaspoon caraway seeds, pounded in a mortar and pestle

1 clove of garlic (optional)

rind and juice of 2 lemons

1 tablespoon of natural yoghurt per portion (optional)

If the carrots are young and fresh simply wipe with a damp cloth. If older, peel them. Grate finely on the old-fashioned grater or put through your Magimix. The caraway seeds can either be pounded to a fine-ground stage in a pestle and mortar, or liquidized in a liquidizer (add a little fresh garlic if you like), but always pass through a sieve. You only want the pure dust with the carrots. Grate the lemon rind on top of the 'powdered' carrots, and then toss them in lemon juice.

Cucumber in Yoghurt

For 4

1 large cucumber

6–8 tablespoons natural yoghurt

1–2 cloves garlic, crushed

a little freshly chopped dill, if available

Wipe the cucumber with a damp cloth and then cut in half lengthwise and remove all the pips. Simply grate the cucumber on an old-fashioned grater or in the Magimix. Combine with yoghurt and the crushed garlic and, if available, a little freshly chopped dill.

New Potato Salad

When I can buy the first of the new season's new potatoes, I know that summer has arrived. In spite of dirty looks from the market stallholders, I delve around picking out the smallest I possibly can and give a charming smile to counteract any scurrilous remarks. As soon as I get home I wipe them with a damp cloth and simmer in salted water, to which I have added a little French dressing (a few parsley or mint stalks in the water improve the flavour, but good potatoes will stand on their own). For me, they are ready when the tip of a sharp knife will pierce them effortlessly, and I drain and serve them as quickly as possible with lashings of butter.

When the potatoes are getting longer in the tooth I tend to heat the French dressing through slightly and have it ready when the potatoes are cooked. Drain the potatoes well, slice fairly thickly, and return to the empty pan. Put on low heat to dry them out and then toss in the warm French dressing. Chopped chives are good, too, with this.

As salads are low in calorie content and filling too (all that munching away tires you out), an extra potato is a delightful cheat!

Spinach and Hot Bacon

For 4

1 lb (450 g) spinach

at least ¼ lb (100 g) de-rinded smoked bacon, finely diced

1 tablespoon walnut oil

I get a fresh supply of spinach twice a week in season, from a local farm, and it is a joy to serve and eat. I wipe each leaf with a damp cloth rather than wash it, and I cut out the stalky veins – which is slightly time-consuming. Roll the prepared leaves up into the shape of a large Cuban cigar, and then slice. Put the sliced spinach into the salad bowl or bowls, or just pop in a small heap onto the actual salad plate.

When you are just about to serve, fry off as much or as little finely diced smoked bacon as you like in a little drop of pure walnut oil and then spoon piping hot on to the spinach. Delicious! When local spinach is at its best, home-grown tomatoes are at their sweetest. Slice the tomatoes and arrange the glittering pieces down two sides of the pile of spinach, put a few thin slices of cucumber on the other two sides and then a generous sprig of watercress alongside some hard-boiled egg and not only is the effect colourful, the taste is divine.

Tomato and Orange

For 4

4 tomatoes, about 2 oz (50 g) each

2 oranges

1 medium onion finely chopped

1 tablespoon chopped parsley

French dressing

lettuce leaves for serving

sprigs of watercress for serving

This salad can be made in the morning and stored in the fridge until you want to serve it.

Skin the tomatoes first. Make a small criss-cross cut with a sharp pointed knife on top of each tomato and then lower each tomato, one by one, on a metal spoon into a pan of boiling water. It is impossible for me to tell you how long to leave the tomatoes in the water as it depends entirely on the type of tomato you are using, their size, and the time of year. Hard, slightly green tomatoes will need up to 8 seconds, fresh new season's red, only 3 or 4. The first one you popped in will tell you if you have soaked it too long or not long enough when you start to skin it. Do this by immediately plunging the tomato into a bowl of very cold water, straight from the boiling water and then, picking at the criss-cross insertion with a small sharp knife, start to peel off the skin. (If you want to remove the seeds as well – and for some recipes you must – cut the tomato in half and scoop out the seeds in one swift movement.)

Stand each orange on its end, having first sliced a small piece off the base so that it stands quite firmly. Then using a very sharp knife, cut down the skin in sections leaving the bare flesh exposed, taking care to remove all the pith. The orange is then cut across the segments into slices.

Arrange in portions of alternate slices of orange and tomato (2 at least per person) on a plastic tray. Leave room between the portions on the tray so that it is easy ultimately to just slide a palette knife under each to serve. Cover each portion with very finely chopped onions and parsley (if you like this combination) and then coat liberally with a good French dressing. Cover the tray with transparent cling film and store in the fridge until needed (do remember to bring back to room temperature before serving though).

Serve on a bed of lettuce garnished with a sprig of watercress and an orange twirl.

SALAD DRESSINGS

Any salad is only as good as the oil and vinegar used in the dressing. You must use the finest wine vinegars (never malt), and the best oils. First pressing Italian olive oil (so green, heavy and rich-smelling) is superb, and French or Spanish olive oils are excellent, but I think the finest is walnut oil. It's horrifically expensive – your breath will be quite taken away when you buy a can – but then you never use all walnut oil in a dressing. To do so would not only be extravagant, but the taste would be far too heavy! The ratio is normally one-third walnut to two-thirds olive oil.

French Dressing

1 pint (600 ml) oil

¼ pint (150 ml) wine vinegar

2 generous teaspoons soft brown sugar

pinch of salt

2 level teaspoons dry English mustard powder

juice of ½ lemon

French dressing must be made with the very finest of ingredients, wine vinegar, walnut and good olive oil.

Using a ¼ pint (150 ml) measure you basically require 4 measures of oil to 1 of vinegar. I make my French dressings in a liquidizer (the end result is a heavier dressing but it's effortless to make). If making 1¼ pints (700 ml) of dressing (and why not? It stores perfectly for well up to a week, and in the summer that is not long when salads are eaten so often), mix together in the liquidizer goblet, the sugar, the salt, the English dry mustard, the lemon juice, the wine vinegar and the oil. Switch the liquidizer on for a few seconds until everything is perfectly combined.

Variations on the Theme

The basic salads of summer can be changed radically by all the delightful things you can actually do with a basic French dressing. Add some chopped chives, parsley, basil or crushed garlic. Use different types of vinegars (red or white wine, or cider vinegar, or herb vinegars). Occasionally, I add a hard-boiled egg to the liquidizer and get a thicker dressing. Finely chopped onions stirred in at the end are pleasant. Finely diced apple added prior to serving is quite nice too, especially if you can incorporate some freshly chopped mint from the garden. Green fennel fronds can be liquidized to add that delicious aniseed flavour. Add a teaspoon of tomatoe purée, a dash of Tabasco or that good old standby, Worcestershire sauce, to give a hot spicy taste. Finely chopped walnuts and pine kernels added at the end make a pleasant change. And, believe it or not, I have even added fresh rose petals to get a most unusual sweet flavour. Bordering on the exotic (if not eccentric), nasturtium petals sprinkled in a dressing or salad are good, as are chrysanthemum petals.

Mayonnaise

2 egg yolks

few drops of fresh lemon juice

$\frac{1}{2}$ teaspoon of dry English mustard powder

$\frac{1}{2}$ teaspoon castor sugar

$\frac{1}{2}$ teaspoon salt

$\frac{1}{2}$ pint (300 ml) best quality olive oil

3 tablespoons white wine vinegar

French dressing is my favourite with any salad, but mayonnaise has so many uses. It is delicious served plain with cold fish and chicken dishes as well as salads, and I always use this basic recipe and method, which makes $\frac{1}{2}$ pint (300 ml).

I find it easier to use an electric hand whisk, but a Kenwood can be used. First of all, combine the yolks thoroughly with the lemon juice and seasonings (it helps to use a warm bowl). Having measured out the olive oil (remembering the better the oil, the better the mayonnaise), gently dip your fingers into the oil and then trail the oil off the fingers into the egg mixture beating vigorously and continuously. At this stage you must literally *dribble* in the oil, and take your time: if you put too much in at once or hurry the making, your mayonnaise could curdle. (If this happens, just add a tablespoon of hot water to bring it round or, in a fresh bowl, beat the curdled mixture teaspoon by teaspoon into a further egg yolk). All should go well, though, if you do exactly as I've described.

When you have incorporated about one-third of the oil (at this stage the mixture will be extremely thick and not at all what you expect mayonnaise to be like), add the vinegar, tablespoon by tablespoon (if you throw in the 3 tablespoons all at once, the mixture becomes very thin – rather like evaporated milk – and difficult to thicken again), and then the balance of the olive oil can be added more quickly.

This mayonnaise might be too thick for you, but can be thinned down with a little warm water or single cream. If too sharp, next time cut down on the vinegar content. If too sweet, leave out the sugar. For changes in final flavours in the final mayonnaise, you can experiment with various vinegars – mint, garlic, and tarragon.

Curry Mayonnaise

1 tablespoon good olive oil

1 oz (25 g) finely chopped onion

1 dessertspoon curry powder

1 teaspoon tomato purée

$\frac{1}{2}$ gill (75 ml) red wine

1 tablespoon apricot jam

$\frac{1}{2}$ pint (300 ml) mayonnaise

4 tablespoons double cream, whipped

Heat the olive oil gently and fry the onion until transparent. Add the curry powder, tomato purée, red wine and apricot jam.

Simmer slowly for about 30 minutes and then pass through a strainer. This liquid is then incorporated into the $\frac{1}{2}$ pint (300 ml) of mayonnaise which has been expanded with the tablespoons of whipped double cream.

MENU

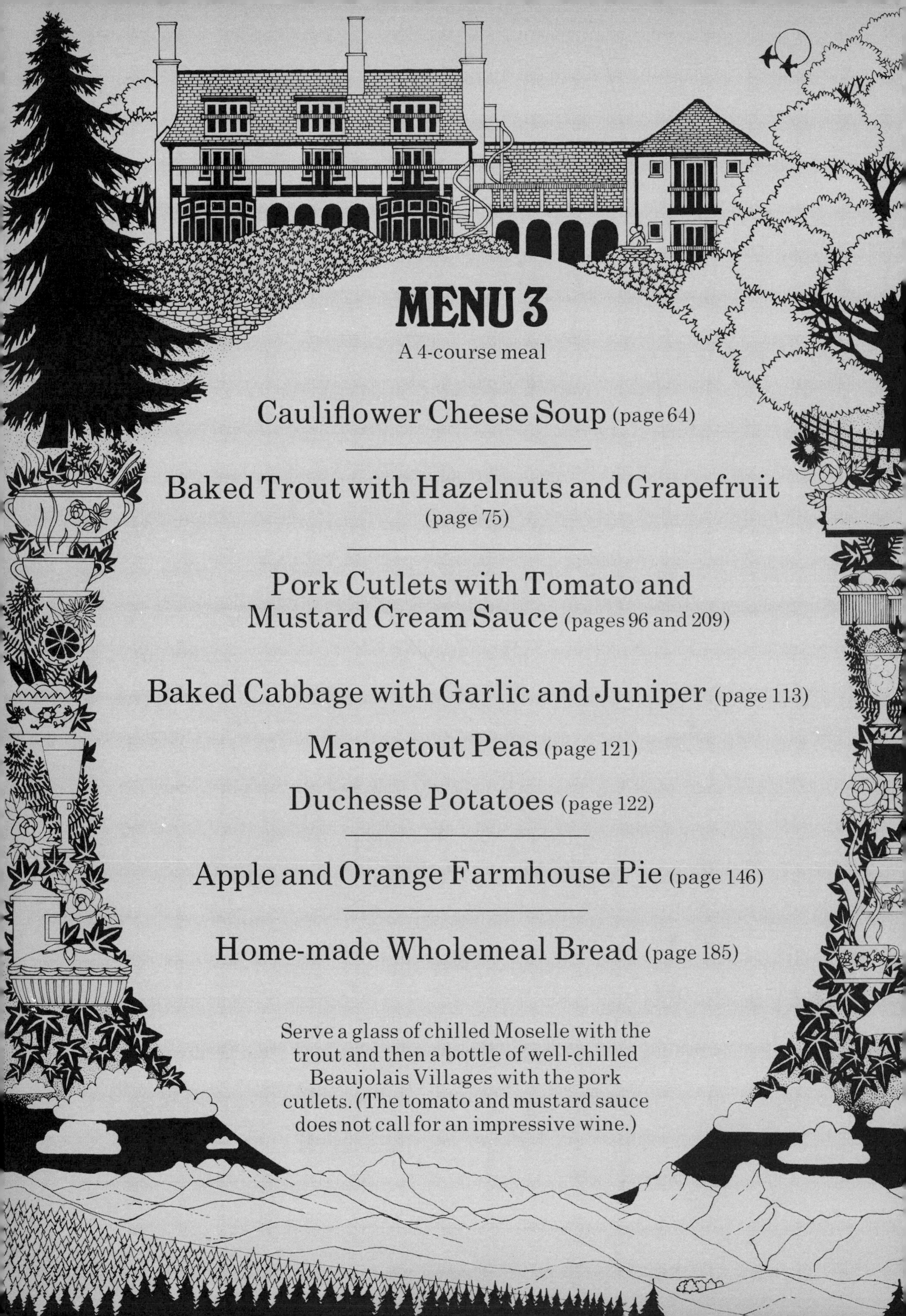

MENU 3

A 4-course meal

Cauliflower Cheese Soup (page 64)

Baked Trout with Hazelnuts and Grapefruit (page 75)

Pork Cutlets with Tomato and Mustard Cream Sauce (pages 96 and 209)

Baked Cabbage with Garlic and Juniper (page 113)

Mangetout Peas (page 121)

Duchesse Potatoes (page 122)

Apple and Orange Farmhouse Pie (page 146)

Home-made Wholemeal Bread (page 185)

Serve a glass of chilled Moselle with the trout and then a bottle of well-chilled Beaujolais Villages with the pork cutlets. (The tomato and mustard sauce does not call for an impressive wine.)

This menu with its additional course only involves you in extra work well before your guests arrive.

Two Days Before

Make the Farmhouse Pastry and chill. Make some stock for the soup (or use some of the condensed stock cubes you have in the freezer). Make the Wholemeal Bread.

Marinate the pork cutlets in wine or cider, and peel the potatoes. Leave them in cold water.

The Day Before

Roll out the pastry, having allowed it time to come to room temperature. Put it into the flan dish, chill it again slightly, then bake it off blind. Leave enough pastry for the lid, and leave to chill until the next day.

The trout can be prepared today too, provided you transfer them to a well-greased baking tray, then cover them with a double layer of transparent cling film and leave them in the fridge. You can also make the soup, but do put it in the fridge, too, when it has cooled.

Arrange the flowers.

Morning

Double check your shopping and the table setting. Put dishes in the warming drawer and prepare the coffee tray.

Check:
the lamps
the heating
the room for coats, and cloakroom
the records and tapes
the flowers

Reduce the cream for the sauce, and combine the mustard and tomato purée, then mix all three ingredients together and put in a double saucepan ready to be heated through.

Drain, dry and seal the cutlets before putting them back in the casserole with the wine or cider poured over.

Chop the cabbage and blend together the garlic and juniper berries. Top and tail the mangetout and leave in iced water. Cook and pipe the duchesse potatoes onto a well-greased tray.

Skin, core and slice the apples, prepare the orange wedges, and place them in the baked pie case. Put lid on the pie, and leave to chill again.

Prepare the Garnishes

For the soup, grate the Cheddar cheese finely and cut some tiny florets of cauliflower which will be fried off at the last minute. Leave these covered in a dish. Chop some parsley with a chopping knife on a kitchen board (*never* in a liquidizer!).

Prepare the grapefruit segments for the trout, and have some watercress or parsley sprigs to hand. Do some savoury salads, too, if you feel you can rise to the occasion. Store these under transparent cling film but do remember to remove in time, so they are not served stone cold on a hot plate!

For the pork, some finely chopped gherkins or gherkin fans are nice, and all you need for the pie are twirls of whipped double cream.

Evening

Put the pork casserole in the pre-set oven 2 hours before you want to eat the main course.

Bake off pie and when cooked, leave in the warming drawer. Butter the wholemeal bread and cover with a damp cloth.

Have the soup ready to heat through, the warmed plates ready and the soup ladle handy. Have the frying pan with oil ready for firstly the cauliflower florets, and then the mangetout.

When your guests arrive, time the reheating of the soup, pop the trout into the oven (minus the grapefruit segments, naturally – but these should be to hand, uncovered).

When about to serve the soup, toss the cabbage off in the oil and transfer it to the oven.

Put the tomato and mustard sauce on now, over very low heat, and have a peep at the trout and cutlets in the oven.

Serve the trout, and put grapefruit segments and chopped hazelnuts on the top. I suggest at this point that you give the cabbage a gentle stir.

Put a gentle heat under the frying pan for the mangetout, and put a teaspoon of tomato and garlic sauce in each duchesse potato twirl. Heat the grill to brown the potatoes. Simply toss the mangetout in the frying pan as you are serving the pork and the other vegetables (don't forget the gherkins).

Take the Farmhouse Pie out of the warming drawer and put into the oven to heat through properly. Before serving the individual

MENU 4

A Gala Dinner

Miller Howe Savoury Apple with Tarragon Cream (pages 29, 57 and 209)

Carrot and Coriander Soup (page 63)

Baked Savoury Sole (pages 71 and 54)

Wolfgang's Austrian Steak (page 91)

Winter Root Vegetables (page 125)

Creamed Potatoes

Irish Coffee Meringue Gâteau (page 157)

or

Port and Claret Jelly with Shortbread

(pages 165 and 194)

Home-made Wholemeal Bread (page 185)

Splash out on a bottle or two of Sancerre to open up the meal and a full bodied Rhône wine for the main course.

The Gala Dinner does take up more time *before* the actual evening of the dinner, but I do hope you will try it. It is rich but satisfying, titillating but not outlandish and – more to the point – relatively easy to serve on the evening as the donkey work has been done beforehand.

Two Days Before

Make the Wholemeal Bread, the stock for the soup, and the Cheese and Herb Pâté for the savoury apple, and the breadcrumbs for the sole.

You could prepare the three root vegetables and get them out of the way, provided you store them in the fridge.

The meringues for the Gâteau can be made now (indeed they freeze very well), and the Shortbread can store for a few days in an airtight container.

The Day Before

Make the soup (which you should be finding very easy by now), and store in the fridge when cool.

Prepare and trim the steaks, and cook them off to the pre-casseroling stage. Make the accompanying sauce.

Make the tarragon essence for the tarragon cream. Peel the potatoes, and leave them in a pan of cold water.

You can prepare the fish too, provided you store them on a well-greased tray; cover them well and store safely in the fridge.

Make the port and claret jellies, and store them in the fridge.

Morning

Prepare, cook and cream the potatoes and store in a buttered double saucepan. Take the pâté out of the fridge and stuff the apples when the pâté has softened. Store in the fridge.

Check your shopping and the table setting. Put the dishes in the warming drawer and prepare the coffee tray.

Check:
the lamps
the heating
the room for coats and the bathroom
the records and tapes
the flowers

Prepare the Garnishes

For this dinner (because you've done so much in advance), you can really go to town on the garnishings. Cover them well and leave in a cool place.

For the savoury apple, you can have celery twirls, orange twirls, egg slices, radish flowers, and red pepper slices.

For the soup, you need croûtons, cream and finely chopped parsley.

With the fish, serve a very small savoury salad garnish of lemon and cucumber slices with a fan gherkin (or just lemon and parsley).

Plenty of finely chopped parsley for the main course (what a boon to cooks parsley is!).

Evening

Put the steaks and sauce in the oven, calculating $1\frac{1}{2}$ hours cooking time.

Take the jellies out of the fridge at the start of the meal.

Have the soup ready to heat through, and the foil parcels of vegetables ready to pop in the oven. Mix the tarragon essence into the cream.

Prepare and lay out the starter with its garnish: place the apples on leaves of lettuce painted with walnut oil, and the other garnishes around. Just at the last minute coat the apples with the tarragon cream, and top with a sprig of mint or fresh tarragon and the tiniest sprinkling of cayenne pepper.

As your guests sit down, put the oven up a bit and pop the sole in before serving the soup.

After you serve the fish there will be a slight pause as you will have to take the steaks out of the oven, remove them to a separate dish while you add the cream and marsala to the sauce and reduce it on top of the stove.

Fill the meringue gâteau with flavoured cream just before serving.

ACT
THREE

ACT THREE

SCENE ONE
DESSERTS

SCENE TWO
CHEESEBOARD

This is where I pull out all the stops. This is where I punch them drunk with enthusiasm. This is when I sit back at a dinner party and say, 'Over to you, I intend to catch up with you on the drink – the coffee is going to be very much self-service!' And everything will have been done beforehand.

I always have a choice of three sweets for my home guests to choose from, knowing only too well that I will be able to finish them myself over the next couple of days. And I do so like to give genuinely enthusiastic diners portions in foil to take home. And why not? Surely entertaining is the simple joy of giving to your friends and sharing in the glow of the effects of good wine, good food and good company. Relaxing, leaving cares of the world behind for a few hours. Switching off (oh yes, I *always* take the 'phone off the hook when entertaining!) and indulging both yourself and your guests.

When the curtain goes up on this, let the scene take over completely. Generous decorations of piped whipped cream; flowers simply but effectively used and where possible, lovely old family dishes to be USED and admired even if eventually they may get broken (at least get some pleasure out of serving your desserts from them instead of continually looking at them in your china cabinet).

Of my three sweets, one is light and easy to digest, one is a little more generous with cream and flavourings, and then a third is just richness and goodness personified. All the guests will make their choice and if, by then, they have lost all their reticence, they will go for a bit of each!

Sweets can be so creative and a course you can really go to town over. I always make certain I have them ready decorated to bring out to the serving table where I always place the plates and serving utensils before the guests arrive. Being trained in stage management comes in very handy here, and I always ask my guests to help themselves, as with the cheese, in case someone hasn't a sweet tooth (or wants *both*!).

So many people mar their performance with the coffee and tea served after a meal. Make certain you have the trays set up, percolator to hand, and be adventurous with your selection of tea. Why is it difficult in so many restaurants in this country (famed for its consumption of tea!) to obtain a pot of tea after a good meal? At times they treat you with scorn and ridicule when you ask. I have a friend who always takes a supply of teabags with her in her handbag and if any difficulty is encountered, orders a pot of boiling water and jug of cold milk and proceeds to 'do her own thing'.

The new coffee filter machines are inexpensive at the moment and certainly, ground percolated coffee puts the finishing touches to your meal. If you have to have the powdered you have to! The only thing I abhor with coffee is those coloured pieces of granite which substitute for demerara sugar – they never seem to melt and sweeten the coffee, and purple, green, and orange blobs in my cup do nothing for my touchy liver at that stage of the evening.

SCENE ONE
DESSERTS

Here I must admit I tend to be extravagant when entertaining as this is invariably the last item my guests will eat before leaving and so the impression must be favourable. Seek out a supplier of free range fresh eggs, use butter in your pastry, good cream for your puds and the finest chocolate available. So many people try to economize with the latter; it invariably shows in the end results.

Essences are often used in this part of the cooking so, when shopping, seek out the good old fashioned well-established firms and avoid some of the newly produced stomach curdling essences. Some of the latter have the immediate effect of making me want to clean my teeth. And don't, whatever you do, resort to rum, whisky and brandy essences. They aren't worth it. If you aren't going to have the genuine stuff, leave it out.

But remember. For the desserts, if you've got it, flaunt it!

Farmhouse Pastry Pies

I feel certain (not that I wish to disillusion you in any way) that the second time you make this pastry it will be better than the first, and by the fifth attempt it will be plain sailing. But do persevere as even on your first attempt I am sure your family will be pleased with the results. By the third attempt your friends will be singing your praises and at the fifth effort even your enemies will admit defeat.

The following recipe gives you sufficient pastry to make one 10 in (25 cm) pie (enough to serve 8), and you can double it up provided you have a big enough bowl; so at one mixing you have sufficient for immediate use, and some to freeze for a future occasion. The following points are relevant to all pastry making but I think them worth repeating, as they really will help with the final product.

1. Butter for pastry should never come straight from the fridge, but should be at room temperature. Thus, when you press your thumb into the lovely golden rectangle the impression stays firmly embedded and there should be no effort to get it there either.

2. Do try to use a large plastic or earthenware bowl about 14 in (35 cm) in diameter with *round* sides. There are several beautiful stainless steel mixing bowls on the market, but most have a definite angle of 65° where the side meets the base, and when making pastry in them, the soft part of the pastry tends to adhere to this whole surround. In a nice smooth half-round bowl there are no corners for this to happen.

3. Before you start rubbing the fat into the flour, spread your hands out in front of you with the palms towards you and open your fingers wide. Waggle your thumbs in and out never letting them touch your fingers. This is the action you have to use; and you scoop up handfuls of the flour and fat into the air and literally let it fall back down into the bowl between the outstretched fingers. If you squeeze and rub the fat into the flour, the end product will be doughy. Your lightness of touch at this stage makes or breaks your pastry! It doesn't matter if you make a slight mess around the working area on your first attempt.

4. When adding the sugar and lemon rind, do not be too meticulous about it being spread absolutely evenly through. The more you try to do this, the more chance there is of you over-working the dough.

5. Spread the lightly-beaten egg yolk zig-zag around the bowl and then, holding the left and right side of the bowl in your hands, slowly shake it as if panning for gold.

6. When you plan to bring the dough together, your hand must act like a gentle scoop, with the back of the hand keeping in touch with the side of the bowl and the palm gently bringing the dough together. Do *not* squeeze it. Hold the bowl at a 45° angle and it will be like a concrete mixer (what an example to give, mind you) rolling the contents round.

7. Chill for a few hours or even freeze.

Cheesecake

My Nan's Tipsy Trifle

A selection of cheeses, and home-made biscuits
to go with them.

Chocolate roulade

8. *Never, never, never* attempt to roll the pastry until it has come back to its former texture at the end of the stage 6. People so often get impatient and start to roll the pastry, and are horrified to find it cracking before their eyes. Remember, it should be similar to the plasticine you used to play with as a child.

At this stage the base is made, chilled, and then baked blind. Roll out the pastry to line the base of your pie, and chill for 30 minutes before baking blind for 30–35 minutes at 325°F (170°C), Gas 3.

9. When filling your pie you – and only you – will know how much liquid your filling has produced or will produce. Tinned fruit, especially, can be a headache for pies due to the syrup content, so I always sprinkle Farola (or semolina) on the cooked base before adding *any* filling and this helps to soak up any liquid but does not, in any way, detract from the joy of eating. If you are going to serve a pie, for goodness sake be lavish with the filling. Having gone to the trouble (and some people when they see the butter content, say *expense*) of making such delicious pastry, why be suddenly mean with the filling, serving a slender pie when a fat one looks so much more appealing! You can also line the cooked base with rice paper which is another way of avoiding a wet bottom! I always sweeten my pies with demerara sugar and, before adding the lid, give a generous sprinkling once more of Farola or semolina.

10. When adding the lid you place the ball of soft dough onto the floured board and give the ball a gentle help on its way by lightly pressing it flatter with the palm of your hand, then lightly roll with your rolling pin from the middle out – both away and towards you always starting from the middle point of the ball of dough. When satisfied that your flat rolled piece of pastry will cover the pie filling, gently place the rolling pin on the pastry lying away from you with the aid of a palette knife, roll the pastry around the rolling pin towards you. On the area where the pastry was lying you put the filled pie base, lift the rolling pin up and place over the part of the base nearer to you and by then rolling away *from* you, hey presto, the top is on. Rather than chopping off the overhanging pieces, ease them up gently onto the inside rim of the fluted flan and then all you have to do is press your thumb around the top all the way round, and the basic pie is completed.

With the odd pieces of pastry left over you can re-roll these and make leaves. Place the first leaf with its base more or less in the middle of the pie top and then go round in a circle to form the base of the pattern you are aiming for and then do a further layer, but this time starting off between two leaves. To get a 'rose' in the middle all you need to do is cut a piece of dough about $3 \times \frac{1}{2}$ in (7×1 cm) and put this on a palette knife and just roll it up like a cartwheel. Put in the centre point of the two layer pattern of leaves.

11. Always chill the pie again prior to cooking.

12. Follow the cooking instructions implicitly. It should be baked at 400°F (200°C), Gas 6, for 20 minutes then for a further 25 minutes

at 350°F (180°C), Gas 4. Keep on looking in from time to time and if some areas are browning faster, loosely cover the pie with foil.

- **12 oz (350 g) sieved self-raising flour**
- **a pinch of salt**
- **4 oz (100–125 g) cornflour**
- **12 oz (350 g) soft butter**
- **4 oz (100–125 g) castor sugar**
- **rind of one lemon**
- **2 egg yolks**

Sieve the self-raising flour, salt and cornflour into a large plastic bowl, and then break up the soft butter into $\frac{1}{2}$ oz (15 g) bits and rub the fat into the flour. Slowly but surely your mixture will begin to resemble breadcrumbs and, at this stage, when you are satisfied the fat is all evenly incorporated into the flour, *stop*. Do *not* overwork it or else your pastry will become heavy.

Add the castor sugar and finely grated lemon rind and just quickly shake together and then zig-zag the lightly beaten egg yolks over the mixing. A light, plastic bowl is excellent here as you have to grab hold of each edge of the mixing bowl and then begin to shake as if panning for gold! If you've got too much egg yolk in one small area you will see an egg-sized piece of damp pastry looking like an oasis in a desert of fine sand! Stop shaking and break this damp ball up and scatter it around so that each and every egg yolk particle can begin to attract the dried butter-flour mixture. The crumbs will become to resemble peanuts, then walnuts, and then larger. Now is the time to stop shaking the bowl and let your hand do the rest (the point in Note 6 should be followed very carefully).

You don't want to make perfect round dough balls at this stage – bouncy, heavy beach balls are no use for light, luscious pastry. It doesn't matter if your ball looks messy or mis-shapen with a few odd areas of damp egg yolk. Wrap each piece in foil, or put them into polythene bags that can be tied. Leave to chill.

Roll out the pastry only when the dough has come back to room temperature. *I can't stress this enough*, as the more plasticine-like the dough, the easier it will roll. If you have to use force to get the pastry to 'stretch', stretch it will, and shrink it will in the cooking! But if you are able to make the base and top of your pie with ease (and this will be simple if you let the dough get to the correct consistency), you will have no headaches whatsoever.

For the base of the pie just follow the instructions given on page 40 for Savoury Quiche Pastry. Don't forget to chill prior to cooking blind. I prefer to cook the base blind for about half an hour and this, again, is explained fully in the section on quiches. When you take it out of the oven the base *may* have risen a little and be a trifle soggy. Don't panic, but wait until it begins to cool a little and then gently ease the foil out and you can commence putting the filling in.

Fillings

Apple and Orange. I always use Granny Smith apples – about 6 to fill the pie. Peel, core and slice them, and arrange in the case with 2 peeled segmented oranges on top.

Black Cherry and Rum. Drain 2 × 10 oz (275 g) cans pitted cherries well and then sprinkle very generously with 2 tablespoons dark rum.

Banana, Walnut and Ginger. You need about 8 bananas for one pie. Skin and slice them and pile quite generously in the cooked base and then use ginger and chopped walnuts according to personal taste – remembering that walnuts are rather bitter when cooked.

Spiced Apricot. Poach about 24 fresh apricots lightly in stock syrup to cover (see page 211) to which you have added 1 tablespoon wine vinegar. Drain well and then when filling the pie, sprinkle ½ teaspoon each of nutmeg, cinnamon and a little ground ginger on, and finish off with a generous tablespoon of wine vinegar (rather like the amount you would dash onto your chips when presented to you in paper at the local fish and chip shop).

Apple and Raspberry. Peel, core and slice 5 apples as in *Apple and Orange* above, and arrange in the flan then add the raw raspberries – about 4 oz (100 g) – remembering that this sort of soft fruit is extremely damp when cooked!

Gooseberry and Juniper. Place 1½ lb (675 kg) gooseberries and place them in the flan. Take 8 juniper berries and grind them with some brown sugar in a pestle and mortar (or liquidizer). You could use dried elderflowers instead of the juniper.

Pear and Stilton. Thin slices of uncooked pear (about 5) are used and then you sprinkle the top with about 2 oz (50 g) crumbled Stilton.

Apple Pie with Cheddar Cheese Pastry

For a 10 in (25 cm) pie to serve 8 people

- **10 oz (275 g) sieved plain flour**
- **a pinch of salt**
- **10 oz (275 g) soft butter**
- **10 oz (275 g) finely grated Cheddar cheese**
- **6 Granny Smith apples**
- **about ½ teaspoon each cinnamon and nutmeg *or* 1 teaspoon allspice**
- **a few cloves, if liked**

Sieve the flour and salt into a mixing bowl and gently work in the soft butter (see the instructions on Farmhouse Pastry Pies, page 144), and then work in the cheese.

This is a very pliable pastry and needs to be well chilled prior to rolling, and lining a 10 in (25 cm) pie dish. Chill again before baking blind for about 30 minutes at 325°F (170°C), Gas 3. Then fill the pie with peeled, cored and sliced apples and a generous sprinkling of spices – cinnamon, nutmeg, allspice or a clove or two, if liked – to provide a contrast in flavour with the cheese pastry. Don't forget to 'dome' the top, or the pie will look mean, then roll out the top and cover as explained in detail under Farmhouse Pastry. Bake your pie at 425°F (220°C), Gas 7, for the first 15 minutes, then reduce the heat to 350°F (180°C), Gas 4, for a further 20 minutes. Check during the cooking time that the pastry is being evenly browned. Serve hot, or it's also good when cooled – the slightly tart, spicy apples contrasting with the savoury, melt-in-the-mouth cheese pastry.

Pancakes

The pancakes (see page 51 for basic recipe), can easily be made in the morning, and provided they are stored under a tea towel can then be used in the evening, with one of these sweet fillings. I would serve 2 pancakes per person as a pudding, and I never serve them with less than 3 oz (75 g) of filling in each pancake.

To warm pancakes through, fill them and then line them up on a well-buttered tin tray and cover with well-buttered greaseproof paper. Give them 10 minutes in a medium oven at 350°F (180°C), Gas 4, and then finish them off, if appropriate to the recipe, by coating with double cream whipped with soft brown sugar and sprinkled with more sugar, and flashing under the grill.

Fillings

1. Calvados Apple Purée (page 211) with whipped double cream on top. Sprinkle with demerara sugar over them and finish off by flashing under a hot grill.

2. Any fruit purée is delicious in a pancake, and they can easily be prepared in the morning. I particularly like to lay the pancakes out flat and put alternately down the middle a portion of fruit purée and then a scoop of ice cream (or Lemon Ice Box Pudding). Roll the pancake up, sprinkle liberally with demerara sugar and then flash quickly under a very hot grill. When you actually then serve this be generous with whipped double cream! You can also experiment by adding grated coconut or well-drained fried breadcrumbs to the purées.

3. Broken pieces of meringue mixed with small slices of banana and finely chopped ginger combined with whipped double cream, then reheated in a very warm oven for about five minutes. Finish off by flambéing with a little good rum.

4. When raspberries and strawberries are slightly past their best they can be liquidized and combined with some fine cake crumbs, cream and castor sugar. Fill the pancakes, warm them through, and serve with a reduction of boiled double cream.

5. Mincemeat combined with vanilla cream ice can also be used for filling a pancake which is then flashed under a very hot grill. The end result of cold ice cream with rich mincemeat and hot pancake is quite superb.

6. Fill your pancakes with a minced mixing of equal parts of walnuts, chopped banana and preserved ginger mixed with a little dark rum. Warm them through and coat with whipped double cream.

7. Try chopped glacé fruits mixed with chopped nuts, or for an occasional extravagance, put a few chocolate truffles in each pancake before flashing under the grill and serving with cream.

8 oz (225 g) good dark chocolate

1 tablespoon spirit of your choice

1 oz (25 g) soft butter
or
$\frac{1}{2}$ tablespoon corn oil

$\frac{1}{2}$ pint (300 ml) double cream, whipped

Éclairs, Profiteroles and Puffs

The recipe for choux pastry on page 43 will make 30–40 éclairs or profiteroles, 8 swans or 6 large puffs. Choux pastry for puddings – whether submarine-shaped éclairs, small balls (profiteroles) or large puffs – should be coated with or dipped in chocolate, using this recipe.

Use brandy, crême de cacao or rum – whatever you fancy.

Place the spirit and the chocolate in the top of a double saucepan. Heat gently, and when combined together, beat in the soft butter or the corn oil. Coat the choux pastry when it is completely cool, and leave the chocolate to set before filling the choux with cream.

The whipped double cream for filling the éclairs or profiteroles can also be flavoured with coffee (I use good old Camp Coffee Essence), or ground hazelnuts (which can surprise your guests!). I have also folded those delicious Italian chocolate beans into the whipped cream, and then filled the éclairs with this mixture: but if you do this, *do* make sure you have a fairly large plain nozzle piping bag or else you will be in trouble.

For choux puffs, use a $\frac{1}{2}$ in (1 cm) plain nozzle to pipe out 6 large rounds on to a dampened baking tray and bake these off at 425°F (220°C), Gas 7, for 20 minutes. Take out and make a hole in the side (remembering that this will be the hole through which you insert the filling), and return to dry out in the oven. Topped with coffee icing and filled at the last moment with coffee-flavoured whipped cream, these are superb.

Fill your swans with raspberries and cream – a good way to stretch an expensive fruit.

Puff Pastry Desserts

The nicest way to serve Puff Pastry Cornets or Milles Feuilles (for the basic recipes, see pages 36–38) is with fruit – whole, fresh, stewed or puréed – and cream.

Puff pastry cornets for desserts normally are served with a blob of nice jam in the tip and then topped up with sweetened and whipped double cream. Any fruit purée can be used, and to provide a contrast in texture, you can fold into the purée some finely chopped up raw fruit. I frequently pipe in any of the mousses (see page 159), and instead of the traditional mincemeat pies, I put mincemeat into puff pastry cornets and serve them with whipped double cream, soft brown sugar and rum to taste. Very, very good indeed (and not only to be served at Christmas!).

Always remember – *please* – to fill your pastry *at the very last minute.*

Rich Egg Custards

This is a *rich* egg custard which looks simple when presented to your guests but which tastes creamy and quite delicious. There is

For 6

2 tablespoons chosen liqueur

2 eggs and 1 egg yolk, lightly beaten

2 tablespoons castor sugar

$\frac{1}{2}$ pint (300 ml) double cream

freshly grated nutmeg (optional)

no skill in preparing it, just a slight extravagance, and if the end result is a sweet that is guaranteed to please your guests, why frown at the quantity of cream you are going to use?

When served with fresh or poached seasonal fruits a few tablespoons of an appropriate liqueur in the custard makes all the difference and turns a schooldays dish – my school custards were made with powdered milk and dried eggs and lashings of nutmeg – into a mouthwatering dinner-party delight.

These quantities will produce just over $\frac{3}{4}$ pint (400 ml), enough to fill 6 individual 3 in (7 cm) ramekins.

Beat the eggs and yolk with the sugar and your chosen liqueur, then pour on the cream. Mix gently and pour into the ramekin. Place the ramekins (and do remember that a light sprinkling of freshly grated nutmeg on the top is tasty) in a baking tray and then add hot water to come half-way up the sides of the ramekins. Bake for 35–45 minutes at 375°F (190°C), Gas 5. Put a knife point in the custard after 35 minutes. If it comes out clean, it is ready. You can serve it straightaway, or it can be left to go cold – just as delicious.

Serve your rich egg custards accompanied by the following fresh, stewed or puréed fruits, and liqueurs. Mix 2 tablespoons of Calvados into your custard mixing and serve it with an apple purée. Mix peach brandy in and serve the custard with fresh or puréed peaches. Pernod-flavoured custard goes beautifully with Kiwi fruit, and try gin flavoured custards with gooseberries.

Bread and Butter Pudding

For 8

12 slices bread, liberally spread with butter

2 tablespoons raisins (preferably soaked overnight in rum)

3 eggs

$\frac{1}{2}$ pint (300 ml) warmed single cream

a little candied peel if you like

rind only of 1 lemon and 1 orange

about 4 tablespoons Negrita rum

Serve me this on any occasion in the cold winter months and I am as happy as a skylark. It is rich, warm, smooth, delicious, and so good for you. I prefer to make it with either the Boiled Lakeland Loaf or All Bran Loaf on pages 187 and 188. You may think this is a dish that should only be served at a lunch or supper party, but why? I can think of no valid reason for this old-fashioned idea and people who have raised their eyebrows when I have suggested they choose it for their pudding after a four-course dinner, are invariably the first to ask for either the recipe or a second helping.

I prefer to make individual portion dishes (this mixing serves 8) which should be well greased with butter and sprinkled with vanilla sugar (see page 194).

Prepare the pud in the morning, and then cook it during dinner. Cut the well-buttered bread into sensibly sized pieces that will fit the dishes you are going to use and layer by layer, fill each with the bread, the raisins, candied peel and lemon and orange rind. Finally, pour over the warmed single cream that has been mixed with the eggs and rum, *and leave to stand for as long as possible.*

Bake in a roasting tray with water to come half-way up the sides of the dishes, for 40 minutes at 375°F (190°C), Gas 5. Leave on one side to cool a little before serving and then just pour a thin layer of single cream on top as you take them to the table. A teaspoon of Rum Butter (see page 212) served on top makes this pud even more sinful!

My Nan's Baked Apple

For 4

4 large cooking apples

2 oz (50 g) each of dates,seedless raisins, sultanas

3 tablespoons Lemon Curd (see page 198)

soft brown sugar

a little double cream

Wash the apples, remove the core and pips with an apple corer, and place on a well-buttered ovenproof dish. Roughly chop the dates, raisins, and sultanas together and combine them with the orange juice and rind and lemon curd. Spoon into the centres of the apples right up to the top. Sprinkle with soft brown sugar and bake at 350°F (180°C), Gas 4, for approximately 40–45 minutes, basting them occasionally during this time.

Serve with more soft brown sugar and the double cream. They are also delicious served with very cold vanilla ice cream.

Galettes

Galettes are made from a pastry similar to Savoury Pastry (see page 38), and it makes lovely desserts. It cooks extremely crisp, is very buttery and tasty and ideal for using with combinations of fruits and other fillings. The recipe is for about 21 individual galettes, using a 3 in (7 cm) pastry cutter.

1 lb (450 g) sieved plain flour

2 oz (50 g) sieved icing sugar

10 oz (275 g) soft butter

3 egg yolks

a little vanilla essence

Sieve the flour and icing sugar on to a baking board and make a well in the centre. Into this flatten out the soft butter, breaking the egg yolks lightly on top, and using the fingers (exactly as described on page 144), bring the butter and egg yolks together. Then, with the aid of a palette knife, continue to make the basic pastry, forming three balls. Leave to chill.

Remove it from the fridge when you wish to use it and allow the pastry to return to room temperature.

Roll out one ball to about $\frac{1}{8}$ in (3 mm) thick and use whatever size cutter you feel adequate (you should get 21 3 in (7.5 cm) in diameter out of this mixing without re-rolling), and place each individual galette onto a tray lined with greaseproof paper. Let the pastry rounds chill well and then cook them off at 350°F (180°C), Gas 4, for 10–25 minutes, according to size. As they cool, sprinkle with vanilla sugar. Fill them at the last minute with one of the following fillings:

1. Any fresh summer fruit, or fruit purée, folded into lightly sweetened whipped double cream.

2. Calvados Apple Purée (see page 211) combined with sweetened whipped cream.

3. Sultanas plumped-up in brandy, mixed with grated chocolate and a little rum-sweetened cream.

4. Peach purée, flavoured with 2 tablespoons peach brandy and whipped double cream.

5. Finely chopped glacé fruits combined with grated chocolate and a little rum-sweetened cream.

See also flavoured cream fillings on page 209.

Chocolate Brandy Roulade

4 eggs, separated

4 oz (100 g) castor sugar

4 oz (100 g) good plain chocolate, chopped

$\frac{1}{4}$ gill (40 ml) brandy

Please see the section on roulades (page 46) for more detailed instructions on method.

Beat egg yolks to a ribbon with the sugar – remembering to get the eggs on the way first before adding the sugar, a little at a time.

In a double saucepan, melt the chopped chocolate (remembering the end result is only as good as the chocolate you use!) with the brandy.

Begin to beat up the egg whites. When the yolk and sugar mixture is ready, transfer this to a large plastic bowl and fold in the chocolate (which you've passed through a sieve to make sure there are no hidden lumps). Fold in one-third of the beaten egg whites, bring the balance of the egg whites back to a firm consistency and then fold these in as well.

Spread in the greaseproof-lined and buttered trays (about 8 × 12 in (20 × 30 cm) in size) and cook at 350°F (180°C), Gas 4, for 15 to 18 minutes. When you have tested the roulades (and they will have a very crisp cracky top!) cover them with clean, dry tea towels and then, in turn, cover these with a tea towel that has been well dampened. You will see steam begin to rise. Leave it now to cool. This settles the crisp top and gives you a delightfully rich dessert. Leave overnight if you can, before turning out, spreading with whipped double cream flavoured with more brandy and sugar – I usually use $\frac{3}{4}$ pint (400 ml) of cream with 3 tablespoons of brandy and 3 tablespoons of castor sugar. Roll up carefully.

To transfer to a serving tray, cut off each end by approximately 2 in (5 cm) and then get two fish slices and insert them at an angle of 45° underneath the 'log' and gently ease onto your display dish, setting the end pieces at a 90° angle either end. I often use an ordinary baking tray lined with foil which I garnish with ferns and, of course, the whole thing is coated with icing sugar. This is a particularly good dish for the festive season.

Chocolate Cherry Brandy Round

8 oz (225 g) chocolate digestive biscuits

8 oz (225 g) good chocolate

8 oz (225 g) butter

2 eggs

3 oz (75 g) castor sugar

continued

This is an easy, rich and filling dish to serve at a supper party and, although not one of my own favourites, the recipe is invariably requested by guests unaware of the sheer simplicity of its making!

Liquidize the digestive biscuits or crush between 2 sheets of greaseproof paper with a rolling pin (do this somewhere cool).

Place the chocolate and butter into a double saucepan to melt and meanwhile put the eggs into the Kenwood and beat for about 8 minutes then slowly, little by little, add the sieved castor sugar.

Remove from heat + continue
whisking until the bowl is clean,
then add the choc. + the grated
orange rind. Lightly whip cream
+ fold half into mixture x
Disolve the gelatine in the orange
juice over heat + add to mousse x
Stir until thickening, then
pour quickly into soufflé case x
Leave in cool place to set x
When firm, press ground [illegible]
round sides + decorate with
remaining cream + candid peel x

2 tablespoons brandy

2 oz (50 g) walnut halves, chopped

2 oz (50 g) finely chopped glacé cherries

Slowly beat the melted chocolate and butter into the eggs and sugar and follow this with the brandy (if feeling generous, a further 2 tablespoons will easily be absorbed by the recipe and the sweet the better for it at the end). Fold in the chopped cherries, crushed biscuits and walnut halves and spoon the mixture into 15 individual cup-cake cases and leave to chill in the fridge.

This is a very rich sweet and when cherries are in season I usually remove the paper from each pud, pipe a twirl of cream on top and decorate with fresh cherries – the joined ones in pairs or threes look quite attractive. You can also serve with chopped preserved ginger in cream or diced pineapple with Kirsch Cream (see below).

Chocolate Crunchies

6 oz (175 g) golden syrup

6 oz (175 g) butter

6 oz (175 g) good chocolate

5 oz (150 g) cornflakes

I blush at times when people say how much they have enjoyed this dessert, as a child of 7 could quite easily prepare it, but as it is so popular – what the hell! This makes 12 of these, which will keep well in the fridge until filled for use.

Melt the syrup, butter and chocolate together in a double saucepan, and then pour over the cornflakes. Mix well so that all the flakes are well covered with chocolate. Press this delicious chocolatey mass into lightly greased ramekins and hollow up the sides (this mixing should give about 12 little cases). Leave to cool and set.

When set, turn out of the ramekins by running a sharp knife round the edge of each 'case'. Fill the hollows with your chosen flavoured cream. For example:

Calvados Cream with Apple Slices (leaving green or red skin on)
Fresh Cherry with Kirsch Cream
Raspberry Framboise Cream with Grated Chocolate
Pineapple with Kirsch Cream

For each mixing of flavoured cream, 1 pint (600 ml) double cream should be whipped with about 2 tablespoons castor sugar and 2 tablespoons of your chosen liqueur.

Chocolate Rum Squidgy Gâteau

8 oz (225 g) chopped chocolate

8 tablespoons dark rum

8 oz (225 g) butter

8 oz (225 g) sieved castor sugar

8 eggs, separated

4 oz (100 g) self-raising flour

4 oz (100 g) ground almonds

This recipe makes two gâteaux – one can be eaten the day it is cooked and the other will keep extremely well in the freezer. Line carefully 2 × 8 in (20.5 cm) sponge tins with good greaseproof paper and preheat your oven to 350°F (180°C), Gas 4.

Put the chopped chocolate in a double saucepan with the dark rum (the best rum for cooking is Negrita which is a blend of East and West Indian spirits made by Bardinet in Rouen). Allow the chocolate to melt but please see that the water in the base pan does not boil too rapidly.

For the topping:

6 oz (175 g) chocolate

4 tablespoons rum

4 oz (100 g) softened butter

½ pint (300 ml) double cream

about 1 tablespoon icing sugar to taste

Cream the butter and sieved castor sugar together and little by little beat in the egg yolks.

Remove the melted chocolate and rum from the heat, allow to cool a little and then beat into the butter, sugar and egg yolk mixing. Now fold in the sieved self-raising flour and ground almonds, followed by one-third of the stiffly beaten egg whites. Beat the remaining egg whites up once more and incorporate them into the mixture.

Divide the mixture between the two prepared tins and bake at 350°F (180°C), Gas 4, for 45–60 minutes. Always test to see if cooked by inserting a skewer into the centre – this should come out completely clean and dry. When cool remove from the tins and take the greaseproof paper off the sides and bottom. Invert the gâteaux and dowse liberally with more rum. One can be wrapped in a polythene bag and frozen at this stage.

When you wish to make up the other, you melt the chocolate for the topping with the rum in a double saucepan as before, and as it cools beat in the soft butter little by little. As this goes cold it begins to set. While this is happening slice the gâteau into 3 horizontally, layer with the whipped double cream to which a little icing sugar has been added (don't forget the rum and butter chocolate topping is rather bitter) and sandwich together again. As the chocolate is setting, pour over the three-layered gâteau letting it run down the sides. With the aid of a small palette knife repeatedly submerged into very hot water, straighten out the edge of the gâteau. You can garnish it with walnut halves or pecan nuts.

Kentucky Chocolate Pie

For the filling:

2 oz (50 g) good dark chocolate

1 tablespoon rum

½ pint (300 ml) single cream

2 tablespoons cornflour

½ lb (225 g) castor sugar

½ teaspoon vanilla extract

2 eggs, lightly beaten

2 oz (50 g) butter

This is a rich sweet which I enjoy cooking, but like eating even more! The recipe was given to me by a friend in North Carolina and when serving it at Miller Howe to people from Kentucky I've been told, 'My, my, one doesn't get Kentucky Chocolate Pie like this in Kentucky'! Serve it in 12 individual shortbread tartlets (see page 194) or pour the filling into a 10 in (25.5 cm) cooked flan case made from Savoury or Farmhouse Pastry (see pages 38 and 144).

Melt the chocolate with the rum in a double saucepan. Take a little of the single cream and make the cornflour into a smooth paste and then slowly add the balance of the cream, the sugar, vanilla extract and the 2 lightly beaten eggs. Transfer to a saucepan, adding the melted chocolate and rum, and cook over a low light stirring *constantly* until the mixture thickens. With care this should take about 8 minutes, but do not have the heat too high. As it cools, beat in the butter and then pour the mixture into the cooked pastry flan or tartlets and leave to chill.

Petit Pots de Chocolat à l'Orange

Or 'Chocolate Orange Cream' (you know what you're getting then!). Very rich, very delicious and very easy to make. This mixing will give you 12 small portions.

6 oz (175 g) chocolate

2 oz (50 g) butter

6 eggs, separated

3 tablespoons orange curaçao, Grand Marnier or Cointreau

Slowly and carefully melt the chocolate with the butter in a double saucepan, or a china basin, over a pan of gently simmering water, stirring from time to time.

Remove from the heat and beat in the egg yolks one by one along with the spirit flavouring. When cold, fold in the stiffly beaten egg whites, remembering to fold in one third first, then whisk up the egg whites again before folding in the balance. Pour into 12 small ramekins and chill well.

MERINGUES

I think the easiest of desserts to make are those from egg whites and sugar – meringues and their endless variations on a theme! Meringue gâteaux look quite stunning on a buffet table but are tricky to cut and serve neatly so I usually prepare individual portion sizes. They freeze remarkably well and, of course, when taken straight from the freezer are much easier to garnish and fill with cream as they are not at all brittle. Meringue nests, pavlovas and 'blobs' store well, too, in airtight containers and are such a handy standby to have in the store cupboard.

The basic recipe is 2 parts of castor sugar to 1 part of egg white. The sugar should be sieved completely free of lumps, and I prefer the egg whites to be taken straight from the fridge and weighed rather than counted. The purists say that eggs hand beaten in a copper bowl gleamingly cleaned first with salt and lemon juice give by far the better meringue. I fully agree with them on this for whites which have to be *folded* into a mixture to strengthen and hold, but when making basic meringues I just do not get as good a result with this orthodox method as I do with the Kenwood Electric Mixer!

What are always needed, however, are spotlessly clean and completely dry utensils, and so do check your mixing bowl, beater, and large spoon or spatula. You also need the right kind of greaseproof paper, which should be silicone treated and of good quality. If you use cheaper paper you will find the meringue sticks to it, and this causes a terrible headache when trying to get it off. (And who wants to make extra work in the kitchen when there is always plenty of it around anyway!) So do buy good quality silicone-treated greaseproof paper or vegetable parchment and line your trays first.

I turn the usual baking trays over and always cook meringues on the true bottoms of the trays as I find when cooking them on the normal side that there is a slight loss of heat caused by the side lip of the tray. Doing them my way the heat swirls round the meringue completely and evenly. Pre-heat your oven to 325°F (170°C), Gas 3.

8 oz (225 g) egg white

1 lb (450 g) castor sugar

Into the bowl place the egg whites and beat on high speed until the mixture is white, foamy and light and then add gently (whilst still beating) 4 oz (100 g) of the sugar. The mixture will be knocked back a little at first but will very quickly come back up to its former peak and you then repeat this procedure 3 more times which will use up all the sugar. Many people say you should fold in the last quarter of the sugar – I have tried both methods and find no valid reason for this, so do it the easy way!

I am not too keen on piping meringue, as I am convinced that when you have the mixture scooped up into the piping bag and you begin to squeeze like mad to get lovely meringue nests, swans, etc, some of the air is knocked out. I just use a large silver tablespoon and literally scoop up dollops (usually about 12) of the rather stiff mixture and plonk them (leaving gaps between each individual portion) onto the greaseproof paper.

For making elegant mouth-watering gâteaux, just divide the mixture into 2 on 2 separate lined baking trays and by lightly holding a palette knife you can gently ease the mixture into a rough round shape, but don't be heavy-handed and knock out the air! There is no need for the gâteaux to be exactly the same size and shape – they look much more homely and edible if irregular.

Bake at 325°F (170°C), Gas 3, for 1 hour, and then turn off the oven, open the door slightly and leave ajar with the aid of a wooden spoon. Leave in the oven for 2 to 3 hours. The end result will be slightly brown meringue, firm and crisp. If you prefer pure white meringues that are a trifle soft, bake at 200°F (100°C), a very Low gas, for 3–4 hours.

I must admit, though, that a meringue basket does look rather grand, and to make this you do have to use a piping bag and nozzle. Mark out on the greaseproof paper 6 even-sized rings. Pipe one fully from the centre, and round, to the extreme edge, but just pipe a strip about $\frac{1}{2}$ in (1 cm) wide round the perimeter for the other five. When baked and cooled you build them up, sticking them together with more little blobs of uncooked meringue mixture, using it like glue, and return to the oven for further baking. If you wish to be frightfully elegant at this stage, measure the height of your basket and pipe out S-shape designs of uncooked meringue mixture and bake these off too. When the basket itself is finally baked, stick the cooked S shapes round the side with further meringue mixing and put back into the oven again. On the occasions when you are building up and out the meringue is cooked off at 200°F (100°C), gas Low, as opposed to 325°F (170°C), Gas 3, which is the temperature for making the 'parts'.

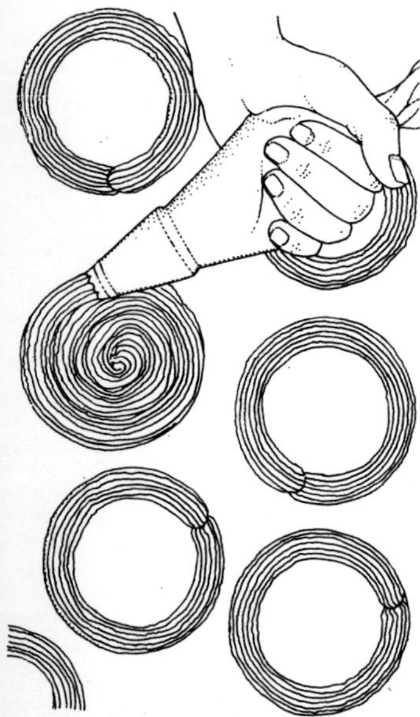

When finished and cooled off, wrap in foil and store in an airtight tin. To prevent this pretty 'serving dish' from going soft you can line the inside base and sides with rice paper before filling with fresh fruit salad, strawberries or, as I do often, mousse mixing on the base. If you have the time and energy you can also line the finished 'dish' with melted chocolate.

Almond Meringue Gâteau

1 lb (450 g) egg whites

2 lb (scant 1 kg) sieved castor sugar

8 oz (225 g) sieved ground almonds

This mixture cannot be piped into nest shapes as the oil in the nuts tends to dampen your artistic piping, and this mixing will give you 4 gâteaux approximately 12 in (30 cm) in diameter.

Beat the egg whites as described previously adding the castor sugar in 4 oz (100 g) stages. This takes a little longer, but 8 oz (225 g) poured onto egg whites is quite a concentrated attack on a mixture that is endeavouring to stand up bravely! Then scatter the sieved almonds on top and, using a large long-handled metal spoon, carefully fold the ingredients together by using a figure-of-eight motion through the mixture with the spoon. Do not be heavy-handed please, or else all your attempts at getting the mixture light will be destroyed in one fell swoop.

Divide the mixture into 4 on the prepared oven trays and coerce into the shape desired by gently using a palette knife as mentioned earlier. Put into the oven at the higher meringue temperature of 325°F (170°C), Gas 3, and bake for $1\frac{1}{2}$ hours. Turn the oven off and open the door, wedging a wooden spoon in to keep it just ajar. Leave for at least 4 hours. Remove from oven and when cool decorate (always best done as late as possible) or wrap in foil and freeze.

Hazelnut Meringue Gâteau

1 lb (450 g) egg whites

2 lb (scant 1 kg) sieved castor sugar

$9\frac{1}{2}$ oz (235 g) sieved ground hazelnuts

This is prepared in exactly the same way as the Almond Meringue Gâteau, and will give you 4 × 12 in (30 cm) gâteaux.

You should use slightly more ground hazelnuts than almonds, because after sieving, there is quite a lot of skin from the hazelnuts left in the sieve.

Coffee Meringue Gâteau

8 oz (225 g) egg whites

8 oz (225 g) sieved castor sugar

6 oz (175 g) icing sugar

3 tablespoons powdered instant coffee

This mixing will give you 2 large gâteaux each 12 in (30 cm) in diameter, serving 12 people.

Beat the egg whites until stiff, then beat in 2 oz (50 g) of the sugar at a time as described under the basic meringue method. Fold in the icing sugar mixed with the coffee (do make sure you use the powder not the coffee granules).

This mixing is rather glossy and not as tough as the normal meringue at this stage and will have fallen a little in the mixing bowl.

Divide mixture into 2 and spread evenly on 2 prepared baking trays, using a palette knife. Bake at the lowest setting on your oven for 3–4 hours. Open the oven door a little and insert a wooden spoon to keep the door slightly ajar and, having turned off the oven completely, leave the 2 gâteaux in for a further hour to dry out.

This meringue is delicious when filled with whipped double cream flavoured with Irish Whiskey and garnished with *fresh* walnuts.

Pavlovas

8 oz (225 g) egg whites

1 lb (450 g) sieved castor sugar

3 level teaspoons cornflour

1½ teaspoons white wine vinegar

These store extremely well in airtight plastic bags or boxes, and can be frozen. There is much debate about the origin, shape, size and consistency of Pavlovas, but I, personally, like my Pavlovas to be rather well done and slightly brown on the outside with just the smallest, gooey, marshmallowey centre.

Beat the egg whites, then beat in the sugar in 4 stages, the same way as for making basic meringues. Then, when you have got all the sugar into the mixing, sprinkle on (still beating away merrily) the cornflour and white wine vinegar (whatever you do, don't use malt vinegar).

The mixture will be quite firm and all you have to do is scoop tablespoon-sized dollops out of the bowl and plonk them onto good silicone-treated greaseproof paper on the baking tray. Bake off at 325°F (170°C), Gas 3, for 1¼ hours, and then turn the oven off. Wedge the door slightly open with a wooden spoon, and leave in the oven for a further 3 hours at least.

In the autumn fill your pavlovas with those luscious juicy tasty blackberries which grow in such abundance in the lanes and byways. When the pavlovas have been in the oven for 20 minutes I take the trays out and carefully scatter lightly toasted flaked almonds on top of each and every one. The 'rusty' tint on the flaked almonds truly reflects the autumn tints outside!

Flavoured Cream Fillings and Accompaniments for Meringues, Gâteaux and Pavlovas

With this type of sweet you can be as mean or as generous as you like with the filling. But if you were to sit down seriously and consider the actual basic cost of the meringue, gâteau or pavlova, I am sure you will quickly realize how inexpensive they are to make. So, be extravagant with the fillings and accompaniments.

The basic filling is of course whipped double cream and fruit, but you can flavour the cream with a liqueur to make it more extravagant – and more delicious. To your lashing of lightly whipped double cream, add 2 tablespoons of sieved castor sugar and 2 tablespoons of your selected liqueur. See the table below which shows which liqueurs go best with which fruit.

apricot	apricot brandy or plain brandy
banana	Crabbies green ginger
cherry	gin
chestnut	brandy
chocolate	rum
coffee	crème de cacao
kiwi fruit	brandy
orange	orange curaçao/Drambuie/Grand Marnier

passion fruit	*nothing*
peach	peach brandy (or see section on basic essences)
pineapple	Kirsch
raspberry	framboise (*very* expensive), brandy a good substitute
strawberry	*nothing* or brandy

MOUSSES

Mousses are light, fluffy desserts ideal for ending a dinner as they are effortless to eat, have infinite variations in flavour, and are relatively inexpensive to make (my basic recipe which will give you between 12 and 15 portions, uses only half a pint of double cream). Mousses can be served on the day after they're made, but I prefer to use them within 12 hours.

I serve mousses in Royal Worcester ramekins (seconds from the sales or from Royal Worcester themselves). They are very pretty dishes and look superb when set off against a simple fern leaf placed on a doyleyed plate. To add glamour to the mousse, if you are serving in a ramekin or glass, first dowse the container with the liqueur appropriate to the recipe.

Mousses can be served by themselves, but are delicious served as fillings in chocolate shortbread tartlets or chocolate roulades. They can be piped into brandy snaps or the mixture may be used for filling gâteaux.

The basic recipe takes approximately 30 minutes to prepare and will give you enough to fill 12–15 ramekins.

Gelatine

Whenever a recipe calls for gelatine, I think it best to deal with that first.

I use powdered gelatine, and the individual portioned packets of $\frac{1}{2}$ oz (15 g) made by Davies's are ideal as they are accurately weighed out. Sprinkle the gelatine on to the base of a small saucepan and then pour all the liquid over at once (don't add the 5 tablespoons tablespoon by tablespoon, but measure out separately and pour onto the powder in one fell swoop). Gently shake the pan round and round until the liquid absorbs the powder (which won't take long) and, if necessary, help it along with the use of a teaspoon. If you use water the powder will melt easily, but it is a different matter if you use three-fifths spirit (as some recipes call for), and takes a little longer. It is *not* a good idea to be over-generous with the spirit in an attempt to get more flavour as when you come to reconstitute the gelatine, you would then have trouble. The contents of the small saucepan will look unsightly but never mind – just leave it to one side.

People have very varying ideas about reconstituting gelatine before using it in a recipe. Some work it in a cup placed inside a pan of simmering water, some dissolve it in a saucepan over a high heat. I find the results of these two methods unsatisfactory as occasionally the water boils up into the teacup resulting in more liquid than I require, or with the intense heat the gelatine sticks to the base of the saucepan rather than integrating into the liquid!

When the time comes for you to incorporate the gelatine into your recipe place the saucepan over a very low light and gently melt the mixture. *At all times* you should be able to take the saucepan off the heat and place it on the palm of your hand without feeling too uncomfortable. This way you will be sure to get every single grain of gelatine incorporated into every drop of liquid. No gelatine will stick to the saucepan and no liquid will evaporate! Have to hand a very fine mesh wire sieve and just before pouring the gelatine into your mousse (or any other dish for that matter), warm the sieve over the gas flame or electric hob then pour the gelatine through this. So often people pour the mixture straight in and should there be the slightest lump of gelatine, it immediately attracts the mixture and starts to form a gluey ball, or else they pass the gelatine through a cold sieve and a thin layer of gelatine is left on the sieve. Use as large a bowl as you can to fold gelatine in with a large spoon, and you can make gentle sweeping figures of eight!

The Mousse

3 eggs plus 2 egg yolks

2 oz (50 g) sieved castor sugar

$\frac{1}{2}$ pint (300 ml) double cream

approximately 5 fl oz (150 ml) flavouring (see individual recipes)

$\frac{1}{2}$ oz (15 g) gelatine with 5 tablespoons liquid as in recipes

The Kenwood will do the work of mixing the basic mousse for you, provided you put the 3 eggs and 2 egg yolks into a warmed bowl and allow the beater to work at the highest speed for at least 5 minutes before you attempt to add any of the sugar. The object of the exercise *isn't* to get an extra portion through good whipping, but the more you multiply the basic eggs in volume, the lighter the end product will be. Add the sugar tablespoon by tablespoon, and altogether this part of the recipe takes about 12 minutes to do.

A common mistake when preparing mousses, is to beat the double cream too far, so that when you come to combine the flavoured cream with the mousse base, it requires quite an effort. The cream should just be whipped enough so it will merge into the mousse and not sink down to the bottom of the bowl! At this stage I would advise you to transfer the mixed mousse mixture out of the Kenwood bowl into a large plastic bowl about 14 in (35 cm) in diameter. This helps to keep the end result light.

Fold the gelatine in last of all and then have to hand a 2 or 3 pint (1 to $1\frac{1}{2}$ litre) jug that has a sensible pouring lip on it. (A perfectly rounded jug is hopeless as you get constant drips and dollops everywhere when you attempt to fill your dishes or containers.) Transfer the creamy mixture to this jug and, as quickly as possible, portion it out. Cover with greaseproof paper and leave to chill in the fridge and decorate at the last minute.

Marsala and almond cake

The start of a Victorian breakfast – Buck's Fizz, grapefruit with crème de menthe, and porridge with whisky, demerara sugar and butter.

Shortbread

Orange Mousse

Add to the basic mousse mixture 1 can defrosted Florida orange juice ($6\frac{3}{4}$ fl oz or 178 ml) with the juice and finely grated rind of 1 orange. Use 3 tablespoons orange curaçao and 2 tablespoons water for the gelatine.

Grapefruit and Pernod Mousse

Add to the basic mousse mixture 1 can defrosted grapefruit juice ($6\frac{3}{4}$ fl oz or 178 ml), and a segment of fresh grapefruit on the base of each dish. Use 3 tablespoons Pernod and 2 tablespoons water for the gelatine.

Crème de Menthe Mint Crisp

For this recipe increase the amount of cream to $\frac{3}{4}$ pint (400 ml) and beat in 2 tablespoons of Crème de Menthe. Chop up some Chocolate Mint Crisp bars finely to provide a difference in texture. The gelatine is reconstituted with 3 tablespoons Crème de Menthe and 2 of water.

I usually half-fill the containers first and then sprinkle the Chocolate Mint Crisp in and then top up with the mousse.

Strawberry or Raspberry Mousse

To get $6\frac{3}{4}$ oz (178 ml) of well-flavoured purée you need 8 oz (225 g) of either fruits liquidized with 2 tablespoons icing sugar and 2 tablespoons brandy which is then reduced on the stove down to just over 5 fl oz (150 ml).

Chocolate Raspberry Mousse

To the basic recipe you add 6 oz (175 g) chocolate melted down with 4 tablespoons brandy. As it starts to set fold in 8 oz (225 g) whole fresh raspberries.

Calvados Apple Mousse

Add to the basic recipe 2 large Granny Smith apples which you have peeled, cored and sliced, and cooked with a little brown sugar and knob of butter until fallen. Pass through a nylon sieve with 2 tablespoons Calvados. As the mousse starts to set, fold in 1 Granny Smith apple that has been finely diced to provide a complete contrast in texture.

CHEESECAKES

When I first started to make Lemon Cheesecake years ago I think I served it on every possible occasion until I began to groan at the very thought of making one. But as it was so popular and always eagerly devoured, I kept asking myself, 'why change a winning horse midstream?' But I did. I evolved numerous ways of using the basic recipe and changing it, and so it is well and truly restored to my repertoire and no matter which version I serve, if there is any left it disappears immediately in second helpings. What better recommendation can I have!

The recipe will make a cheesecake that will fit in a 10 in (25 cm) cake tin (always use one with a loose bottom), and you will have 8–10 portions.

For the base

1 × 10 oz (300 g) packet chocolate digestive biscuits

2 oz (50 g) melted butter

The Base

Use plain or milk chocolate digestives, whichever you like best. Liquidize the biscuits in a blender to crumble them, but only put a few in at a time and then drop the others, broken up, through the hole at the top (the machine will jam if you place the whole lot in at once). If you don't have a liquidizer, break the biscuits up onto a piece of greaseproof paper and then cover them with a further piece and firmly push a rolling pin to and fro until you have even crumbs.

Turn the crumbs out into a bowl and fold in the melted butter. Line the base and sides of the cake tin with greaseproof paper and spread the chocolate mixing on the base. The back of your hand is the best thing to use as you will be able then to get the mixing right round the base and spread fairly evenly. Cook this in a medium oven at 350°F (180°C), Gas 4, for about 20 minutes and then leave to cool.

For the cheesecake

9 oz (250 g) Philadelphia cream cheese

3 eggs, separated

2 oz (50 g) castor sugar

½ pint (300 ml) double cream

½ oz (15 g) gelatine with 5 tablespoons of liquid

The Cheesecake

Prepare the gelatine as outlined in the section on *Mousses* (page 159) and put to one side.

Lightly beat the egg yolks and beat these into the cream cheese with the sugar and then double cream. Add the relevant flavourings (see the individual recipes). Fold in the stiffly-beaten egg whites. Now reconstitute the gelatine (see page 160) and pass through a warmed sieve into the mixture and carefully fold in. Pour the mixture on to the cool biscuit base and place in the fridge to set.

Lemon Cheesecake
Fold in the juice and rind of 2 lemons to the basic Philadelphia cheese and cream.

Strawberry Cheesecake
Liquidize 8 oz (225 g) strawberries with 1 tablespoon brandy and 1 tablespoon icing sugar. Line cooled base with extra whole strawberries and fill with half the cheese mixture. As it sets, spread further strawberries on top and then cover with the remaining cheesecake mixture.

Cheese, Apple and Celery Cheesecake
Finely chop, peel and core 2 Granny Smith apples, and sprinkle them with the juice and rind of 1 lemon. Finely chop 2 good sticks of celery, and grate finely 4 oz (100 g) of strong Cheddar cheese. Fold the apples, lemon juice and rind, celery and cheese into the cream cheese mixture with 1 teaspoon salt.

A teaspoon of horseradish is nice in this recipe and a tablespoon of freshly chopped chives, if available, are delicious.

The gelatine should be let down with 2 tablespoons cooking brandy and 3 tablespoons of water (but you don't *need* to use the brandy!).

Bilberry Cheesecake
Drain a 10 oz (275 g) can of Polish bilberries, keeping the juice. Line the biscuit base with half the bilberries and top with the cheesecake cream. Chill. Reduce the liquid from the bilberries by half and, if necessary, thicken with a pinch of arrowroot. Combine this with the other half of the bilberries and decorate the top of the cheesecake when set.

Crème de Menthe Chocolate Cheesecake
Chop finely a 4 oz (100 g) bar of Chocolate Mint Crisp, and reconstitute the gelatine with 3 tablespoons of Crème de Menthe and 2 tablespoons of water. Add a further 2 tablespoons of Crème de Menthe to the basic cheesecake mixing. Half line the cooled crumb base with the mixing and as setting, sprinkle over the mint crisp, and then top off with the balance of the cheesecake mixture.

Coffee, Rum and Pecan Cheesecake
Add 2 tablespoons Camp Coffee essence to the basic cheesecake mixing, and reconstitute the gelatine with 3 tablespoons Negrita Rum and 2 tablespoons of water. Line the cooled crumb base with about 2 tablespoons chopped pecan nuts (walnuts can also be used but they are much more bitter) and then put half the cheesecake mixing on top. When nearly set, add a further layer of pecan nuts and top off with the balance of the cheesecake mixture.

You could also make an Irish Whiskey Coffee Walnut Cheesecake in the same way.

Banana Rum Cheesecake

Use sufficient ripe bananas to give you 5 oz (150 g) when mashed well with a silver fork. Beat this purée into the basic cheesecake recipe and reconstitute the gelatine with 3 tablespoons of Negrita Rum and 2 of water. Line the cooled crumb base with half of the mixing. Place further sliced bananas through the middle of the cheesecake. Finish off with the remaining cheesecake mixture.

Carrot, Ginger and Nut Gâteau

(served with Preserved Ginger and Natural Yoghurt)

- **approximately 1 lb (450 g) carrots**
- **6 eggs**
- **6 oz (175 g) castor sugar, sieved**
- **4 oz (100–125 g) very finely chopped almonds**
- **2 oz (50 g) finely chopped walnuts**
- **3 oz (75 g) ground almonds**
- **1 teaspoon baking powder**
- **½ nutmeg, grated**
- **¼ teaspoon ground ginger**
- **2 tablespoons ginger syrup**
- **4 pieces preserved ginger**
- **10 oz (275 g) yoghurt**

Grease, flour, and sugar 3 cake tins 8 in (20 cm) in diameter, to serve 8 people. Preheat the oven to 350°F (180°C), Gas 4.

Peel, top and tail the carrots, and grate them very finely (the end result will be approximately 12 oz (350 g). Place the eggs in a Kenwood bowl and beat at a high speed for about 8 minutes, then start to add the sieved sugar little by little.

When satisfied with the egg and sugar mixture, gently fold in all the other ingredients using a large metal spoon. Divide the mixing into the 3 prepared tins, gently patting down with a palette knife. Bake in the preheated oven for 20–30 minutes. Do not turn out the cakes until cooled.

Two can be used immediately to make a gâteau and the third will freeze for future use. Lightly soak one of the gâteaux with the syrup from the preserved ginger and then line with thinly sliced preserved ginger. Use the second gâteau as the top and, at the last moment, liberally pour over natural yoghurt sweetened with a little castor sugar.

Apple Curd Cake

The following recipe will fill one 8 in (20 cm) flan tin lined and baked blind with Savoury Pastry (see page 38).

- **4 oz (100 g) butter**
- **4 oz (100 g) castor sugar**
- **2 eggs, lightly beaten**
- **3 Granny Smith apples**
- **juice and rind of 2 lemons**

Cream the butter and sugar together thoroughly until white and fluffy and then little by little beat in the eggs. Coarsely grate the apples, and leave on the polished green skin. Place the grated apple in a tea towel, and then gently squeeze out the juice. Fold the grated apple into the sugar, butter and egg mixture along with the grated lemon rind. As you begin to fold the lemon juice in, the mixture will slightly curdle.

Spread the mixture evenly in the baked pastry case in the flan tin, taking no heed of the slightly separated watery effect certain areas may have. Place the flan tin on a double thickness of aluminium foil which you can then coerce up some way round the edge of the flan tin (what you are trying to do is set up a 'bath' to catch the overflow from the cake filling as it cooks).

Cook for 30 minutes, and then turn off the oven and leave to cool. It will look and feel rather sloppy in the middle. Remove from the oven. Eventually, when cold, remove it from the fluted flan tin.

As you will get 8 good portions from this, you can decorate it with 8 spokes of piped double cream running from the centre. Place in the middle of these spokes thin wedges of unpeeled Granny Smith apples which have been dipped in a mixture of lemon juice and white cooking wine. Mint leaves are a further attractive garnish.

Port and Claret Jelly

- **¾ pint (400 ml) cold water**
- **8 oz (225 g) cube sugar**
- **2 tablespoons redcurrant jelly**
- **half stick of cinnamon**
- **¾ pint (400 ml) claret**
- **½ pint (300 ml) port**
- **2 tablespoons brandy**
- **just under 1 oz (25 g) powdered gelatine**

This is a very light, tipsy-like dessert, requiring little or no effort of digestion. Served in silver goblets on a doyleyed plate with a head of a seasonal flower (not too scented, mind you) and a piece of shortbread, you have a simple, but quite divine ending to your meal.

In one clean saucepan put the cold water with the cube sugar along with the redcurrant jelly and cinnamon. Bring to the boil.

In a second clean saucepan, pour the claret, port and brandy. (The claret doesn't have to be Château Haut Brion Pessac 1966 or the Port, Taylors 1960. Rough Vin Rouge from Bordeaux will suffice and so will Taylors Mesquita Port, and Napoleon Cooking Brandy is fine.) On top of the alcohol mixture as it comes to the boil sprinkle just under 1 oz (25 g) of Davies's gelatine. Then leave both pans simmering for 10 minutes.

Pass the contents of both pans through a fine sieve into a large jug, stir swiftly and as it is cooling, pour into dishes or goblets. These quantities make 12 adequate portions (don't forget the jelly is rather intoxicating so don't give enormous helpings, and you don't have to serve a dessert wine with the sweet, or probably even offer a liqueur!)

This recipe can be easily adapted to the tipple of your choice provided you do not stray from the actual quantities. In the winter Ginger Wine Jelly is rather pleasant (make up your mixture from Crabbies Green Ginger to the strength you personally like), and this particular jelly is rather nice if you put a spoonful of home-made mincemeat in the base.

Campari and Orange is quite nice but I forbid Gin and Lime at Miller Howe as on one occasion the cook put ¾ pint (400 ml) gin to half a pint of lime juice and the result wasn't funny at all!

Biscuits to Accompany Jellies and Cream Ices

- 4 oz (100 g) butter
- 4 oz (100 g) castor sugar
- 4 oz (100 g) sieved plain flour
- 4 egg whites, stiffly beaten

Cream together the butter and sugar and fold in the sieved flour. Then fold in the stiffly beaten egg whites. Using a ¼ in (5 mm) plain nozzle, pipe the mixture onto oiled baking trays, covered with greaseproof paper.

This mixture makes 48 biscuits, approximately 2½ in (6 cm) long. Bake at 375°F (190°C), Gas 5, for 15–20 minutes.

6 eggs, separated

8 oz (225 g) castor sugar, sieved

$1\frac{1}{2}$ pints (scant litre) double cream

plus flavourings (see each recipe)

enough Marie Sweet biscuit crumbs to form base and topping

Ice Box Puddings

Throughout this book I seem to be continually saying, 'This is so easy to make'. With the following variations on the basic theme of Ice Box Pudding nothing could be more accurate or truthful; they are made in a very short space of time, they store quite well in the freezer, and virtually come right out on to the dessert plates. Using a little imagination, you'll be able to find endless further variations of your own.

Place the egg yolks into a warmed Kenwood bowl. Start to whisk at a high speed adding the sieved castor sugar little by little. This is the basic 'mousse' mixing for the Ice Box Pudding and so see that you really get a good basic working. Never just put the yolks and sugar in the bowl together and turn the machine on. This would make the pudding very heavy.

When you are satisfied that the volume will increase no further, beat in the flavouring of your choice. Meanwhile whip the double cream lightly to just running consistency, and bring these two mixtures together in a large plastic bowl with a long-handled spoon. Then fold in the stiffly-beaten egg whites (remembering to incorporate one-third first and then the remaining two-thirds)!

Liquidize some Marie Sweet biscuits and line the bases of either individual ramekin dishes or clean 1 lb (450 g) loaf tins. Pour the basic pudding mix on to the crumbs in the dishes or tins and then coat the top quite liberally with a further lining of crumbs. Put immediately into the freezer for at least 12 hours. Take the puddings out of the freezer just as you are about to serve the main course of your meal, and then the pudding will be easy for you to cut or slice if you have used a loaf tin, and soft, rich and creamy to eat.

Lemon Ice Box Pudding

Add the finely grated rind and strained juice of 2 lemons to the basic mixing.

Orange Ice Box Pudding

Add the finely grated rind and juice of 2 oranges to the basic mixing. A touch of Orange Curaçao liqueur doesn't come amiss when sprinkled over just before serving to your guests.

Coffee Ice Box Pudding

Add 2 tablespoons very strong coffee to your basic mixing.

Van der Hum Tangerine Ice Box Pudding

Add 6 tablespoons Van der Hum (a South African liqueur made from *naartjes*, a type of tangerine) to your basic mixing and top with de-seeded wedges of tangerine or satsuma or mandarin.

Honey and Brandy Cream Ice

8 egg yolks
8 tablespoons warmed honey
1 pint (600 ml) double cream
8 tablespoons brandy

This sweet is simple to make and I like it best when winter colds and sore throats are around, as it's so smooth and soothing.

Beat the 8 egg yolks in a warmed Kenwood bowl for about 5 minutes until they have expanded as far as possible, and then slowly drip in the warmed honey. Carry on beating for a further 5 minutes. Meanwhile, lightly whip up the cream with the brandy and then just fold the two mixtures together.

I prefer to put the cream ice in individual pots as they can be taken straight from the freezer and eaten, with no waiting for them to 'come round'. *But* don't leave them in the freezer for longer than 5 days as they become a little rubbery after a time. Who wants to keep them that long anyway?

Orange Water Ice

For the syrup
1 pint (600 ml) cold water
grated rind and juice of 3 oranges
6 oz (175 g) cube sugar
For the ice
1 egg white
2 tablespoons double cream

This is an extremely light and clean sweet with which to end a meal. Though it has a little cream in it to give it a lift, this can be left out.

The day before you want to serve it, make an orange stock syrup.

Bring the water, orange juice and rind and sugar to the boil and then gently simmer for 12 minutes. Turn out into a plastic bowl and when cold, freeze. The next morning, bring out of the freezer and leave at room temperature for about 45 minutes and then break it up into a Magimix. (You can use a Kenwood hand electric beater, but do be careful as it can be a lengthy job and you don't want to strain the motor and burn it out!) Beat until the mixture is quite smooth. Drop in the egg white and beat again for a few seconds. Then add the double cream and beat once more. Return to the bowl and freeze.

Lemon Water Ice

Make a lemon ice in exactly the same way but, naturally, substituting lemons for oranges. If you are lucky enough to have any Eau de Vie de Marc de Bourgogne, 2 tablespoons of that added with the egg whites makes a lot of difference and a teaspoon of the stuff added just when serving is super.

Frozen Coffee and Almond Yoghurt

To serve 4

- **2 tablespoons Camp Coffee essence**
- **2 tablespoons soft brown sugar**
- **$\frac{1}{2}$ pint (300 ml) natural yoghurt**
- **2 oz (50 g) ground almonds**
- **2 egg whites**

Mix Camp Coffee essence with the brown sugar and beat into the yoghurt. Fold in the ground almonds. Stiffly beat egg whites and fold in. Pour into ramekins and freeze for at least 3 hours.

Frozen Summer Fruit Yoghurts

To serve 2

- **5 fl oz (150 ml) natural yoghurt**
- **2 tablespoons puréed summer fruit**
- **1 tablespoon icing sugar**
- **1 egg white**

To each 5 fl oz (150 ml) carton natural yoghurt you need 2 tablespoons puréed summer fruits (strawberries, raspberries, black, white or red currants, and in autumn, blackberries). Always remember to sieve the raspberries and currants after liquidizing to remove all those pips.

Combine the yoghurt with the fruit purée and icing sugar and fold in the stiffly-beaten egg white. Pour into ramekins and freeze for at least 3 hours.

Frozen Peach Yoghurt

To serve 2

- **2 large ripe peaches**
- **grated rind and juice of 1 orange**
- **5 fl oz (150 ml) natural yoghurt**
- **1 tablespoon icing sugar**
- **1 egg white**

Blanch, peel and stone the peaches and liquidize with the grated rind and juice of the orange, the yoghurt and the sugar. Fold in the stiffly-beaten egg white. Pour into ramekins and freeze for at least 3 hours.

SCENE TWO
CHEESEBOARD

One of my rare pleasures is ferreting around local country markets on market day seeking out *fresh* cheese as opposed to the inedible, rubbery polystyrene wedges processed and prepacked in polythene which are so prevalent these days. I even spend a great deal of time and care purchasing the 7 lb (3.2 kg) blocks of cooking mousetrap cheeses and clearly remember us all in the kitchen falling head over heels in love with a suddenly discovered wedge of cooking cheese from Ireland. As soon as the seal was broken on the packet, so everybody stopped what they were doing and looked towards the oblong shape laid bare on the kitchen table. Not much was used that day in our cooking but most of it was devoured in nibble bits by all and sundry working and coming through the kitchen.

Some of the prepacked cheese slices remind me of what I think recycled bicycle tyres must taste like! The odour they give off when being grilled is offensive, and the havoc they cause in your mouth when dished up on hamburgers make me realize they would be better used as a fixative for one's denture plate (for those of us who have such things) rather than an embarrassment to the palate.

Personally, I love to serve and eat the *Blue Cheshire Cheese* which is becoming so popular these days. Do try and seek this out from your supplier as it has such a definite, appealing flavour: to some sharp, biting and soapy (what a compliment to pay a cheese, say I!), to others rich, sour, strong and distinctive!

A white, crumbly, sharp *Lancashire* cannot be beaten, but is becoming increasingly difficult to find. How can the large manufacturers of cheese sleep at night when they have the audacity to push on to the public mini-wrapped packets of nougaty dough?

Dolcelatte at its prime is the only imported cheese I relish and frequently buy and – of course – the good old day-by-day standby is the English *Stilton*. Vary they do as the seasons come and go, both in appearance, texture and taste, and any bottom bits of Stilton I cream with a K-beater and beat in as much port as I possibly can. This I then pot and serve with lamb cutlets and, occasionally, with scones for afternoon tea.

However, for me, no matter what cheese I serve, provided it is in prime condition, it is the fact that I take the trouble and time (and what better gift can you give your friends than the latter?) to make my own biscuits. Sweet they are, sometimes with a light touch of curry powder providing a delightful surprise to the palate. I do urge you to make them for your next dinner party and if your cheese is served with a radish flower, celery twirl, a couple of grapes and small wedge-cut apple – what a delightful way this is to end a dinner party.

Cheese Biscuits

2 oz (50 g) Parmesan cheese, grated

2 oz (50 g) Cheshire cheese, grated

2 oz (50 g) soft butter

2 oz (50 g) sieved plain flour

pinch of cayenne pepper

These go marvellously with consommé and any cream soup with tomato in it, as well as with cheese. The basic dough can also be used for lining individual pastry cases: ideal for putting fishy or savoury dishes in. See my notes on Making Biscuits, too, on page 193.

Mix all the ingredients together, and the fat in the cheeses themselves with the butter and flour will form the dough. Roll out onto greaseproof paper and, using a 2 in (5 cm) cutter, you will make approximately 20 biscuits which should be baked for 10 minutes at 375°F (190°C), Gas 5.

Wheatmeal Cheese Biscuits

12 oz (350 g) wheatmeal flour

4 oz (100 g) Quaker oats

4 oz (100 g) lard, flaked

4 oz (100 g) butter, flaked

8 teaspoons castor sugar

2 teaspoons baking powder

$\frac{1}{4}$ teaspoon salt

1 teaspoon curry powder

4 tablespoons milk

A Kenwood bowl with a K-beater is ideal for this recipe but, whatever you do, do not overwork. The Kenwood takes the strain out of this recipe, but if left switched on, the end result will be biscuits as tough as old boots and rubbery as the thickest crêpe soles.

Put all the ingredients into the Kenwood bowl, and mix together. (You may need more or less milk to bind the mixture.) Roll out onto greaseproof paper and cut into shapes. A 2 in (5 cm) cutter will give you approximately 70 biscuits. Chill prior to cooking, and then bake for 15 minutes at 350°F (180°C), Gas 4.

MENU

MENU 5

A dinner for a very special occasion

Courgette and Fennel Soup with Cream and Toasted Almonds (page 64)

Salmon Mayonnaise (page 73)

Salads in Season

Roast Local Farmhouse Duck and Grapefruit Segments (page 104)

Baked Red Cabbage (page 113)

Parisian Potatoes (page 123)

Cream Water Ices (page 167)

Home-made Biscuits (page 165)

Home-made Wholemeal Bread (page 185)

Serve Sancerre with the salmon, claret (the dryer the better) with the duck, and Muscat Beaumes de Venise (if you can get it) with the dessert.

A very special menu, but still easy if you organize yourself very carefully – but remember that you *must* eat the duck at the allotted time, so you should also organize your guests carefully!

Two Days Before

Cook off the stock syrup (see page 211) for the water ices and, when cool, freeze. (How about doing two separate mixings, i.e. one lemon and then one with a fruit purée?)

Make the Wholemeal Bread and the Biscuits to accompany the ices.

The Day Before

Make the soup, using one of your own concentrated stock cubes from the freezer.

Remove your ducks from the fridge and see they dry out well.

If you are going to be rushed for time on the actual day, start the baked red cabbage now, but only partly cook through.

Morning

Check your shopping and set the table. Prepare the coffee tray and put the plates and dishes in the warming drawer.

Check:
the lamps
the heating
the room for the coats and the cloakroom
the tapes or records
the flowers (this should all be second nature by now!)

Prepare the Parisian potato balls and leave in a bowl of cold water.

Cook off the salmon and leave to cool. Make the mayonnaise. Wipe, stuff and prepare the duck for roasting.

Make the water ices, and return to the freezer.

You could even, when the salmon is cool, portion it out now, provided each plate is tightly covered with transparent cling film (don't coat with the mayonnaise until the last minute).

Prepare the Garnishes

For the soup, chop the very inside heart of the root fennel and garnish each bowl just before serving with a twirl of whipped cream, the chopped hearts and the lovely feathery fennel tops. Toast the almonds (but don't forget about them!).

For the salmon mayonnaise, prepare a savoury salad from as many or as few seasonal salad vegetables as you like (see page 215).

Cut the grapefruit segments and store in a covered bowl.

Evening

Set the oven and roast the ducks, allowing $1\frac{3}{4}$ hours, remembering to remove excess fat at intervals.

See you have chilled glasses with appropriate serving plates for the water ices. Have a saucepan with oil and butter in it ready for the Parisian potatoes. Slice and butter the Wholemeal Bread and cover the plate with a damp cloth. Have the soup in a double saucepan ready to re-heat.

When your guests arrive, warm through the soup before garnishing and serving (pop the toasted almonds into the oven meanwhile so that they are warmed through as well). Gently start the Parisian potatoes, perhaps using some of the duck fat instead of oil.

Check the duck occasionally. Coat the salmon with mayonnaise and garnish just before taking to the table. Put the partly cooked red cabbage into the oven to finish cooking (but do remember that the oven is very high, so only cook it for a short time).

Finish the Parisian potatoes just before serving with the duck and the red cabbage.

Remove the cream water ices from the freezer just before serving.

MENU 6

A classic Christmas lunch or dinner

Miller Howe Savoury Cheese Peach with Bacon (page 55)

Roast Local Farm Turkey (page 105)
and Cranberry Sauce (page 106)

Rich Old-Fashioned Stuffing (page 102)

Winter Root Vegetables (page 125)

Purée of Sprouts (page 113)

Chipolata Sausages

Mincemeat Puff Pastry Cornets (page 36)

Home-made Wholemeal Bread (page 185)

Serve sparkling white burgundy or champagne as your guests arrive, a glass of chilled dry Madeira with the starter, and a good red burgundy with the turkey. (I don't think you or your guests will have the capacity for anything further with the mincemeat puff pastry cornets!)

This Christmas meal is *so* easy to serve and all the work – yes, I *do* mean *all* – can be done beforehand. On the day, it is simply just a matter of putting things in and out of the oven and under the grill.

Two Days Before

Make the Cheese and Herb Pâté and pipe it into the peach halves. Cover with the Croûton topping, and store in the fridge.

Put the carrots, onion and quartered apple inside the turkey along with the butter, and store the bird, covered, in a cold place (or the fridge). Make the stuffing and store in the fridge.

Prepare and par-cook the 3 winter root vegetables and put into their separate foil parcels. Cook and purée the sprouts and store them covered, with the winter root vegetables, in the fridge. Make the sauce reduction of red wine and orange juice.

I haven't included potatoes in my menu, but if you feel the meal isn't the same without them, peel them now and leave in cold water.

Make the puff pastry cornets and the Wholemeal Bread.

Morning

Check everything and set the table. Prepare the coffee tray and put the plates and dishes in the warming drawer.

Check:
the lamps
the heating
the room for the coats and the cloakroom
the tapes or records (try and find a nice Christmassy one)
the flowers

Put the champagne or white burgundy in the fridge, with the Madeira, and leave the red burgundy out at room temperature (*not* next to a roaring fire!). Bake the croûtons.

Evening

Four hours before you want to eat the turkey, put the muslinned bird into the oven and leave (basting only once) to cook at 350°F (180°C) Gas 4. If you want potatoes, drain them and cook them (preferably in duck fat) under the bird for about 1 hour. Thereafter the oven temperature is the same for everything that goes into the oven.

Ten minutes before you want to eat the starter, put the cheese peach and the croûtons separately into the oven along with the bacon rolls and the stuffing in its separate dish. At the last minute, flash the peaches under the grill, and serve garnished with a small savoury salad.

As you serve the starter, put the chipolatas and the winter root vegetables in their foil parcels into the oven. Start warming up the sprout purée in the double saucepan and the sauce for the cranberries. Put the cranberries into the oven on a baking tray.

While you carve, pop the chipolatas under the grill, take out the stuffing, and pop the cranberries into the warmed sauce.

Warm the cornets in the oven and warm the mincemeat separately. Fill the cornets at the very last minute and serve with whipped cream.

Merry Christmas!

ONE
ACT
PLAYS

ONE ACT PLAYS

VICTORIAN BREAKFAST
MATINEE PERFORMANCES

Afternoon Tea

High Tea

MENU

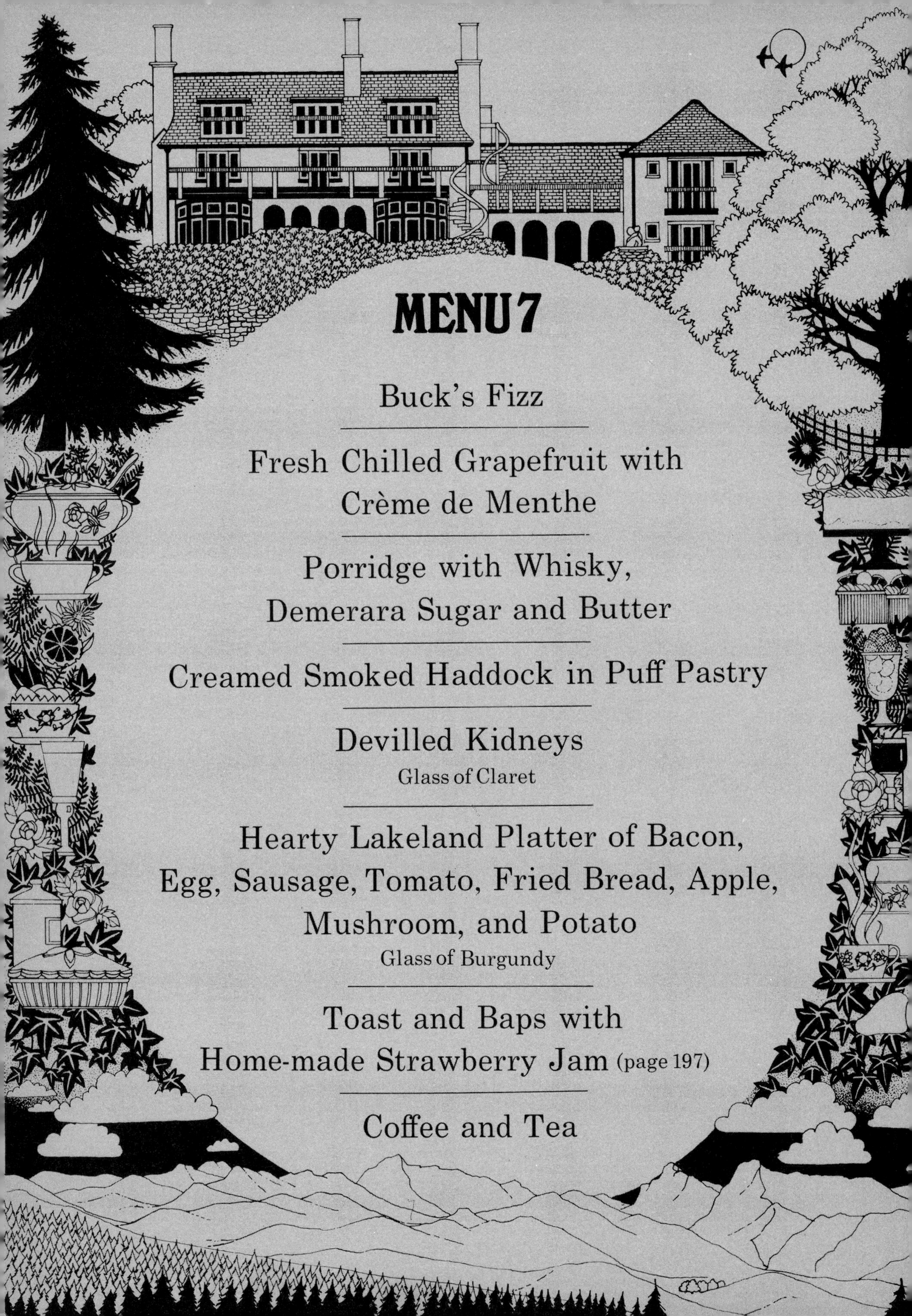

MENU 7

Buck's Fizz

Fresh Chilled Grapefruit with
Crème de Menthe

Porridge with Whisky,
Demerara Sugar and Butter

Creamed Smoked Haddock in Puff Pastry

Devilled Kidneys
Glass of Claret

Hearty Lakeland Platter of Bacon,
Egg, Sausage, Tomato, Fried Bread, Apple,
Mushroom, and Potato
Glass of Burgundy

Toast and Baps with
Home-made Strawberry Jam (page 197)

Coffee and Tea

VICTORIAN BREAKFAST

Sunday is my day off during the season and I occasionally decide to invite guests round at 11.30 for 12.00 midday and serve a relatively easy 6-course meal. It is popular as it allows everybody (including myself) to sleep in longer than usual, have a quick skim of the newspapers and then slowly socialize. Very civilized indeed.

To serve this meal successfully you want to do as much preparation as possible beforehand, and be really and truly organized for when the guests arrive.

Make sure you have the table attractively laid with cutlery, napkins etc, the day before and have one good sensibly-sized double saucepan ready for the prepared porridge and another for the smoked haddock.

You will need plates decorated with doyleys and some flowers for the grapefruit, liners for the porridge dishes, warmed plates for the smoked haddock, plates with doyleys only for the devilled kidneys (provided you intend to serve them in small dishes) and, of course, warmed plates for the Lakeland Platter. Don't forget to set your marmalade and honey out in preserve dishes along with your butter portions and whatever you do, see the coffee machine is prepared and the teapot is to hand well before the arrival of the guests.

I greet my guests with a Buck's Fizz which I make up of half a glass of fresh orange juice topped up with sparkling white Burgundy (instead of the traditional champagne), and this certainly gets them all smiling. I serve a small glass of inexpensive claret with the kidneys and then everybody thinks it daringly different to sup glasses of a hearty Beaujolais with their fried platter! If it sounds revolting, I can assure you it isn't!

Fresh Chilled Grapefruit with Crème de Menthe

Per person

1 grapefruit

1 tablespoon Crème de Menthe

sprig of fresh mint

Criss-cross around the 'equator' of the grapefruit so that it falls into two attractively 'vandyked' halves. Remove the segments from each half and fill *one* half with *all* the flesh. Serve the half grapefruit on a plate decorated with a doyley and a fern, and some sprigs of fresh mint add colour. Just before serving, sprinkle generously with chilled Crème de Menthe.

Porridge with Whisky, Demerara Sugar and Butter

Per person

approximately 2 oz (50 g) oats (but see my method

generous $\frac{1}{4}$ pint (150 ml) milk

a pinch of salt (optional)

$\frac{1}{2}$ tablespoon demerara sugar

$\frac{1}{2}$ tablespoon whisky

knob of butter

Use any commercial oats – even the quick ones which 'cook in a minute'. The amount the manufacturers recommend for 2 generous servings will serve 4 portions (don't forget this is a 5-course breakfast!). Use all milk instead of water.

Whatever the quantity of the oats, they are always the better for soaking overnight in the milk. Cook the oats slowly in the milk (adding a little salt if you like) for the length of the time stated on the packet, and when cooked, keep warm in a double saucepan.

Serve the porridge in attractive soup cups or bowls. Sprinkle generously with the demerara sugar, and a good helping of whisky (I use malt which, to many people, is sacriligious!), and finish off with a generous knob of butter.

Creamed Smoked Haddock in Puff Pastry

Per person

a $3\frac{1}{2}$-in (9-cm) vol au vent (see page 36)

2 oz (50 g) creamed haddock filling (see page 77)

Make up a $\frac{1}{2}$ batch of puff pastry (see page 34) and roll it out to $\frac{1}{8}$ in (3 mm) thickness. Cut into circles with a fluted cutter, chill and then bake blind at 425°F (220°C), Gas 7. When ready to serve, split each round in 2 (don't forget to throw away any soggy pastry) and gently warm through again.

Lightly pack the fillets of smoked haddock in sufficient milk to cover them, and simmer slowly until the fish is cooked. (See page 77 for fuller instructions). Make a cheese sauce with the milk, and at the last minute, combine the flaked fish with the sauce. After warming through in a double saucepan (about twenty minutes) fill the pastry with the smoked haddock and brush the lid with melted butter just before serving. A wedge of fresh tomato either side of the pastry looks attractive and a large sprig of fresh parsley completes the scene!

Devilled Kidneys

Per person

1 kidney

1 dessertspoon chopped onion

1 oz (25 g) butter

$\frac{1}{2}$ teaspoon French mustard

1 tablespoon brandy

Prepare the kidneys carefully, making sure that the skin is removed and the core is taken out.

Sauté the finely chopped onion in the butter and add a little French mustard. Pop in the kidneys, and seal well and then turn down the heat and simmer slowly for about 3 or 4 minutes.

Flambé with cooking brandy (turn up the heat and add the brandy which will catch fire and flame for a minute or so). Put the kidneys into individual warmed dishes and sprinkle with chopped parsley.

Hearty Lakeland Platter

Per person
1 rasher bacon
1 sausage
1 slice apple
½ tomato
1 triangle fried bread
2 medium mushrooms
about ¼ potato, sliced (depending on size)
1 egg

For this you need 4 baking trays (or as many as you can fit into your oven).

1. Lay rashers of your particular brand of smoked bacon on the tray (if you prefer to leave the rind on make small snips all along the edge to stop the rasher from curling up).

2. Lay out (and prick) your favourite sausages.

3. Core and peel an apple and lay slices on a well-buttered tray.

4. Cut the tomatoes in half, brush with melted butter, and season with salt, sugar and freshly ground black pepper.

These are then ready for cooking in an oven set at 350°F (180°C), Gas 4, in the following order:—
Sausages about 30 minutes
Bacon about 15 minutes
Apple about 10 minutes
Tomato about 5 minutes

The *fried bread* can be done earlier. Cut however many portions you want, soak them in melted butter, and bake in the oven until slightly brown and crisp. Leave aside in the warming oven on kitchen paper.

Mushrooms should be skinned and prepared and then at the last minute tossed off in butter.

Potatoes should be partly boiled first and then fried off in butter at the last minute too.

Eggs accordingly to taste (scrambled are often the easiest for 6 or more people).

MATINEE PERFORMANCES
Afternoon Tea

In the old days at matinée performances, we used to order those delightful wooden trays lined with a linen napkin and with beautiful china, which were passed along the aisle in the interval. There would be lovely fresh tomato sandwiches, or the famous cucumber ones, a lovely fresh cream cake (éclair or meringue was my favourite) and a piece of buttery shortbread. All you get now is a plastic tray, tea-bag tea, and a bit of mangy fruit cake in cellophane. Oh, how style has gone out of our lives!

In my household, *everything stops for tea*, and has done since I was a child. Afternoon tea plays a great part in life in the North of England where I live and was brought up, and is a constant source, to me, of many happy childhood memories. I vividly remember the living-room at my grandmother's house prior to the Second World War. It sported a gleaming open black-leaded hearth with a sparkling oven on one side and two open fire hobs at either side of the burning grate. The kettle was continually on the boil as it was 'open house' for the busy neighbours, friends and family, and there was invariably something cooking in the oven or on the hob.

There would be teacakes, scones, Chelsea buns, spiced cobs, home-made bread and butter, and, of course, home-made preserves, gingerbread, shortbread, biscuits, macaroons, parkin, 'fly' cake, frangipane, sponge cakes, rock buns: all played their part in the order of the day for afternoon tea.

The cloth on the table was always stiffly starched and when 'company' was present, with napkins to match. The endless pot of tea was forever being refilled and recharged and the actual tea used was a constant source of change. Liptons, Typhoo, Brooke Bond (bought I am sure for the stamps which were religiously saved and stuck onto a card to be redeemed for so called 'luxury' items beyond the normal resources of my Nan) and on feast days and holidays, a pinch of china or green tea. Nowadays on my frequent travels I always seek out the tea of the country I am visiting. A recent favourite is a mint tea bag I discovered being sold by that doyenne of homely English cooks now living in New York – Rona Deme at Country Host on Lexington Avenue (but, it is, I must admit, a poor imitation of my very favourite tea for a hot summer's day – Moroccan mint tea).

I am rather old-fashioned in my making of tea. In traditional fashion, I warm the pot first with a little boiling water (I prefer china to stainless steel or silver) and then, after putting in the tea (one heaped teaspoon per person) I take the pot to the kettle which is still boiling. As the gush of boiling water hits the leaves they unfurl quickly to give out their delicate flavours.

As a firm believer in titillating the palate as much as possible (and being anything but conventional), I have used slices of fresh lime rather than lemon with china tea in the winter, I grate the minutest piece of nutmeg into the tea pot with the tea leaves. You may well raise your eyebrows but I will never refuse a cup of tea at any time of the day or night. I very much like to ring the changes, so my store-cupboard at home never has less than twelve assorted teas in it; I take a pinch of this and a pinch of that like an alchemist mixing a devilish brew.

One special tea-party I gave at home recently for a charity was a huge success as I made china tea and served it in tall glasses liberally filled with ice, fresh mint, and four or five rose petals. The taste was most unusual, and very pleasant, but more important still, the drink itself proved thirst quenching and cooling! But my own favourite, as I mentioned, is Moroccan Mint Tea. To make this, simply pour 1 pint (600 ml) of boiling water over 8 large sprigs of fresh mint (including the stalks), coarsely chopped. Infuse for 3 minutes and then strain.

Serve it hot with some rose petals and a few more sprigs of fresh mint, or cold, poured over lots of ice cubes (if the latter, don't forget to add a little sugar first).

In Morocco this is served very sweet, and I have also had it sweetened with delicious honey. Even for my sweet taste, this tends to be rather sickly.

BREAD, SCONES AND CAKES

Provided you have an ample supply of airtight containers (or better still, a freezer), it is best to have one really good baking session every so often. It is much more economical in both time and money to organize it this way, you will get a lot of fun and pleasure (I hope) from cooking some of the following recipes, and your guests will be delighted with the results!

Wholemeal Bread

For me the smell of newly baked bread straight out of the oven is sensual; so is the taste of hot, steamy bread, buttered so that the butter immediately melts and soaks right in. But working with yeast initially can have so many snares to trap the unwary, and you can have as many failures as successes. For me, anyway, it has only been constant care and practice that has enabled me to bake a consistent bread, whether it is Rich Vienna, Cob, or French. I doubt, anyway, if there is a single further word to be written on this fabulous subject since Elizabeth David published her simply splendid book called *English Bread and Yeast Cookery* (published by Allen Lane) which is a sheer feast of information and interest.

Do not be depressed, however, for *my* Wholemeal Bread can be made by a child of 6, and greedily consumed by a family of as many in as many minutes! There is no messing about with basic doughs, no need for rising, knocking down or kneading. It keeps for up to 10 days in a bread tin, up to 20 wrapped in greaseproof paper and foil in a fridge, and it freezes beautifully. Toasted for breakfast or for a snack it is tasty. Cut wafer thin for sandwiches whilst not exactly soft, the texture and taste will enhance any filling.

Notes

You require one large bowl and then a Christmas pudding bowl for starting off this recipe as they have to stand in a warm place for 8 minutes. I usually use the warming drawer of my oven or a gas oven that has a permanent gas jet in, or a very warm airing cupboard will do.

The water can come straight from the hot tap *provided* you draw off what is needed before it reaches the very, very hot stage!

Commercially bought yeast these days is made in factories on a base of molasses and water, whereas it used to be formed from potatoes and sugar. Although modern fresh yeast is reliable and works much faster, you must be careful how you store it. In a cool larder or fridge, fresh yeast will keep for 2 to 3 weeks *provided* it was in prime condition when you purchased it. You can also freeze it, when it will last for up to 5 months. When I do this though, I tend to freeze it in 2 oz (50 g) portions, wrapped in transparent cling wrap, and when I take it out of the freezer, I grate it to help it on its way.

If you cannot obtain fresh yeast – and somehow it is becoming increasingly difficult to buy in the shops – and have to use the dried yeast, do remember it is *twice as potent* as the fresh so use only half the quantity with a pinch of castor sugar in the warm water you will need to reconstitute the yeast. You will find it good to use but, for me, the flavour of dried yeast never really cooks out.

The Method

It is important that you mix thoroughly the black treacle and initial amount of warm water, otherwise you will find yourself with three separate layers, i.e. yeast, water, treacle, when bringing the flour into contact with the yeast mixing.

After leaving the yeast to rise at first before you proceed with the next stage, make certain the yeast has come up like a good head on a pint of Guinness, and then add the other amount of water which should be at the same temperature.

Having put the dough into the bread tins, make certain it is well knocked down by either using a spatula or by actually knocking the base of the tin rather hard on to a work surface. Cover with dampened greaseproof paper when returning for the 30-minute rising. Do, however, remember that the dough does rise and rather have too little in the tin than too much, for should the latter be the case the dough will come over the top and down the sides and not eventually find its way down into your stomach. Such a waste!

If you like bread with soft crusts, as the bread is cooling out of the oven, wrap it in a dampened cloth, but I do think the crisp crusts are best. Good for the teeth and for the taste as you really have to chew on the bread, savouring the molasses! One very odd point about this bread, mind you, is that when it is toasted it does tend to burn along the outside edge. The same applies if toasting under a grill or in one of the modern pop-up toaster machines and I can't for the life of me think why!

1 lb (450 g) wholemeal flour

$\frac{1}{4}$ oz (10 g) sea salt

2 tablespoons black treacle

$\frac{1}{8}$ pint (75 ml) warm water

1 oz (25 g) fresh bakers' yeast

$\frac{1}{2}$ pint (300 ml) warm water

Grease 2 × 1 lb (450 g) loaf tins.

In a warmed bowl, mix the flour with the salt – I prefer to use sea salt as the final flavour is so much better, but run of the mill kitchen salt may be used.

In the other bowl (I use a china Christmas pudding one as I said), mix the treacle thoroughly with the $\frac{1}{8}$ pint (75 ml) warm water. Crumble the yeast on top of this liquid.

Place both bowls in a warm place and leave for about 8 minutes. When the yeast in the small bowl has become frothy add $\frac{1}{2}$ pint (300 ml) warm water to the wet mixture, combine with the flour, and mix.

Put the mixture into the prepared tins, pat down, return to the warm place for about 20–30 minutes until the dough has risen by about one-third volume. Bake in a pre-set oven at 400°F (200°C), Gas 6, for 40 minutes. Turn out and leave to cool.

All Bran Loaf

1 large cup All Bran

1 large cup castor sugar

1 large cup mixed fruit

1 cup milk

1 heaped cup self-raising flour

This is practically the very simplest thing you could make for afternoon tea – but it is so delicious – and it stores extremely well for 7 to 10 days. (Use a standard 8 fl oz (225 ml) cup.)

Mix together the All Bran, castor sugar and mixed fruit and work to a dampish consistency with milk. Leave overnight. In the morning, fold in the self-raising flour. Put the mixture into greased and floured loaf tins and bake in a pre-set oven at 350°F (180°C), Gas 4, for 45 minutes. Leave to cool before turning out. Slice and put plenty of butter on before serving. It is also delicious toasted.

Boiled Lakeland Loaf

1 cup water
1 cup sultanas
1 cup castor sugar
4 oz (100 g) butter
1 teaspoon bicarbonate of soda
1 egg
2 cups of self-raising flour

(Use a standard 8 fl oz (200 ml) cup.)

Boil together the water, sultanas, castor sugar and butter for 10 minutes and then beat in the bicarbonate of soda (beware at this stage as it tends to froth up rather so use a saucepan large enough to allow for this to happen).

When cool, lightly beat the egg, beat it in and stir in the self-raising flour. Bake in the pre-heated oven at 350°F (180°C), Gas 4, for 1¼ hours.

Lemon Bread

6 oz (175 g) butter
10 oz (275 g) castor sugar
4 eggs, lightly beaten
5 oz (150 g) self-raising flour
5 oz (150 g) plain flour
4 oz (100 g) chopped walnuts
rind and juice of 2 lemons

This recipe will bake 2 loaves, if you use 1 lb (450 g) loaf tins. If you have good non-stick tins, there is no need to prepare them, otherwise I suggest you line the tins well with good greaseproof paper.

Pre-heat the oven to 350°F (180°C), Gas 4.

Cream the butter and sugar together well until white and fluffy, and then gradually beat in the lightly beaten eggs. Fold in both the flours and chopped nuts and then add the juice and rind of the lemons. Mix well.

Turn into prepared tins and bake for about 1 hour.

Batter Gingerbread

6 oz (175 g) self-raising flour
½ teaspoon mixed spice
2 oz (50 g) demerara sugar
2 teaspoons ground ginger
2 oz (50 g) butter
2 tablespoons treacle
2 eggs
¼ pint (150 ml) milk
1 teaspoon bicarbonate of soda

This 'cake' is the better for keeping but rarely has the opportunity to prove it as it is so popular. My recipe is a bastardized version of the one originally given by Margaret Costa in her lovely *Four Seasons Cookery Book* (now available again from Macdonald and Jane's) and it makes 2 × 1 lb (450 g) loaf-size cakes. Line the tins with greaseproof paper if they are not non-stick.

Place all the ingredients in a Magimix with the exception of the milk and bicarbonate of soda. Combine vigorously and then pour in the milk which you have brought to just below the boil. Add the bicarbonate of soda and blend until nice and bubbly. The result is like a runny pancake batter, which you pour into the prepared tins and bake at 350°F (180°C), Gas 4, for just over an hour.

1 lb (450 g) soft butter

1 lb (450 g) castor sugar

1 lb (450 g) eggs (weighed out of their shells)

1 lb (450 g) sieved self-raising flour

Fairy Cakes and Sponges

The old-fashioned pound cake recipe is the one I always fall back on here, i.e. one pound butter, sugar, eggs (weighed out of their shells!) and self-raising flour. This will make 6 × 8-portion sponge cakes and 12 fairy cakes!

The important requirement is soft butter. I always use Kerrygold – but we all have our own personal likes and dislikes. People ask if margarine can be used instead of butter? Of course it can and, in some ways, it is better for the figure as it contains less cholesterol, but in no way is it as good for the tastebuds! The eggs, in my opinion, should be at room temperature and lightly beaten together first.

But the actual creaming of the butter and castor sugar are next in importance. A warm bowl helps and you can use either a Kenwood Chef or a Kenwood Hand Mixer. (I prefer the latter as you can really work your way round and into the mixing and see just where it requires an extra boost!) I use a large plastic mixing bowl measuring 12 in (30 cm) diameter by about 6 in (15 cm) deep. Start off by combining the butter and sieved castor sugar with the palm of your hand and then whisk and whisk and whisk until the mixture is practically white and extremely light in texture.

The lightly beaten eggs should then be added a little at a time. Allow them to be well mixed in and absolutely disappear before adding more. If you add too much egg too quickly, the mixture will split which, in my opinion, isn't a sin, but you then have to fold in carefully some of the flour and continue mixing with much greater caution.

When the butter and sugar mixture has taken up all of the egg, divide it into four and turn out into three further bowls. To the first one you can add 4 tablespoons drinking chocolate powder made up to 4 oz (100 g) with the sieved self-raising flour – and you have two chocolate sponges. To the second you add 4 tablespoons desiccated coconut with 4 tablespoons sultanas that have been soaked in 2 tablespoons brandy, along with 4 oz (100 g) of self-raising flour, and this makes 2 further 8-portion cakes. To the third you add 4 tablespoons crushed banana with 2 tablespoons of finely chopped ginger and 2 tablespoons of ginger syrup with 2 tablespoons mixed chopped walnuts plus the 4 oz (100 g) self-raising flour. The fourth mixing has just a little vanilla essence added before you stir in the 4 oz (100 g) sieved self-raising flour and this can make either 2 further sponge cakes or will produce 12 individual small fairy cakes.

Do, however, always turn out into large bowls and use a large metal spoon for folding in. By doing so you will not knock back the mixture and the end result will be the lighter. Other additions to the basic recipe can be instant coffee powder (not granules), a few tablespoons of purée of strawberry or apricot jam, and diced apple with diced glacé cherries make an interesting filling.

The sponge tins should be 8 in (20 cm) by $\frac{3}{4}$ in (2 cm) deep, coated liberally with melted butter and then floured and sugared (and, as far as I am concerned, seldom washed!). The cakes normally take 20 minutes to cook in a pre-heated oven at 350°F (180°C), Gas 4. When I take them out of the oven I leave them for about 15 minutes and then turn them out on to a wire cooling tray.

The fillings need not necessarily just be plain whipped cream. The chocolate sponges are the better for a tablespoon of rum whipped into the cream with a tablespoon of castor sugar and then the cake coated with chocolate icing and walnut halves. The coconut and sultana sponges can be 'jammed and creamed' and not necessarily iced – just have the tops liberally sprinkled with icing sugar through a sieve. For the cakes with banana, ginger and walnut, a little nutmeg in the cream is quite tasty.

Marsala and Almond Cake

- **8 oz (225 g) castor sugar**
- **8 oz (225 g) butter**
- **4 eggs, lightly beaten**
- **10 oz (275 g) sieved self-raising flour**
- **pinch of salt**
- **4 oz (100 g) ground almonds**
- **6 tablespoons Marsala (if Marsala is not available use a sweet sherry and change the name!)**

This mixing will fill an 8 in (20 cm) square tin which has been lined with a double layer of greaseproof paper. Set the oven to 325°F (170°C), Gas 3.

As mentioned earlier when writing about pound cakes, this cake is the better if you spend some time and care in really beating the sugar and butter together until light and white and creamy, and then slowly adding the egg mixture a little at a time. Then all you do is gently fold in the flour, salt, almonds and delicious Marsala. Bake at 325°F (170°C), Gas 3, for 45 minutes and then turn off the oven, cover the cake with foil and leave it in the oven for a further 45 minutes.

When cool, turn out the cake and prick deeply on top and base so that you can sprinkle liberally with further Marsala. I find this cake is very popular and really loved by elderly people as it has a richness to it that is easily digestible, and a lot of my older friends would rather I make them one for Christmas as opposed to my very rich Christmas Cake (but perhaps they don't *like* my Christmas Cake!).

Éclairs

The basic mixing on page 43 will give you 40 × 3 in (7.5 cm) éclairs that are dainty for a tea party, iced with coffee or chocolate icing and filled with whipped cream at the last minute. They are piped using a $\frac{1}{4}$-in (5-mm) plain nozzle and take about 15 minutes in a pre-heated oven at 425°F (220°C), Gas 7. They freeze extremely well and are so handy to have in case of unexpected people calling for a cuppa.

Whipped Cream Cake

8 fl oz (225 ml) double cream

3 eggs, lightly beaten

8 oz (225 g) sieved self-raising flour

8 oz (225g) castor sugar

½ teaspoon salt

1 teaspoon vanilla essence

This is an extremely rich type of sponge cake, but made with whipped double cream and no butter. It rises well and is filling. When soaked liberally with liqueurs or spirits it is good served as a dessert, but I prefer it for afternoon tea, filled with whipped cream and either jam or soft fruits.

In a large bowl, whip the double cream until fairly stiff and then fold in the gently beaten eggs. Using a large metal spoon, gently fold in the sieved self-raising flour, sugar, and salt along with the vanilla essence. Pour into 2 greased and floured 8 in (20 cm) cake tins and bake in the pre-heated oven for 30 minutes at 350°F (180°C), Gas 4.

Scones

2 lb (scant 1 kg) self-raising flour

12 oz (350 g) very soft butter

generous pinch salt

6 tablespoons sieved castor sugar

sultanas to taste

4 eggs, lightly beaten

milk or sour cream to mix

They are so easy to make and I usually do a 2 lb (1 kg) mixing which will give approximately 40 scones. If you aren't going to use them all at once, they are best frozen uncooked.

Pre-heat the oven to 425°F (220°C), Gas 7.

Sieve the self-raising flour into a large plastic bowl (mine is 12 in (30 cm) in diameter and 6 in (15 cm) deep) and break the soft butter up into 1 oz (25 g) pieces. Very gently – and carefully – bring the butter and flour together. When I'm doing this, my thumb never touches my fingers; I simply just put my eight fingers down in the bowl, scoop up as much as I can and allow it to gently fall through my open fingers. It soon starts to come together and resembles fine crumbs, *but* do not overwork.

Add the salt, castor sugar, sultanas and the lightly beaten eggs and start to bring together, using the outstretched palm of your hand. Do not squeeze and do not knock out any of the air.

It is virtually impossible to say exactly how much milk or sour cream you need to get the mixture to the right consistency as so much depends on how soft the butter is, how warm the room is, etc, but the mixture should not be too soft (or your scones will spread in the eventual cooking) or too dry (or they will not be as light). When you are satisfied with the mix, turn it out onto a lightly floured board and, using a palette knife, cut it into diamond shapes. *Do not* roll the mixture out and then cut into delightful scalloped circles and then economically re-roll to get a few more, as many people do. If you do this, your scones are bound to be heavier.

Put on to trays and bake for approximately 10 minutes.

To ring the changes, savoury scones can be made by substituting grated cheese and crushed coriander or curry powder for the sugar and sultanas. Even chopped prunes may be used instead of sultanas, or try diced dried apricots. Occasionally, I include a smattering of desiccated coconut or a few ground almonds. Do not be set and staid in your approach! Experiment!

Farm Fruit Cake

6 oz (175 g) wholewheat flour

6 oz (175 g) plain flour

3 teaspoons baking powder

a pinch of salt

2 teaspoons ground nutmeg

5 oz (150 g) butter

4 oz (100 g) soft brown sugar

8 oz (225 g) sultanas

4 oz (100 g) mixed peel

2 oz (50 g) glacé cherries, chopped finely

juice and rind of 1 lemon

4 eggs

$\frac{1}{4}$ pint (150 ml) milk

blanched almonds for top of cake

Use a 10 in (25 cm) round cake tin and double-line it with greaseproof paper. Pre-heat the oven to 350°F (180°C), Gas 4.

Mix the flours with the baking powder, salt and nutmeg, and rub in the butter. Fold in the sugar along with the sultanas, mixed peel and cherries. Add the rind and juice of the lemon, then add the eggs that have been beaten lightly with the milk.

This forms a paste which you put in the prepared cake tin and bake in the pre-heated oven for $1\frac{1}{2}$ hours.

Smooth Velvet Cake

This mixing will fill 3 × 9 in (23 cm) cake tins.

8 oz (225 g) butter

10 oz (275 g) castor sugar

2 whole eggs plus 2 egg yolks, lightly beaten

5 fl oz (150 ml) natural (or flavoured) yoghurt

1 teaspoon vanilla essence

10 oz (275 g) self-raising flour

Set the oven at 350°F (180°C), Gas 4.

Cream the butter and sugar until white and fluffy and then add the beaten eggs little by little. Stir in the yoghurt with the vanilla essence and carefully fold in the self-raising flour. Turn out into the 3 prepared cake tins and bake for 25 minutes.

GENUINE
Herb Tea

MAD
CKLES
HOME
REL

Orange mousse

BISCUITS

However simple the meal or informal the occasion, a sparkle is added when home-made biscuits are served. It is a touch to show that you have given the one thing that is so valuable in this day and age – your time. And if you do decide to go mad, you will be thoroughly amazed at the number of biscuits you can turn out in a couple of hours devoted to biscuit-making.

The doughs can be used immediately, or chilled, or frozen. The cooked products keep amazingly well for quite a long time provided they are stored in airtight containers and, believe you me, they prove a godsend on numerous occasions and, of course, are way ahead of the mass-produced biscuits which seem continually to go up in price and taste less and less like the buttery, rich delights you bake at home!

What I usually do in the winter, when I cook at home like any other normal person, is to spend one half morning up to my eyes with everything needed for biscuits. Several recipes I double up. Cook off one-third, chill one-third clearly labelled, and freeze the other third. It is a relatively simple task then, when the tins begin to empty, to cook off a few more biscuits when the oven is finished with, after cooking lunch one day.

Also, what nicer gift is there for a friend in this day and age of over-priced gift-wrapped chocolates than a box of assorted home-made biscuits?

Points to Watch when Making Biscuits

Soft butter is a great help when making the doughs, and measure out your ingredients accurately.

Double-check the oven temperature. Domestic ovens can be as temperamental as the most fiendish prima donna – particularly when cooking biscuits. Of course, you look into the oven (or on élite models turn on the light and lovingly gaze through the glass door) but you are only seeing the tops! What I find infuriating is when the tops are cooked, the bottoms (particularly those on trays placed on bottom shelves) are sometimes burnt. Just over half-way through cooking most biscuits, gently open the door and 'top and bottom' your trays.

A lot of people are then too hasty in the storing of their biscuits and pile them into containers whilst they are still hot. Always wait until the biscuits are stone cold and, seeing that you have taken time to prepare, shape and cook the biscuits, show a little care in the storing. Don't just slide the trayfuls into containers any old how. Stack the biscuits neatly, then you will be able to use one and all and not end up with a tin quarter full of broken bits.

1 lb (450 g) sieved plain flour

pinch of salt

8 oz (225 g) Farola

8 oz (225 g) castor sugar

1 lb (450 g) softened butter

Shortbread

The above ingredients will give you 2 trays 8 × 10 in (20 × 25 cm) of shortbread. Put everything into the electric mixer (I use a Kenwood Chef) and let the beater *slowly* do the work for you.

Spread the mixture into 2 tins as above (or only use 1 and use the balance of the 'dough' to make individual tartlets – in which case you must always chill the tartlets for about 30 minutes before cooking). Cook in a low oven at about 250°F (130°C), Gas ½, for about 1 hour. (The individual tartlets, if you make these instead, should be lined with a cake paper and beans.)

When cooked and cooling, sprinkle liberally with vanilla sugar (see note below). To ring the changes, mixed spices and ginger may be added to the mixing, but I prefer the shortbread to be as near the original Scottish recipe as possible.

Vanilla Sugar
Every kitchen should have tucked away in a cupboard a small tin of this, as it has so many uses and does enhance so many biscuits etc. Simply find an empty tin and place inside 2 or 3 vanilla pods and fill the tin up with castor sugar. To sprinkle the sugar on, I use a large salt shaker (that you find in fish and chip shops) as the top comes off freely when you wish to fill up the container and when shaken the vanilla sugar comes out in force.

4 oz (100 g) sieved plain flour

3 oz (75 g) desiccated coconut

1 oz (25 g) castor sugar

2 oz (50 g) well-crushed cornflakes

4 oz (100 g) butter

Iced Coconut Biscuits

Mix all the dry ingredients in a bowl, pour on the melted butter and mix thoroughly together. Cover a baking sheet with greaseproof paper, and spoon out about 16 walnut-sized biscuits. Flatten each gently with a palette knife. Leave a little space round each one, but they do not spread much. Bake for 20 minutes at 350°F (180°C), Gas 4. When cool, top with plain white icing (12 oz (300 g) icing sugar made up to the correct consistency with water).

1 oz (25 g) sieved icing sugar

8 oz (225 g) sieved castor sugar

6 oz (175 g) ground almonds

3 egg whites

a drop of almond essence

about 36–40 whole almonds

Macaroons

Pre-heat the oven to 300°F (150°C), Gas 2, and line the baking tray with rice paper.

Mix the sugars and ground almonds together in a mixing bowl and make a well in the centre. Into this drop one egg white, and using a silver fork, work it into the sugar until you get a stiff smooth paste. Then gradually work in the other egg whites until the paste is soft and smooth. Flavour with almond essence.

Put the mixture into a piping bag with a star nozzle, and pipe approximately 36–40 dainty-sized biscuits onto the rice paper. Before putting in the oven, dust with extra castor sugar and decorate each biscuit with a whole almond. Bake for 30 minutes until firm and golden. Take out and leave to cool, then trim off surplus rice paper and store in an airtight container. These biscuits are deliciously nutty and chewy.

Banana Oatmeal Biscuits

This makes about 50 biscuits.

6 oz (175 g) butter

6 oz (175 g) castor sugar

1 egg, lightly beaten

6 oz (175 g) plain flour

½ teaspoon bicarbonate of soda

1 teaspoon salt

½ teaspoon grated nutmeg

½ teaspoon powdered cinnamon

2 bananas, peeled and mashed

10 oz (275 g) oatmeal

2 oz (50 g) finely chopped peanuts

Pre-heat oven to 350°F (180°C), Gas 4.

Cream the butter and sugar until light and fluffy, and then beat in the egg. Sieve in the flour, bicarbonate of soda, salt and spices, and fold in the bananas, oatmeal and peanuts. Mix well.

Line a baking tray or trays with greaseproof paper. Using two teaspoons (one for scooping and one for scraping the mixture off onto the trays) spread heaped teaspoons of the mixture on the trays allowing about 2 in (5 cm) between each biscuit as they will spread in the cooking.

Bake for 15 minutes and then transfer to a rack to cool. Remember to do this as quickly as possible, otherwise the bottoms of the biscuits will continue cooking with the heat of the tray and sometimes their bottoms get slightly browner than one would like.

Coconut Chocolate Fingers

4 oz (100 g) good dark chocolate

6 oz (175 g) desiccated coconut

6 oz (175 g) castor sugar

3 oz (75 g) chopped glacé cherries

3 oz (75 g) butter

2 eggs, lightly beaten

Set the oven at 350°F (180°C), Gas 4.

Line a Swiss roll tin measuring 12 × 8 in (30 × 20 cm) with greaseproof paper and lightly oil it. Melt the chocolate gently in a double saucepan and spread this out thinly with a palette knife to line the greaseproof paper, and put in the fridge to set. Put the desiccated coconut, castor sugar and glacé cherries into a bowl. Melt the butter and, when it is cooling, add to the lightly beaten eggs. Combine with the dry ingredients in the bowl and then spread the mixture over the set chocolate. Bake for 25 minutes. Leave overnight in the tin and then cut into fingers. (Well, not necessarily overnight, but you do want the chocolate to set on the base, don't you?)

Almond Biscuits

This should give you approximately 25 biscuits.

- **1 egg**
- **6 oz (175 g) icing sugar**
- **finely grated rind of 1 lemon**
- **6 oz (175 g) ground almonds**
- **1 teaspoon baking powder**
- **drop of vanilla essence**

Set the oven at 350°F (180°C), Gas 4.

Beat the egg and icing sugar together until the mixture is fairly white (with an electric hand whisk this will take about 5 minutes). Add the finely grated lemon rind and fold in the ground almonds, baking powder and a little vanilla essence. This resulting paste will be *almost too stiff to handle.* Roll up into a roll $1\frac{1}{2}$ in (4 cm) diameter, wrap in greaseproof paper and chill for 1 hour. Cut off thin biscuits $\frac{1}{4}$ in (5 mm) thick, and place on a baking tray lined with greaseproof paper and bake for 15–20 minutes.

Miller Howe Fork Biscuits

- **10 oz (275 g) sifted self-raising flour**
- **4 oz (100 g) castor sugar**
- **8 oz (225 g) fairly soft butter**
- **grated rind of one large lemon**

Place all four ingredients into a Kenwood bowl and use the K beater. Mix slowly until the ingredients come together. At this stage the dough can either be put in the deep freeze or kept in the fridge for up to a week.

When required, bring up to room temperature and form into small balls which are flattened out onto a baking sheet using the back of a fork dipped in cold water. Bake at 350°F (180°C), Gas 4, for 10 minutes. As they are cooling, sprinkle with vanilla sugar (see page 194). When cold, store in air-tight containers.

Florentines

- **$3\frac{3}{4}$ oz (100 g) butter**
- **$3\frac{3}{4}$ oz (100 g) castor sugar**
- **4 oz (125 g) ground almonds**
- **2 oz (50 g) finely chopped glacé cherries**
- **rind of 1 orange**
- **1 tablespoon double cream, whipped**
- **8 oz (225 g) dark chocolate**

These are so expensive to buy and are looked upon as a luxury item, but when made at home they are far from expensive and so professional! The basic points to observe, mind you, when making florentines are to measure the amounts *exactly* and never cook more than 4 at a time in the oven (you *could* put 4 in and then 5 minutes later a further 4 so that you are taking them out at more frequent intervals but, at first, just cook off 2 at a time so that you can get the hang of bringing them together and finishing them off).

Pre-heat your oven to 300°F (150°C), Gas 2, and test the temperature with a thermometer!

Melt the butter in a saucepan, add the sugar, bring to the boil and cook this mixture for approximately 1 minute. Remove from heat and add all the other ingredients except the cream and the chocolate. When the mixture has cooled a bit, stir in the cream.

At your first attempt, take a level dessertspoonful of the mixture and place it on a baking tray covered with a sheet of oiled greaseproof paper and, allowing room for it to spread, place a further spoonful on the same tray. Put in the pre-heated oven, and bake for about 10 minutes.

You now need a large biscuit (or fried egg) cutter for, as you take the tray out of the oven, you will see that the mixture has spread and will occasionally have left wide holes in its middle. You use the cutter at an angle of 45 degrees and gently, but quickly, drag the mixture back to what looks like a reasonably shaped biscuit and return to the oven for a few more minutes. Remove again and if it has spread a little more, use the cutter to form the final shape you require.

Leave them for two or three minutes before attempting to take them off the tray. Then swiftly slide a palette knife underneath each biscuit (which will be beginning to harden by now) and remove to a cooling tray. When you have developed this knack you will be able to do them, as I said, in batches of 4 at 5-minute intervals.

When they are cold and crisp, turn them face down and coat with melted chocolate. Leave to set and then put into air-tight containers as soon as possible, interleaving them with greaseproof paper so they do not stick together. Served with soft creamy puds, they provide such a delicious contrast in flavour and for tea they are very more-ish indeed!

HOME-MADE JAMS AND PRESERVES

In the season at Miller Howe jams are made when required from what is readily and economically available on the market. They're all soon eaten! Preserving is worthy of a whole book to itself, but here are a few hints on what we do in the hotel.

Always wipe or wash the fruit first, and take off the stalks. A thoroughly clean pan is always needed for jam making and I invariably give mine a rub with half a lemon and a teaspoon of salt and then rinse well under cold water.

Strawberry and Raspberry Jams

These require $3\frac{1}{2}$ lb (1.6 kg) sugar to a full 4 lb (1.8 kg) fruit but *no water at all.* The strawberries take about 15 minutes over a simmering heat after they have come back to the boil, and raspberries about 5 minutes. Simply add the fruit to the pan and begin to cook and then add the sugar and stir from time to time. Leave to cool and when half cold pour into clean warm jars. Cover and seal.

Damson Jam

For 4 lb (1.8 kg) damsons, melt 3 lb (1.4 kg) sugar with 1 pint (600 ml) water, and then add the damsons. When the mixture comes back to simmering, cook for about 30 minutes. Pour into clean warm jars and, when the jam has cooled a bit, cover and seal.

Gooseberry Jam

Top and tail the gooseberries, then follow the quantities and instructions for Damson Jam.

Home-Made Lemon Curd

4 oz (100 g) butter

8 oz (225 g) castor sugar

grated rind and juice of 2 lemons

4 egg yolks

Lemon curd is a preserve I can never have too much of as it is rich, tart, and – however contradictory it may sound – sweet! I use it for filling simple jam tarts for tea or just plain on bread and butter or scones, or with Calvados Apples in Galette Pastry.

Melt the butter, sugar and lemon rind and juice together in a china or pot bowl set over a saucepan of simmering water and beat until quite smooth. Then beat in the egg yolks and continue cooking until the mixture will coat the back of your wooden spoon (i.e. when you take the spoon out of the mixture run your index finger along the middle of the back, and the indentation remains there quite clearly). Do not overcook, as the mixture sets and thickens further when cooling.

Do take your time with this recipe and don't allow the water to boil fiercely, otherwise you will have speckled bits of cooked egg yolk which would spoil an otherwise smooth lemon curd.

Pour into pots and serve. This will make about 1 lb (450 g).

MATINEE PERFORMANCES
High Tea

High tea is even more of a tradition in the North of England, and reminds me so much of my childhood.

My grandfather used to come home from the shipyard in the evening at about 5.45, and everything was geared to his homecoming. Even the dog (a lovely black-and-white spaniel called Terry) used to become impatient around 5.30, and would spontaneously take my grandfather's slippers through from the wash-house to the hearth for them to warm. When my grand-dad came in through the backyard gate the dog rushed to greet him, relieving him of the local evening paper, and then carried his slippers through, one by one, from the warmed hearth to the wash-house where John would be washing and getting out of his overalls. We had all had our tea before this as John liked to eat in peace and quiet. On fine days we were sent to play in the yard and back street, and on wet days allowed in to the front parlour to play the old HMV gramophone.

For his high tea, added to the goodies we had consumed at afternoon tea, he might have poached haddock with poached eggs, fried cod with parsley sauce, faggots, buttered eggs, belly pork with baked beans, grilled liver and bacon, tripe and onions, bubble and squeak with home-made chutneys, Welsh rarebit wickedly enhanced with a drop of Guinness, cold meats and salads and always, but always, home-made pickled onions. Then he would dip into the Tipsy Trifle!

Buttered Eggs

You must have a very clean saucepan for this, so give it a rub over with salt and lemon, and wipe it out just before you start to cook. See that your guests are well and truly seated before you get on with the cooking and by the time they have exchanged small talk for 3 or 4 minutes the dish will be ready.

I allow myself 1 oz (25 g) of butter for each egg I am going to use and this I bring up to simmering point having beaten the eggs separately with freshly ground black pepper and a pinch of nutmeg. Pour the egg mixture into the simmering butter and, using a wooden spoon, continually stir and beat the mixture. As the eggs begin to come together with the butter, reduce the heat slightly. In fact, I take the pan off the stove after about 2 minutes and whisk the mixture with an electric hand whisk before returning to the heat.

As the mixture begins to thicken, remove from the heat and beat again with the hand mixer. Serve immediately. Chopped fresh chives are lovely thrown in at the last minute. Should you slightly overcook the eggs, pour in a couple of tablespoons of cream and beat well. Do remember that the eggs go on cooking for a short while in their own heat after they have been removed from the stove.

For me Buttered Eggs are a trifle too rich for breakfast, but I have served them with Danish lumpfish roe for brunch, and in small quantities they make an ideal, tasty and simple starter or high tea dish – served with triangles of croûton, in puff pastry cases with small pieces of smoked salmon, in ramekins lined with warmed Mushroom Pâté, on top of buttered nutmeg spinach, or in gougères.

Pickled Onions

2 lb (900 g) button onions

2 tablespoons kitchen salt

1 pint (600 ml) malt vinegar

$\frac{1}{2}$ oz (15 g) sea salt

$\frac{1}{2}$ oz (15 g) pickling spice

6 cloves

$\frac{1}{4}$ oz (10 g) black peppercorns

2 oz (50 g) demerara sugar

I talk about onions elsewhere (see page 118), but for me the queen of onions is the pickled one. I never go to a local market without coming back home with a few jars of pickled onions if there are any available, and they are becoming more and more scarce. Each year the staff and I go to the finest farmhouse for food in the land – Mrs Johnson's at Tullythwaite House – and I am sure she must shudder when our visit looms up, as we devour bottles of her fine onions with our meat-laden high tea salads. Nobody, but nobody, can pickle onions like she can and one day she might part with her recipe, but if you want to tackle your own, here's how I would do it.

Pickling onions – or button onions as they are often called – are the round small bulbs that are picked before the onion starts to develop. Take your onions, and to peel them quickly, simply remove their tops and tails (take care with their tails as you just want to remove the minute roots) and then pour over them sufficient boiling water to cover and leave to soak for 4 minutes. Drain immediately and slip the skins off (do this as quickly as possible as the skins come off much more easily if the onions are still warm).

Spread the peeled onions out on a large tray, sprinkle them generously with kitchen salt and leave overnight. Next day rinse them well and pat dry with kitchen paper. Mix all the other ingredients together in a large saucepan and boil for 10 minutes. Add the onions and bring the mixture back to the boil. Remove immediately from the heat, take out the onions and pack them into well-washed, sterilised jars. Reheat the vinegar mixture, pour over the onions in the jars, leave to become cold, and cover.

Although you'll be tempted to pick and sample to see how they are 'coming along', leave well alone for at least 4 weeks. They should then be well and truly pickled.

Date Chutney

2 lb (900 g) stoned dates

1 lb (450 g) onions

2 oz (50 g) sea salt

1 pint (600 ml) malt vinegar

1 teaspoon ground ginger

3 oz (75 g) allspice berries

1 lb (450 g) brown sugar

(With grateful thanks for being introduced to this delicious dish by my good friend Margaret Costa.)

Put the dates and peeled onions through a mincer.

Bring to simmering point $\frac{1}{3}$ pint (200 ml) of the vinegar and to this add the salt, ginger and the allspice (the latter being securely tied in muslin!) and the minced dates and onions. Simmer over low heat until thick. Meanwhile dissolve the sugar in the rest of the vinegar and then add to the thickened mixture in the pan. Simmer again (without a lid) until thick and when cool, pot and seal.

Piccalilli

1 lb (450 g) frozen sliced runner beans

1 large cauliflower

2 cloves garlic

a little salt

1 cucumber

1 lb (450 g) onions

$2\frac{1}{2}$ pints (1.4 litres) malt vinegar

1 teaspoon nutmeg

1 lb (450 g) castor sugar

2 oz (50 g) English dry mustard

6 oz (175 g) sieved plain flour

1 oz (25 g) turmeric

Made once a year (normally when we are quiet in the closed period, from January to March) the following recipe doubled up lasts us through the season as it is sparingly used – a teaspoon on one of the cheese dishes, a smattering with a packed lunch, the odd splash on to thick bap cobs served for a quick snack, with cold meats at high tea.

Make piccalilli when you have a good supply of clean jam jars to hand and you will be surprised at how economical this dish turns out and how grateful your friends are for this surprise gift!

First of all prepare the ingredients: pound the garlic to pulp with a little salt; skin and dice the cucumber (removing the seeds and pith in the middle) and skin and chop the onions. Break off the flowers only of the cauliflower – do not use the stalks. Put 2 pints (1.1 litre) malt vinegar on to simmer in a large pan and into this place the onion and cauliflower. Bring to the boil and simmer for 10 minutes. Add the sugar, cucumber and defrosted runner beans and cook for a further 10 minutes.

Meanwhile, mix the mustard, flour, nutmeg and turmeric to a smooth paste with the rest of the vinegar and then slowly add this to the cooked vegetable mixture. Blend well, stirring constantly and cook for a further 5 minutes.

When cool, pot in sterilised jam jars. Cover with small rounds of greaseproof paper and then top off with transparent cling film, using rubber bands to secure them.

My Nan's Tipsy Trifle

Everybody, but everybody, has their own version of a trifle, the very worst being those made with packet jelly and canned fruit and which make such a revolting rude sound as your spoon starts the attack (rather as if you are walking over a tennis court in water-filled galoshes)! Prejudiced I obviously am, but Sunday afternoon high teas at my Nan's were always made the more exciting by the prospect of Tipsy Trifle (which was always eagerly attacked by the otherwise teetotal Tabernacle minister who seemed to become tipsy on his liberal second helping)! Sponge cakes made from the Pound Cake recipe (see page 189) provide the base for my trifle and these are sliced and then spread with strawberry jam (page 197) and whipped double cream. If you're over-generous with the sponge at this stage, you'll end up with a heavier trifle which will require more 'tipsy' to soften it. It's up to you. I'm usually rather heavy-handed with the combination of brandy and Marsala (one-third brandy to two-thirds Marsala).

Strain the juice from a small can of apricot halves and liquidize the apricots. Top the trifle sponge with this purée.

A rich egg custard made with 1 pint (600 ml) single cream, 8 eggs, and 2 oz (50 g) castor sugar now completes the sweet. Beat the eggs and sugar together while warming the single cream. Add the warmed cream to the egg and sugar mixture and stir vigorously, return the pan to a low heat and stir constantly until the mixture begins to coat the back of your wooden spoon. Don't go too far or the eggs will curdle and remember the custard thickens on cooling. Pour on to the trifle or trifles and leave in the fridge when cold.

Decorate as lavishly or as meanly as you like. See the photograph for some ideas.

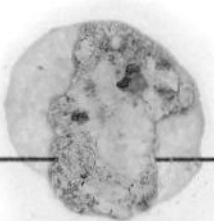

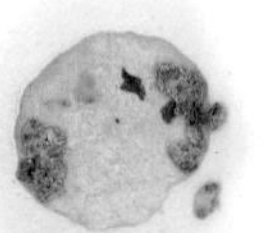

PROGRAMME NOTES

SAUCES
GARNISHINGS
HERBS

SAUCES

So often I've been told that 'Sauces make or mar a meal', and I'm sure that many beginning – let alone experienced – cooks quake with fear when they are confronted with sauces. But although they *are* important, the sauces in this section are *so* simple and delicious that you can't fail to be successful.

The basic white sauce made from the roux is a joy for me to make as, although it takes a bit of time to slowly add the milk and beat to get that special satin-sheen, once this technique is mastered you will be able to experiment with numerous other tasty sauces. People tend to get scared when the sauce continues to look lumpy after each addition of milk, but you will soon get the smooth texture back with further beating.

The Hollandaise Sauce is simple to do as well, but for this you do need a Magimix or a liquidizer. Gone are the days of beating madly for ages, with your right hand (and your left making signs of the cross so that the ruddy thing didn't curdle!).

The basic cream sauce is, I do assure you, the very simplest one to make and although you might find it expensive on the pocket, it's very rich on the palate and I'm sure you and your guests will go into raptures over it along with the several variations.

Basic White Sauce

1¾ oz (45–50 g) butter

¾ pint (400 ml) milk

a pinch of salt

1½ oz (40 g) sieved plain flour

A basic white sauce, once mastered, can enhance your cooking like nothing else. When entertaining, it can be made earlier on in the day, and it also freezes well. For creamed dishes a good basic guide is to double the amount of the filling to the actual sauce (for instance, 2 cups of diced meat to 1 cup of cream sauce).

It is easier to thin a sauce down rather than thicken it up, and so I always make a fairly thick basic pint (600 ml) of white sauce, as follows:

Melt the butter in a saucepan (a deeper, narrower saucepan is better than a wide one), and put the milk on to warm through with the pinch of salt in another pan. When the butter has melted and is bubbling away, add the sieved flour all in one go and, using a wooden spoon (make sure it has a curved back), stir vigorously until the mixture is smooth.

Do not overcook or burn at this stage and make certain that your milk is quite warm. I use a small soup ladle to add the warm milk to the basic roux (the flour and butter mixing) – and do remember to add a little at a time (about ⅛ pint or 75 ml) and never, never, *never* add more until the milk has been absorbed and the mixture is creamy.

The first addition of warm milk to the hot roux will produce quite a fierce heat so be prepared to start to beat the mixture immediately. When all the milk has been absorbed at this initial stage, I find it best to slightly tilt the saucepan to an angle of 45° and beat the living daylights out of the mixture before starting to add further warm milk.

Some people use a wire whisk, but I still stick to my old wooden spoon. You can make a sauce quite quickly with a whisk, but that isn't the point of the exercise. The slower you do it, giving you more beating time, the shinier your sauce will be and the more the flour will be cooked out. There is nothing worse than getting a floury flavour in a sauce, and this happens when you have rushed the making. If you follow my instructions, the sauce should be smooth and lump-free (don't take fright each time you add further milk and your smooth sauce momentarily looks hideous again!); however, I always pass my finished sauce through a fine sieve before adding the flavouring.

Store the basic sauce in a double saucepan, covering the top of the sauce with a used butter wrapping paper to prevent a skin from forming.

At this stage the sauce will be of a good coating consistency (in other words, when you take the wooden spoon out of the mixture and you run your finger along the back, wiping off a streak of sauce, the section you have wiped will stay clean and the top and bottom 'layers' will cling to the spoon). It might be too thick for your requirements, so all you need do is add some more milk – or better still, a little cream.

Once you have mastered the art of making a basic white sauce you can ring the changes according to your mood and palate, and some of the following suggestions may appeal to you. They are all based on the basic $\frac{3}{4}$ pint (450 ml) recipe for white sauce.

White Wine Sauce

I suppose wine sauce is the most popular of the white sauces, but don't just add a couple of tablespoons of wine to the basic sauce. Put half a bottle of white wine (not a Montrachet '71 naturally, but the better the 'plonk' the better the sauce) into a saucepan with four black peppercorns and reduce it over a low heat to a couple of tablespoons. This means you are virtually getting a grape essence. It is rather 'tacky' at this stage, and what I usually do is use the top of a double saucepan to reduce the wine and then sieve the sauce into it (having fished out the black peppercorns, of course) and by beating for a few minutes, the flavour is soon imparted.

Cheese Sauce

To the basic white sauce mix, I add about 4 oz (100–125 g) grated cheese. Cook until the cheese has melted into the sauce and I often flavour naughtily at the end with $\frac{1}{4}$ gill (35 ml) Kirsch or brandy.

Mustard Sauce
Add 2 tablespoons of *Moutarde au Meaux* to the white sauce. As well as being tasty, the lovely specks of seeds make the sauce look very appealing.

Tomato Sauce
Add 2 tablespoons of basic Tomato purée (see page 124) to the basic white sauce.

Curry Sauce
I normally use the apricot jam, curry, wine and onion mixture mentioned on page 132 and then, after passing this through a sieve, reduce it over a simmering heat to 2 tablespoons. Add to the basic white sauce.

Parsley Sauce
I like parsley sauce to really taste of parsley and I add *lots* to the basic white sauce so that it is the colour of Kendal green mentioned by Shakespeare in his famous Battle of Agincourt speech.

Herb Sauce
Herb sauces are all to do with personal taste, so you must always experiment – but do be *bold*.

Shrimp Sauce
Liquidize 8 oz (225 g) shrimps and pass through a strainer. This makes a lovely-tasting sauce, and a touch of anchovy essence enhances the flavour.

Blender (or Magimix) Hollandaise

4 tablespoons fresh lemon juice

2 tablespoons white wine vinegar

12 oz (350 g) butter

6 egg yolks

2 teaspoons castor sugar

a pinch of salt

Heaven forbid, say the old school of chefs, throwing their hands up in disgust! But they should just try it! I *always* use this method when entertaining at home, as it is quick, reliable and never curdles.

The recipe can be halved but *not doubled* in the type of blender normally found in home kitchens.

Place the lemon juice and vinegar in one small saucepan and the butter in another. Put both on the stove – to heat the lemon juice and vinegar to bubbling point and to completely melt the butter, without burning.

In the blender goblet or Magimix, blend the egg yolks, castor sugar and salt for literally 2 seconds, just to break up the yolks and incorporate the other two ingredients.

When the vinegar and lemon juice mixture is boiling, gently trickle into the blender which is whizzing at high speed. (I find it better to use a jug with a sensible pouring lip. Pouring from a pan is awkward, and your mixture sometimes dribbles down the side of the pan on to the lid and sides of the blender.)

When all the vinegar is absorbed, do the same with the melted foaming butter and, lo and behold! You have a smooth, rich, tangy Hollandaise.

I have occasionally combined this basic Hollandaise sauce with Calvados Apple Purée (see page 211) and served it with grilled pork chops at a barbecue.

Puréed avocados combined with Hollandaise go deliciously with Baked Halibut (see page 69).

To coat breast of chicken, fold finely-diced raw red peppers into the basic Hollandaise.

Variations on Hollandaise

In season, a handful of lovely fresh watercress liquidized with a couple of tablespoons of dry white wine and then passed through a sieve is very tasty (but do not despair if you think it looks slightly curdled: watercress is full of iron and Vitamin C, and does not always, when puréed, blend in smoothly with the Hollandaise). But oh, it does taste so good.

Two tablespoons of commercial tomato purée may be combined with the basic Hollandaise but, better still, when tomatoes are inexpensive, make your own purée by simply simmering away on the stove (see page 124).

Purée of apple (about $\frac{1}{4}$ pint or 150 ml) with Calvados as a flavouring is nice, and I also like to occasionally fold into the Hollandaise fine strips of various vegetables that I have simply blanched in simmering water. Grated horseradish (1 tablespoon), 4 tablespoons finely chopped walnuts, $\frac{1}{4}$ pint (150 ml) pear purée with a little brandy – these are all other ideas you may use. Chopped fresh herbs can also be combined with the Hollandaise, and curry powder, too, if you like it.

Your *own* personal taste buds come to the fore here as it is important for you to get to know the taste of the basic Hollandaise. (It may be that you might want to add more lemon, for instance.) Once that is established, you can branch out on your own and investigate all sorts of different tastes!

Blender (or Magimix) Béarnaise

Prepare in exactly the same way as for Hollandaise but use 2 tablespoons of tarragon wine vinegar instead of the white wine vinegar and, naturally, be generous with finely chopped *fresh* tarragon.

Serve with breast of chicken done with limes and bacon, or with a plain grilled steak which you all know how to cook.

Basic Double Cream Sauce

Good high-fat-content double cream makes superb sauces that are rich, nutty and succulent. For 6 people you will need 1 pint (600 ml) of double cream. Pour it in to a large pan with a $\frac{1}{4}$ teaspoon salt, and

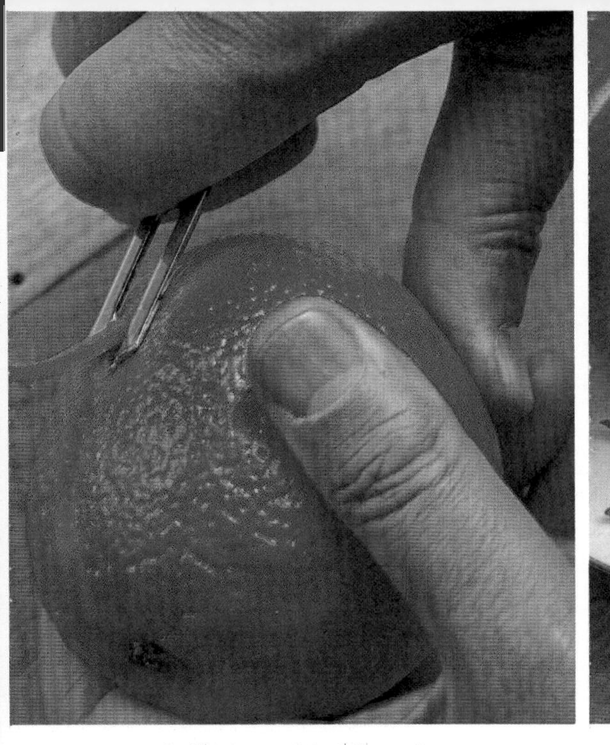

1. Score around the fruit evenly

2. Don't throw away the parings!

3. Cut half-way through the fruit

4. Slice the fruit and make your twirls

Cucumbers and lemons look particularly good
pared for garnishings

1. Cut celery into 2 in (5 cm) strips

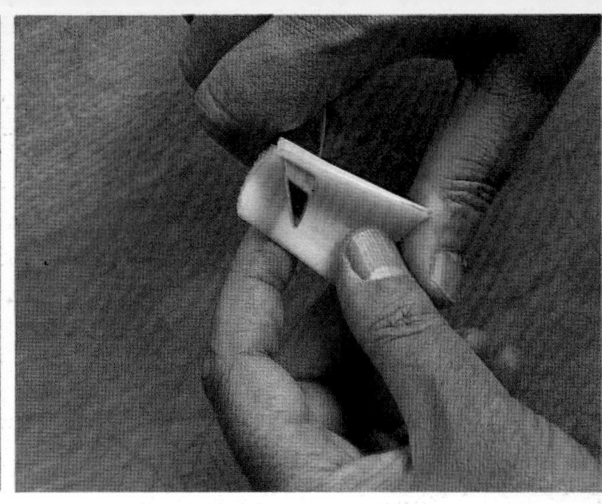

2. Cut in one-third of the way towards the middle

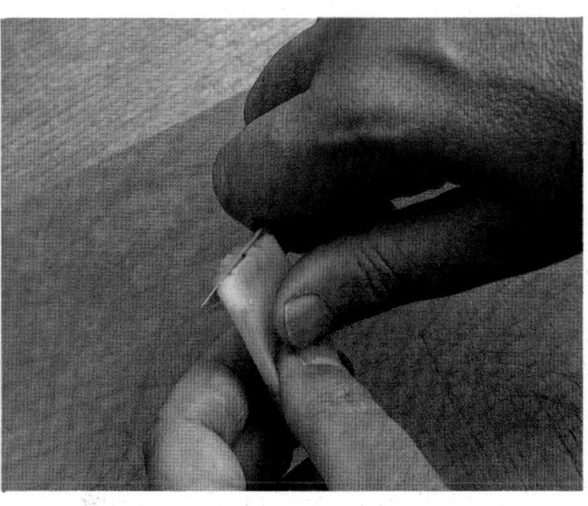

3. Slice *through* these tiny cuts

4. Your finished twirls

1. A sharp knife is vital

2. Pull zig-zag halves apart carefully

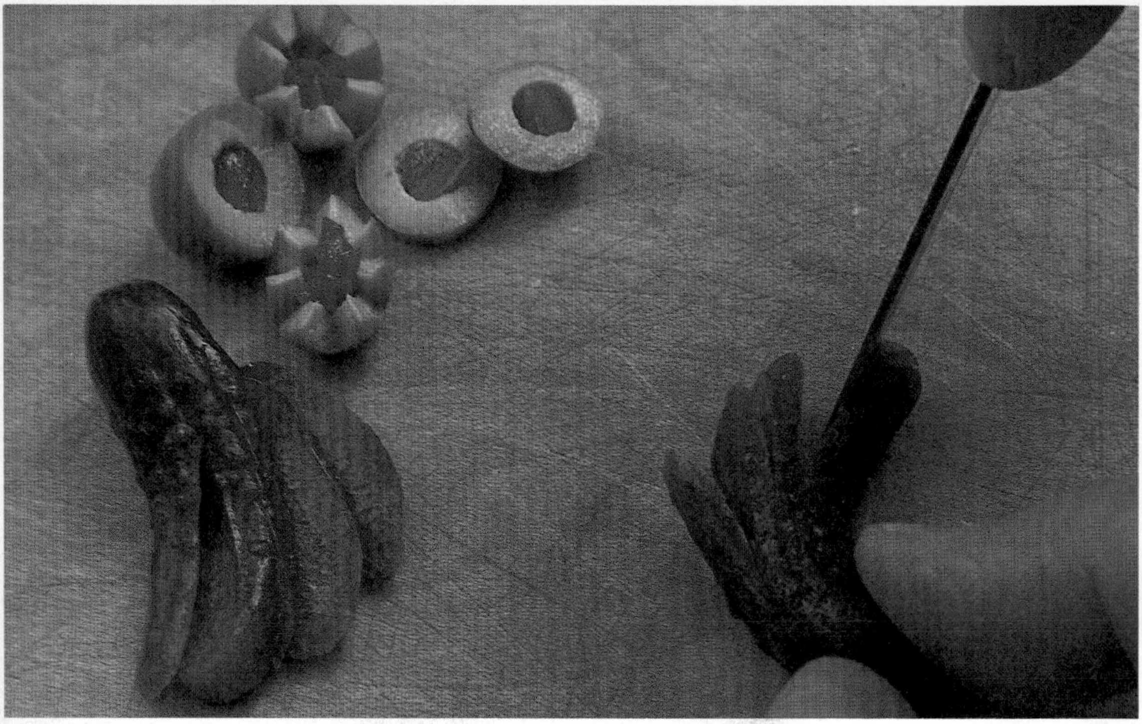

1. Make several cuts the length of gherkin. and fan out

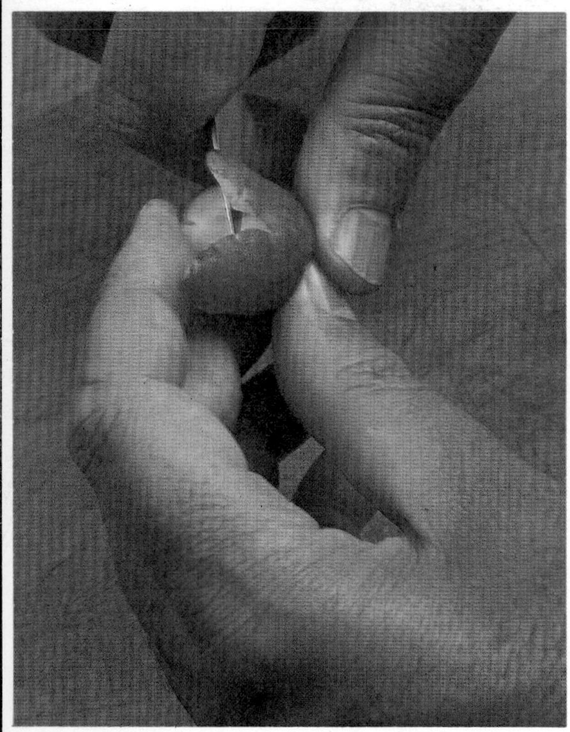

1. Slice two-thirds down into each radish as shown

2. Before and after iced-water immersion

How to make gherkin fans and radish roses

put the pan over a low heat. Leave until the cream has reduced by half. Do be careful as cream has a nasty habit of suddenly, with too much heat, coming right up the pan and over the edge, making a mess of your stove and causing you devastating, costly losses! The cream should become a nutty brown and slightly bubbly round the edges.

This reduction, when mixed with flavouring, makes a superb classic sauce which can then be kept warm in a double saucepan at the side of the stove. The flavourings I list below are in proportion with each original 1 pint (600 ml) of double cream.

Calvados Apple

Add about $\frac{1}{4}$ pint (150 ml) well-reduced Calvados Apple (see page 211) to the reduced cream to make this rich and flavoursome sauce, to serve with pork cutlets and plain baked halibut.

Marsala

Reduce $\frac{1}{4}$ pint (150 ml) Marsala down to a tablespoon in a small saucepan, then add the reduced cream. Stir well.

This mixture when combined with some Mushroom Pâté is an absolute winner for stuffing pancakes or using in between strips of rough puff pastry to make a savoury Mille Feuilles.

Tomato and Mustard

Combine 1 tablespoon of English dry mustard powder with 2 tablespoons of good tomato purée. Beat until smooth and then gradually beat in the reduced cream. Serve with pork cutlets.

Watercress

Liquidize a bunch of watercress with a tablespoon of white wine and pass the mixture through a fine sieve into the reduced cream sauce. Serve with breast of chicken.

Brandy

Reduce $\frac{1}{4}$ pint (150 ml) brandy down to a tablespoon in a small saucepan and then add the reduced cream. Stir well, and serve with Christmas pudding and mincemeat puff pastry cornets.

Flavoured Essences and Creams

Basic essence

2 eggs

4 oz (100 g) castor sugar

$\frac{1}{4}$ pint (150 ml) chosen vinegar, or liqueur (see below)

Basically, this is a simple method of imparting strong flavours to lightly whipped double cream, and it can be used for both sweet and savoury dishes. The basic essence can be made long before it is needed and stored in a screwtop jar in the fridge for a few days, but it is best to lightly whip the double cream as late as possible before folding in the essence.

Instead of a double boiler, in this case I prefer to use a pudding bowl and a saucepan. Make sure that your bowl fits comfortably into the pan, and that its bottom isn't sitting on the base of the saucepan (you want *indirect* heat). The water should come half-way up the pudding bowl when it sits inside the pan.

Break the eggs into the basin in the pan, add the sugar and beat these two together lightly. Trickle in the vinegar or liqueur, beating all the time. Set over a medium heat and, when the water in the base is beginning to bubble, turn the heat down slightly and stir the mixture continually with a wooden spoon. *Do not overcook.* Set on one side.

To make the savoury (or sweet) cream, very lightly beat up 1 pint (600 ml) double cream. Pass the cold essence through a fine plastic sieve, and mix into the cream, using a large metal spoon. You want a rich coating consistency. If you have over-beaten the cream, and the end result is more of a piping consistency, pipe it by all means, but it is better thinned down with either single cream or a little milk to get the right consistency.

Garlic Vinegar
A basic essence made from garlic vinegar mixed into double cream goes well with poached leeks.

Mint Vinegar
A basic essence made from mint vinegar mixed into double cream goes well with a savoury apple.

Tarragon Vinegar
A basic essence made from tarragon vinegar mixed into double cream goes well with savoury apples, pears, and peaches.

Drambuie
A basic essence of Drambuie mixed into double cream goes well with Chocolate Rum Squidgy Gâteau (see page 153).

Basic Tomato Sauce

¼ pint (150 ml) olive oil

2 medium-sized onions, finely chopped

6 plump, fresh cloves of garlic

fresh basil, tarragon, and marjoram to taste

5 lb (2½ kg) fresh ripe tomatoes

This is a sauce which is ideal to make when there is a glut of tomatoes. It can be kept in the fridge for up to a week but can be frozen most successfully and lasts you for months.

Heat the oil in a large saucepan, add the onions and fry until golden brown, and then add the chopped garlic along with the herbs (don't be too rash with these, or the herbs will dominate).

Add the quartered tomatoes and bring to the boil. Cover the saucepan and leave to simmer for about an hour. Look at the contents periodically and stir gently with a wooden spoon. The juice from the tomatoes should have evaporated by now and you will be left with a thickish mixture. Pass everything through a sieve and, if you are not satisfied with the texture, return to the stove to reduce further. Season to taste prior to cooling and storing.

Miller Howe Tomato, Onion and Garlic Sauce

1 lb (450 g) tomatoes

2 oz (50 g) butter

2 medium-sized onions, finely chopped

2 fat cloves of garlic

½–1 teaspoon salt

When tomatoes are in full season it is a good idea, as I've said earlier, to make sauces or purées etc in large quantities and store them in the freezer. But at all times of the year, this simple sauce enhances simple food such as baked cod, filled puff pastry cornets etc. It is as easy to make as the basic tomato sauce, but just tastes more strongly, obviously, of garlic and onion.

Skin and de-pip your tomatoes (see page 130) and chop them roughly.

Melt the butter in a saucepan and lightly fry off the finely chopped onions. Then crush the garlic cloves with the salt, and add to the onions. Cook for a few minutes. Add the chopped tomatoes, leave the saucepan uncovered, and cook gently until the mixture is thick and fairly dry, stirring from time to time.

Basic Stock Syrup

2 lb (900 g) preserving or cube sugar

1 pint (600 ml) water

Simply dissolve the sugar in the water over a low heat in a very clean saucepan and infuse at first over this same low heat. Then turn up the heat and allow the liquid to simmer for about 15 minutes. Now you can poach your fruit in it.

If you wish to have a tangy flavour, you can add 3 tablespoons of wine vinegar whilst simmering.

Aspic

For me, gone are the days of making my own aspic as the Swiss powdered aspic is very good provided you do not actually follow the instructions given on the tin or packet. When they say add a pint (600 ml) of water to so many tablespoons of the powder use one-third sherry, marsala or wine and two-thirds water, and you will be surprised at the difference this makes. Simmer the aspic according to the instructions and then leave to set. When I start to coat anything with aspic it is best brought out of the fridge in its firm jelly form and put into a small saucepan over a very low heat and barely brought back to a coating consistency. Laborious as it may sound you should coat your pâté, tomato, egg or whatever, with a *minute* amount and then return to the fridge to set and bring out again and repeat the process, gradually building up layers of aspic. Rather time-consuming and messy you might think, but I find it rather relaxing!

Calvados Apple Purée

This sauce, one of my favourites, can be stored in the fridge, or frozen, and has a multitude of uses. It's delicious as part of a galette, or mixed with a little sweetened cream and put inside a meringue gâteau with wedges of raw apple. Accompanying most

2 lb (900 g) Granny Smith apples

$\frac{1}{2}$ teaspoon cinnamon

1 oz (25 g) butter

$\frac{1}{2}$ tablespoon soft brown sugar

Calvados

pork dishes it is less mundane than plain apple sauce, and I like it with duck. A curried vegetable soup is enhanced by a teaspoon on top as you are about to serve it and it is nice combined with raw apples when making a Farmhouse Apple Pie. Pancakes or scones are ideal accompaniments, and with a rich egg custard it is a feast for an invalid!

Lightly butter a flameproof casserole dish, and peel, core and thinly slice the apples and mix with the cinnamon, butter and soft brown sugar. Place in the casserole and bake in an oven set at 375°F (190°C), Gas 5, for about 40 minutes, stirring from time to time with a wooden spoon.

When the apples have fallen, bring out of the oven and place the casserole over a high heat. Be as generous as you can with the Calvados, which you heat in a soup ladle and then flame over the apples. Pass through a plastic sieve and use, or store.

Brandy (or Rum) Butter

4 oz (100 g) butter

4 oz (100 g) castor sugar

3 tablespoons brandy

My personal helping of Christmas pudding is never complete without a dollop of brandy butter as the sole accompaniment. Likewise, mince pies are all the nicer when, having been warmed through prior to serving, you prise open the lid and pop a very small blob of rum butter in. You can serve butters with scones at afternoon tea, and both would be nice with mincemeat-stuffed puff pastry cornets.

Both butters are extremely simple to make, and store and freeze well.

Simply cream the butter and sugar well together and then beat in the brandy a tablespoon at a time. Do remember to really work at the butter and sugar mixing as you want it light, fluffy and creamy.

For rum butter, to the same quantities of butter and sugar as above, add the grated rind and juice of $\frac{1}{2}$ a lemon and 3 tablespoons Negrita rum. The method is the same.

GARNISHINGS

For me, a plate of food should look exciting to the eye when set in front of a guest. With a little imagination, a fair bit of time beforehand, and little extra expense, this can be easily achieved.

Garnishings and side salads are two of the things I prepare in the morning. During any preparations for a dinner party, there always comes a time when you feel you must sit down for 5 minutes to rest your tired feet and aching back, and this is the best time to do your garnishes. With a cup of coffee (or better still, a glass of wine), and a good programme on the radio or stereo, you will, I hope, have a lot of pleasure trying out some of the ideas below (and do look at the photographs).

All garnishings, once made, should be placed on trays (be careful not to have distinct clashing flavours too near), and then covered generously with transparent cling film.

Basically, the only tools needed are one good small, sharp, stainless-steel knife and a scorer – I find the Victorinox Swiss utensils by far the best to use in a kitchen.

Oranges, lemons and limes (among others) look so much prettier sliced, when you 'score' the skin for a delightful cartwheel effect. Don't throw away the pieces of scored skin as quite often they can be cut in half and used to good effect in savoury salads – rather like blades of grass growing! Always wipe your fruit before you start.

If you want any of the slices for making twirls, after scoring the sides, hold the fruit up and run a sharp knife down from top to bottom half-way through. As you cut each slice it will fall and you will immediately see how it will twirl.

Cucumber can benefit equally well from scoring, and perhaps looks the prettiest of the lot with its dark green and pale yellow stripes.

Gherkins can be made into attractive fans. Take a small, sweet pickled gherkin, and let it find its own position on your cutting board. Then, with a sharp knife, make about five insertions three-quarters of the way down from top towards the base. All you have to do then is fan it out with your fingers.

Olives are simple to cut for olive slices, but with a little patience and a good, sharp-pointed knife, you can do a zig-zag cut round the 'equator' and, lo and behold, you have two halves that certainly look more attractive than just two plain halves of stuffed olive!

Parsley is an absolute *must* to garnish almost everything, and adds such a good finishing touch, both fresh and deep-fried. Other fresh herbs (see under *Herbs*) may be used too – particularly when they are flowering.

Walnuts and pecan nuts are useful to have, and I serve them a lot as you will see from the recipes throughout the book.

Maraschino cherries (not my favourite garnish, mind you) are good standbys and certainly add a splash of vivid colour!

Red and Green Peppers can be cut into very thin strips and are useful for both taste, texture and colour. They can make 'basket handles' too: cut a thin circular slice off the whole pepper, clean out the seeds and pith and cut in half so that there are 2 arcs. They can be served stuck into a tomato stuffed with Cheese and Herb Pâté to look like a basket handle.

Strawberries and raspberries make a delicious garnish in the summer, both whole, or the strawberries sliced.

Onions can be cut into very thin rings which look and taste good.

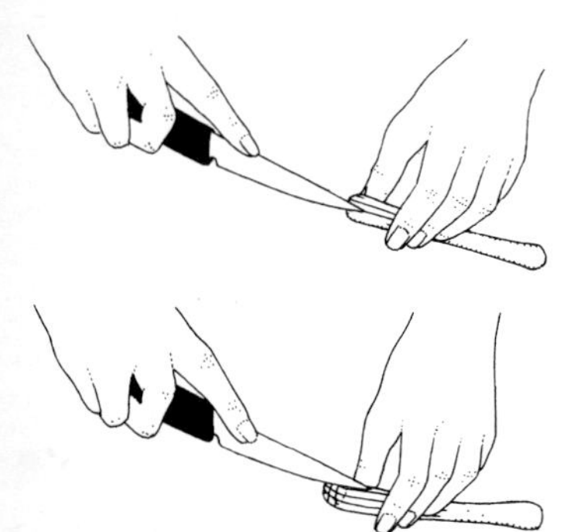

Spring onions make an effective garnish. Top and tail each spring onion, remove the outer layer of skin, and then with a sharp knife make as many little cuts as possible two-thirds of the way down each one, but keeping the bulbous base intact. These should then be left to soak in iced water (add further ice cubes if you have any to spare) and they fan out beautifully. (If you become aware of a peculiar smell in the kitchen, there is no need to start looking in cupboards and down sinks – the smell comes from your collection of spring onions left to soak!)

Radish twirls are very simple to do and look so professional. Top and tail each radish after washing and turn them up topsy-turvy – in other words, on the plate they will be facing you with their true bottoms up! This is quite sensible, really, as the broader top, when cut horizontally, gives you a broader base to sit the flower on. Take the radish between the thumb and first finger of your non-working hand and, with a sharp-pointed knife in the other, slice two-thirds of the way down 8 times, approximately, to give you a leafy effect. To help the leaf on the way just as you have finished doing the downward slice in the radish, fold the cut section gently towards you before going on to the second leaf. These will open up when soaked for a time in cold iced water.

Eggs, hard-boiled and sliced, make good bases for radish flowers, and also serve well as garnishings on their own, but do be careful boiling them. It isn't a job to be taken lightly.

Celery twirls are very useful. Wash and wipe your sticks of celery and cut into 2 in (5 cm) strips. You then cut down – along the grain of the celery – as many lines as possible in one-third of the way towards the middle. Repeat this at the other end, so that you have a lot of tiny cuts in at both ends, but the whole is kept securely together by the uncut middle.

Now you require a lot of patience, as you have to slice *through* these tiny cuts so that you will have a double fringe effect at both ends of the piece of celery. Put the cut pieces into cold water with some ice cubes and they will twirl out beautifully.

Savoury Salads can be done at this stage of your cooking day too, as they are essentially a garnish, provided you put them onto clean plastic trays and cover them with transparent cling film.

Wipe and dry one lettuce leaf for each serving, and lay on the tray. You could lightly coat it with walnut oil. A savoury salad, however, is easier to serve if you use a blob of cream, cream cheese, soured cream, or Cheese and Herb Pâté as the basis for building the garnishings. Having got this far, you could put an orange twirl across the dollop in the middle and then at one side a fan gherkin (lodged in the cream again) and at the other, a radish twirl. Put a sprig of parsley alongside the radish flower, and perhaps a strip of the lemon rind – taken off with a scorer – near the base of the gherkin.

Imagination, imagination is all that is needed. Little onion rings, olive slices, all the finicky things you can think of which do, I know, take time at this stage but, invariably, produce gasps of appreciation when placed in front of guests. Sometimes they can't imagine how you have calmly left the dining table and gone out and – within minutes – brought in the next dish beautifully garnished, whereas in fact you have used one palette knife to put the meat or fish on to the plate and then added the garnish. Lo and behold, you are a genius!

But do remember *never* serve the garnishings straight from the fridge. Allow them to regain their flavour at room temperature while still covered.

HERBS

I find no two palates seem to agree on the use of herbs so, right from the start, you are on your own! Any end result is going to be the one that suits *your* personal palate, and you can only hope that your guests agree. Basically, what you have to use more than anything else is *common sense*! Too much of one herb, or too many, will, of course, overpower the basic flavour of the food you are cooking and, yet again, too little will do nothing to enhance the dish. The only thing I can say honestly, is experiment in your own kitchen on your own family before trying the dishes out on guests.

I vividly recall those glorious Sundays of the early sixties when the *Sunday Times* colour supplement cookery column was written by Robert Carrier. He did a superb piece on herbs one week, spices another, and I'm sure he set many of us on the road to more adventurous cooking. Gardening is something that plays no part whatsoever in my leisure interests, but cooking without fresh herbs outside the back door is unthinkable!

Do not be too set in your ways about the use of herbs. There are other herbs besides rosemary, for instance, that will go with lamb. In fact, I like rosemary with pork, a meat which traditionally just goes with sage. I have found that dill, basil and tarragon are all delicious with pork as well, and I often use a combination of five herbs in butter when roasting lamb, chicken or veal.

I am constantly being told by friends that herbs are easy to grow, but I seem to have had little success. The herb garden at Miller Howe, which seems to flourish on rough treatment handed out by Tom, Bobbie, Phillip and I, is ransacked frequently when our normal suppliers are out of stock.

Bay leaves. Not one of my favourite herbs. I normally use them for lining savoury terrines, putting them underneath the bacon lining so that they can be discarded before slicing the terrine.

Chives. Their distinctive onion flavour is delicious in cheese pâtés or stuffings, nice in salads and super for garnishing many soups. Their purple ball flowers also look so attractive used as a garnish – or even as a table flower.

Fennel. The tops of ours grow extremely well, but the bulbous base never seems to come to anything! This aniseed flavour is delicious with many fish dishes and goes well with pork. I cannot grow dill, so I often substitute fennel.

Lovage. With its strong celery flavour, this makes a delicious soup served hot or cold. The dried seeds are good mixed sparingly into the Wholemeal Bread recipe (see page 185). Start experimenting with $\frac{1}{2}$ teaspoon to 1 lb (450 g) flour.

Marjoram. Use this when making chicken or duck liver pâtés to give you an unusual flavour. Freshly chopped in salads, it adds a warmth to the dish.

Mint. There are endless varieties of mint, and endless uses apart from accompanying boiled new potatoes, or lamb. It's delicious in iced tea, and lovely when stuffed generously into the cage of a roasting chicken. Use it in some farmhouse pies (apples and some of the summer currants), and it's good used as a garnish for Halibut cooked in Yoghurt (see page 70).

Parsley. There are basically two kinds – curly and flat. The flat is superior in flavour, but is so difficult to grow here (I can't get it to take anyway), and the curly has various strains.

As a garnish for a dish, there is nothing quite so attractive or so simple. Try deep-frying large pieces as an accompaniment to egg or mushroom dishes. Chopped as late as possible and just sparingly sprinkled over vegetables or salads, it adds a distinctive flavour.

Rosemary. This is good with lamb, but do try it with pork. Remember though that the leaves are prickly and sharp and don't soften in cooking, so chop them finely first.

Sage. In my opinion sage is the simplest herb to grow, and it has several uses. I like it finely chopped and sprinkled over calves' liver which I am marinating in lemon juice and, of course, it should always be placed in the roasting tray when you are cooking pork.

Savory (Summer and Winter). It has a strong peppery tang which can kill a dish (the winter one in particular), so be careful not to use too much. Use it when roasting lamb, or a small amount can be used when boiling potatoes.

Tarragon. Another favourite of mine which goes very well with chicken and kidneys. It is also delicious when used in chicken stuffings made with the chicken livers.

Thyme. A strong distinctive flavour. A herb which I use with caution as too much can too easily kill all other flavours. Mostly used in stuffings.

There is absolutely no comparison between the flavour of dried and fresh herbs but if you do have to resort to purchasing the dried varieties do so in as small quantities as possible, and as often as possible. *Use half the quantity of dried herbs to that recommended for fresh.*

I have also frozen basil, chives, mint and tarragon, to give me some of the sun of the summer during the winter months. Remove the herbs from the stalks, chop very finely and squeeze them into ice-cube containers. When frozen take out of the containers and wrap individually in transparent cling film and store in the freezer *clearly marked.*

EPILOGUE

How does one write an epilogue for a cookery book? In the old days of rep. after the Monday show when we had played to a full house of 'two for the price of one', we always used to say, 'Thank you for coming, and if you've enjoyed the show tell your friends, and if you haven't, shut up!' And I say the same now. There will be some things in this book with which you disagree, there will be some recipes you find strange and not to your taste one bit: but those you like, *do* try them on your friends, and when they ask for the recipe, tell them about this book – not mentioning its bad points, please!

I consider myself lucky to have found the joy of cooking (although rather late on in life), and I am constantly bewildered – sometimes slightly depressed – at the volume of knowledge I still have to collect. Even after cooking a recipe many times, I can become conscious of a way of improving it, and could kick myself for not having realized it earlier. But that is cooking. So much to learn. So much pleasure to give. So exciting. Don't always stick to my recipes here, but using them as a base, branch out on your own and do variations on these themes and, if you have the time, let me know how you have got on! I have yet to come across a person keen on food who is not a nice person (however clichéd that may sound)!

I am so lucky to be surrounded by a marvellously loyal staff – seven are in their eighth year at Miller Howe – and that enables me from time to time to up roots and go off travelling and eating. I know they enjoy my absence as much as I, but we are always glad to see one another again after a parting as I then pass on to the cooks all my new ideas and we get cracking once more with new recipes. It is, for me, quite remarkable that my three main cooks – whose average age is only 25 – show such enthusiasm for their work. If things go well the adrenalin flows, and if bad the depression is evident. Cooking is certainly caring. Cooking is basically confidence. But, oh the warm glow of satisfaction that comes over you when you reach the end of a meal you have prepared, cooked and served for your guests. For us at Miller Howe, this pleasure is equivalent to the ovations I have seen given time and time again to performers at the final curtain call. Well worth the hard work, well worth the moments of doubt, fear, hesitation and anxiety. Even if our audience is satisfied we, ourselves, know night after night what minor (occasionally major) slips have been made, and endeavour to iron them out on the next repeat performance of that particular dish.

In fact, when it is all over and you are taking your curtain call, hang on eagerly to the slightest form of criticism anybody may be giving, for that is how you learn. Each evening as I go round every single table at Miller Howe, the cooks and I know only too well what kind of a performance we have given on that particular evening. Table after table say nice things – and I am honest enough not always to agree with them (!) – but it is when somebody says, in a very kind way, something valid, critical, a personal judgment, that my night is made. It puts me on my mettle and makes me think. A complacent cook is not really a creative one. Likewise an actor or actress. Always try and turn out a better performance next time and improve each dish each time you make it.

My staff and I consider ourselves very fortunate at being able to devote so much time to what we enjoy so much, and through it give pleasure to many people . . . and make a good living out of our efforts. We hope your performances improve and that you share our love of our art and profession.

INDEX

The **bold** figures denote actual recipes